THE POLICING MACHINE

T0049296

The Policing Machine

ENFORCEMENT, ENDORSEMENTS,
AND THE ILLUSION OF PUBLIC INPUT

Tony Cheng

The University of Chicago Press   Chicago and London

The University of Chicago Press, Chicago 60637
The University of Chicago Press, Ltd., London
© 2024 by The University of Chicago
All rights reserved. No part of this book may be used or reproduced in any manner whatsoever without written permission, except in the case of brief quotations in critical articles and reviews. For more information, contact the University of Chicago Press, 1427 E. 60th St., Chicago, IL 60637.
Published 2024
Printed in the United States of America

33 32 31 30 29 28 27 26 25 24   1 2 3 4 5

ISBN-13: 978-0-226-83063-6 (cloth)
ISBN-13: 978-0-226-83065-0 (paper)
ISBN-13: 978-0-226-83064-3 (e-book)
DOI: https://doi.org/10.7208/chicago/9780226830643.001.0001

Library of Congress Cataloging-in-Publication Data

Names: Cheng, Tony (Criminologist), author.
Title: The policing machine : enforcement, endorsements, and the illusion of public input / Tony Cheng.
Description: Chicago ; London : The University of Chicago Press, 2024. | Includes bibliographical references and index.
Identifiers: LCCN 2023015917 | ISBN 9780226830636 (cloth) | ISBN 9780226830650 (paperback) | ISBN 9780226830643 (ebook)
Subjects: LCSH: New York (N.Y.). Police Department. | Police-community relations—New York (State)—New York. | Police-community relations—Case studies. | Police administration—New York (State)—New York.
Classification: LCC HV7936.P8 C545 2024 | DDC 363.209747/1—dc23/eng/20230505
LC record available at https://lccn.loc.gov/2023015917

♾ This paper meets the requirements of ANSI/NISO Z39.48-1992 (Permanence of Paper).

CONTENTS

The Machinery of Police-Community Relations

November is prime time for fundraisers in New York City. As 2018 neared its end, I got invited to an event called Excuse to Dance. Given all the stresses in the world, a Brooklyn neighborhood group affiliated with RALLY had invited the community to unwind with a dance party at its annual appeal for funds. RALLY stands for Reforms Advancing Long Lives for our Youth—a pseudonymous citywide coalition of two hundred neighborhood groups mobilizing to hold police accountable, reduce police violence, and get justice for victims of police violence. The night's theme contrasted with RALLY's past two months' work in Brooklyn, where it had been fighting cases generated by copwatchers at the West Indian Day parade; marching against white supremacy, gentrification, and police brutality; and recruiting donations and volunteers each day to fulfill even basic administrative tasks in the "office"—a semi-dedicated space tucked into the Brooklyn RALLY director's apartment. Rather than a celebration per se, this night was intended as a much-needed respite from the daily grind of pursuing police transformation. Organizers of the inclusive event charged a sliding-scale admission, advertised cheap alcohol, and promised not to turn anyone away.

But I had to decline my invitation; I was already committed to attending another fundraiser across town. As the RALLY crowd was gathering, I was heading into the Caribbean Breeze Ballroom. Its bright exterior lights were visible from afar—and on this night the green and orange of its neon signs mingled with the flashing red and blue lights of three New York City Police Department vehicles that were illuminating the venue's entryway. Inside, I was struck by the grandeur of the event: guests dressed in suits and gowns gathered around cloth-covered, numbered tables adorned with fresh floral centerpieces and socialized when they weren't visiting an abundant buffet offering everything from steak and shrimp to Jamaican beef patties. In contrast to RALLY's Excuse to Dance, the Fifty-Fifth Precinct Community Council—one of the resident-run boards established in the 1940s in every New York City police precinct to strengthen police-community relations—called its fundraiser an Awards Dinner Dance celebration. Tickets cost ninety dollars a head.

The two events may have overlapped in the time they were held, but likely not in the guests they attracted. I attended the Awards Dinner Dance at the invitation of Jeffrey Rosen, one of the evening's honorees. In fact, that night he would be receiving his second Community Service Award from the Fifty-Fifth Precinct Community Council. The director of security at Brooklyn Gardens, an apartment complex spanning multiple city blocks, fifty-six-year-old Jeffrey had offered me the ticket when I interviewed him a week prior. He had proudly taken me on a tour of the security system he created for the complex, showing me the basement room where he'd set up eleven flat-screen televisions, each capturing a different angle on the property—inside elevators, on sidewalks, and in stairwells, laundry rooms, and courtyards (Jeffrey Rosen, interview, October 31, 2018). He also explained the new walkie-talkie and security guard sign-in systems that he coordinated. A white former correctional officer and private security guard, Jeffrey was enthusiastic about his innovations. Before I left, I asked him about a series of plaques displayed on the wall of the basement room. That was when he invited me to join him as he received another.

As Jeffrey schmoozed the ballroom during cocktail hour, he periodically checked back in at our table with announcements like, "I was just talking to a one-star chief, two-star chiefs, and they said they've seen such a change in Brooklyn Gardens. They can't even remember the last time [there was trouble]—they don't have any issues anymore!" (field note, November 2018). The police and community relations going on around me seemed inconsistent with the idea that the two were in any way at odds. At one point during dinner, an NYPD Community Affairs officer stopped by the table and asked Jeffrey to donate three turkeys to the Domestic Violence Unit (a little something to help recent victims at Thanksgiving). Jeffrey immediately grabbed his cell phone to leave a voice message for his supervisor, asking whether he could use the company credit card for that purpose. In another moment, in talking with the NYPD's then commissioner, James O'Neill, he was quick to praise the Neighborhood Coordination Officers (NCOs) assigned to Brooklyn Gardens' piece of the precinct, bragging to O'Neill, "If you look at their arrest numbers, they're amazing!" (field note, November 2018). The commissioner scribbled the two officers' names on the back of a business card and tucked it into his suit jacket.

The NCOs were the most visible change under the Neighborhood Policing initiative the NYPD began rolling out in 2015. Soon thereafter, the *New York Times* published an op-ed written by Commissioner O'Neill's predecessor, William Bratton, as he closed his forty-six-year policing career and reflected on its culmination in a package of reforms. He wrote how Neighborhood Policing, one of the primary reforms, represented a sort of through line in his long career: "My youthful vision of neighborhood policing on the streets of Boston's Fenway as I began my career is becoming a reality on the streets of New York as I end it" (Bratton 2016). He described incoming Commissioner O'Neill as the "principal architect" of Neighborhood Policing, the person who would "bring it to full flower," providing New York City cops with the time, training, and resources to provide the kinds of localized police services that build trust and promote safety.

This was a rather rosy way to describe the rise of Neighborhood Policing. The actual catalyst for the program had been the July 17, 2014, murder of Eric Garner at the hands of NYPD Officer Daniel Pantaleo, who used a banned chokehold to subdue Garner on a Staten Island sidewalk, suffocating him. Allegedly, Garner had been selling loose cigarettes. Through line or not, Neighborhood Policing came into the city's zeitgeist when, two weeks later, then Mayor Bill de Blasio hosted a roundtable discussion on police-community relations (City Hall Press Office 2014). Just under a year afterward, the NYPD announced the Neighborhood Policing program, and months later, it was up and running. The NYPD's chief of department (the department's highest-ranking uniformed officer), Terence Monahan, recalled in a televised interview, "2014, everyone knows what happened around the world—law enforcement, we had the Eric Garner incident, you had the Ferguson incident, and there was a lot of tension going on with the cops. That's when we made the switch to Neighborhood Policing" (Monahan 2019).

Neighborhood Policing was a response not exactly to Garner's murder but rather to the rising public demand for police transformation occurring in multiple cities across the country. In New York, the public pressure came from above and below. Bottom-up pressures included increased street protests demanding police accountability—a message police associate with life-threatening, antipolice sentiments and threats. Commissioner O'Neill, the architect of Neighborhood Policing, described how the "Ferguson case" and the "Garner decision" led to "three weeks of protests against the NYPD that culminated in the assassination of Officers Wenjian Liu and Rafael Ramos" (Flamm 2019). Note that Michael Brown and Eric Garner are characterized not as victims or as people; their deaths are not even characterized as incidents. They are reduced to a "case" and a "decision," nothing more than pretense behind the unruly protests and the "assassinations" of two NYPD officers. Police are presented here as the victims.

The NYPD was pressured from the top down as well. Institutional reform became a political mandate, but Neighborhood Policing was only one of a number of potential reforms on the table. Included in the package of reforms put forth by elected officials were initiatives to require the NYPD to submit quarterly reports on use of force incidents; require officers to identify themselves and their justifications during police stops; and require appointed, independent monitors in cases of grand jury declinations to indict in episodes of police-involved civilian deaths (Mays 2015). Commissioner Bratton dismissed these additional reforms as "overkill" (Jorgensen 2015) and "unprecedented intrusions into the [NYPD's] operational management" (Mays 2015). Instead, he put his confidence in Neighborhood Policing, which he promised would "change many aspects of how cops and community interact—and thereby address many of the concerns that underlie the bills we're considering today" (Mays 2015). Barely a week after that program was announced, Bratton and the NYPD were already leveraging Neighborhood Policing as evidence that enough reforms were already under way. It was a tactic to resist more fundamental changes to policing in favor of reforms to how policing was administered across individual interactions.

Neighborhood Policing added a new layer to the machinery of police-community relations. A couple years after its launch, I was at the Fifty-Fifth Precinct Community Council's 2018 fundraiser as the awards portion of the evening commenced. Among the first handed out was the Appreciation Award, granted at the sole discretion of the organization's president, Lela Pessod. It turned out to have not one but eleven recipients: each and every NCO in the precinct, plus their supervisor. When I asked President Pessod how she'd made her choice, she said simply, "Because I think they're doing a good job. . . . I just wanted them to know that we—as a people here, the council—we do appreciate what they're doing for the community and the hard work that they put into it" (Lela Pessod, interview, March 7, 2019).

The Community Service Award came next. The Fifty-Fifth Precinct's commanding officer announced Jeffrey's selection: "For your steadfast and tireless dedication to provide a safe living environment for the residents of Brooklyn Gardens, the Fifty-Fifth Precinct Community Council, President Lela Pessod, and I present to you the Community Service Award." The award proceedings were imbued with the political networking and stakeholder partisanship that characterized the entire event: Jeffrey received his award from Alisha Grey, the seventy-three-year-old African American tenant association leader of Brooklyn Gardens and newest member of the Fifty-Fifth Precinct Community Council. As the Awards Dinner Dance wore on, I was reminded that Neighborhood Policing was precisely the reason why RALLY had decided to give its community the "Excuse to Dance."

How do police departments resist institutional change? That's the question at the core of this book. As public scrutiny of the police intensifies, police departments must increasingly navigate and manage pressures in the broader public sphere. The institutional imperative to manage such pressures indicates that police monopoly on legitimate violence is too often assumed, with comparatively less attention paid to the violent consequences of police legitimation. At the same time, in the interactions described above, police were not acting as law enforcers. Their interactions with community members like Jeffrey were targeted, but the tools of exchange were *awards* rather than *arrests*. Their city council testimony and public media statements after Garner's murder, for example, focused on departmental changes intended to ensure accountability internally, obviating external oversight. Their initiatives created constituencies and community meetings, new titles and new layers of obfuscation, rather than transparency, public accountability, and lasting institutional changes to policing. These are strategic politics, and in these pages I will outline their processes and consequences for communities and contemporary American policing.

—

The police killings of the 2010s sparked an extraordinary call to action against the ongoing harms that American law enforcement brings to minoritized communities. One way this call to action has taken shape is in the Movement for Black Lives: a network, platform, and policy agenda for legislative changes ranging from community reinvestment to local control over local institutions. Despite the politics surrounding specific policies, the concern that unites them is the thin line between police conduct and misconduct. Police officers have always vied for the position to *set* this thin line: official reports document justified uses of force; union representation and courtroom strategies enshrine legal victories and favorable precedent; and civil settlements pay out city funds (taxpayer dollars) without meaningful consequences for the officers involved. When these forms of control failed, police departments could ultimately reestablish legitimacy by ostracizing individual officers and reframing the instance as an isolated case of misconduct.

But as intensifying demands for transformative change problematize each of these practices and the institution of policing itself, police departments must rely on a new set of strategies to secure public legitimacy and preserve the organizational independence to determine what constitutes policing. Police today thus seek to build a base of power around another thin line—not that between police conduct and misconduct but rather the one entrenching and empowering police to hold back the tide of lawlessness in society. Doing so requires mobilizing supporters for which neighborhood problems should be prioritized, how police (rather than other actors) can resolve them, and ultimately, what the conditions of police accountability should look like.

For nearly two years, I collected an array of data from ethnographic observations to Freedom of Information Law documents and Twitter data, systematically studying how the NYPD, the largest police force in the United States, differentially interacts with community members, their complaints, and the neighborhood groups organizing channels to amplify particular visions of policing. I not only observed this variation; I experienced it. Over the course of eight months, the

NYPD repeatedly denied my interview requests, either explicitly by email or tacitly through silence, to speak with neighborhood officers, precinct commanders, and deputy commissioners. These denials generated the unique set of public data sources—from amplified sound permits to social media posts—that inform this study. But I also learned that the NYPD did not deny everyone's requests. Instead, the department denied mine over concerns that it would interfere with ongoing "official" evaluations of departmental initiatives with partnering institutions. These are not merely methodological points; they instantiate the book's core argument.

This book argues that thinking about police as central actors within urban politics—not just criminal justice—reveals a surprising reality: the police-community relationships that already exist are precisely what impede the potential for police transformation. I advance this argument by showing how America's largest police force engages in a political organizational behavior I call the *Policing Machine*. The Policing Machine describes how police cultivate political capital through a strategic politics of distribution—the discretionary distribution of public resources and regulatory leniency toward constituents, alongside coercive force against alternative voices. Political capital can be thought of as stocks of influence earned through relationships, which can be mobilized to achieve political goals such as legitimacy or power (Bourdieu 1986; Ocasio, Pozner, and Milner 2020). Police mobilize their accrued political capital to induce public endorsements from constituents—resident testimonials, collaborative events, community awards, and other signs of public support—to demonstrate that institutional changes are unwanted by those they are sworn to serve and protect. The Policing Machine provides the conceptual framework and vocabulary to make sense of an otherwise seemingly disparate set of practices that police departments and officers deploy to transform relationships into capital that quells dissent.

The problem with the Policing Machine is that it creates an *illusion* of public input. It establishes a social order wherein community preferences toward police emerge either on a stage coordinated by police or through struggle imposed by police, depending on how those preferences align with the police's pursuit of political capital. On one level, these internally controlled processes of generating and curating public input and optimizing legitimacy are common across many organizational types. Corporations, for instance, leverage testimonials to maintain legitimacy with clients and independence from shareholders. However, police have a unique capacity in this regard. As city resources have become concentrated within criminal justice agencies, police's coercive power is increasingly reinforced by non-coercive forms of control aimed at shaping the landscape and representation of public support. One outcome is that under the Policing Machine, police seek to control all the neighborhood groups organizing channels that amplify public input on police. The complaints that police can represent or repurpose as endorsements of their services are given a platform, while those demanding police transformation must compete with police and their partners to be heard. Under the Policing Machine, police thus permeate informal social controls, not empower them; this transforms investments in police-community initiatives into mechanisms for concentrating power *in* police at the expense of equal protection within and across communities (Gascón and Roussell 2019; Herbert 2006).

The Policing Machine thus establishes an urban political regime where police accountability is reorganized: police claim accountability to the subset of the public they structurally empower, not the democratically accountable institutions designed to regulate them. As police amplify certain constituents as the "authentic" representatives of local demands and decide which (and how) demands are aired, police accountability comes untethered from city officials, regulatory policy, and even legal precedents. The Policing Machine is about police contestation, whether successful or not, against both on-the-ground protesters and the reform-minded politicians seeking changes that might undermine cops' institutional mandate, professional expertise, and personal identities as police officers. Ultimately, analyzing how police pursue incentives, strategies, tools, and relationships to advance the Policing Machine compels us to rethink the promise of public input for achieving democratic governance over police departments.

THE THEORETICAL SIGNIFICANCE
OF THE POLICING MACHINE

Dominant ways to understand persistent cycles of controversial violence and democratic initiatives have involved doubling down on institutional design: if only the optimal community board, input process, or other democratic initiative could be designed and implemented, the thinking goes, then we can finally achieve democratic governance over police departments (e.g., Ponomarenko 2019; Rahman and Simonson 2020). But focusing on institutional design without articulating sufficient theories of organizational behavior threatens to repeat the "surprise" of when the promise and practice of democratic initiatives diverge.

Answering two fundamental questions would be helpful toward articulating a theory of organizational behavior. First, if police genuinely seek public legitimacy, why do they consistently engage in actions that would seemingly undermine such a commitment? Second, if police are, in fact, primarily law enforcers, how do we understand police investments in tools, strategies, and relationships that do not necessarily enhance enforcement capacity? The answers to these questions are critical, because together they begin to provide an affirmative theory of police motivations that identifies the incentives to which legitimacy-enhancing initiatives repeatedly succumb.

Core to the Policing Machine are two realities of police and policing that help answer these questions: (a) police are *legitimacy optimizers*, not legitimacy maximizers and (b) police are not only law enforcers but also *political mobilizers*. Conceptualizing police along these axes prompts a different diagnosis: gaps in the implementation of democratic initiatives are not operational shortcomings but rather the revealed preferences dictated by institutional priorities. Throughout this book, I will emphasize the politics of policing—not "just" its inequalities—and the ways police pursue those politics through event permits, social media posts, and other tools and strategies not typically associated with law enforcement. This analysis of the machinery of police-community relations allows us to uncover why police invest millions of dollars in community initiatives even when the associated crime control gains are tenuous (Crank 1994; Gill et al. 2014).

These analytic steps situate police as central actors within urban political systems, operating well beyond their criminal justice role. These insights reflect the generative potential of applying a political sociology lens to the study of policing that expands beyond the questions about enforcement capacity and its consequences as traditionally prioritized by criminology, economics, and law. At the same time, introducing these conceptions of police is not just an academic exercise. They are part of the Policing Machine framework, which provides a language for understanding the motivations for why and methods by which police resist institutional reforms.

Police as Legitimacy Optimizers

While police power is technically authorized by law, its successful exercise is more proximately rooted in an infrastructure of public support. Police must actively and iteratively build this infrastructure of media partners, elected officials, community members, and other allies to actually initiate and defend instances of otherwise controversial enforcement practices. For this reason, existing institutional theories would posit that during moments of crisis or change (Dobbin 2009; Edelman 1990, 1992), police seek to maximize their public legitimacy in order to reinstitutionalize themselves. Legitimacy is the "generalized perception or assumption that the actions of an entity are desirable, proper, or appropriate within some socially constructed system of norms, values, beliefs, and definitions" (Suchman 1995, 574). Organizations of all types seek to enhance legitimacy with external regulators, local policy makers, organizational peers, and the public at large (DiMaggio and Powell 1983; Meyer and Rowan 1977; Selznick 1949).

For example, police departments often "accede to the demands of other actors on whom departments depend for legitimacy, and with the receipt of legitimacy, the continued flow of resources for organizational survival" (Crank and Langworthy 1992, 339). Restoring a department's legitimacy in crisis moments often means firing its police chief in a ritualistic act of public degradation (Crank and Langworthy 1992). Legitimacy is also central in explaining why police departments adopt policies to align with changes in the law (Grattet and Jenness 2005). In fact, a staple set of police reforms today focuses on interventions that enhance procedural justice—changes premised on the idea that if police treat individuals with more dignity, fairness, and respect, then perceptions toward police will improve, benefiting police legitimacy, public compliance, and public safety (Tyler 2004; Peyton, Sierra-Arévalo, and Rand 2019).

But existing institutional theories insufficiently capture the considerations of police departments. Police may want public legitimacy but not at the expense of organizational independence. Autonomy over the decisions that shape daily work is a fundamental imperative for institutions and their actors. Police may be unwilling to cede organizational independence to gain public legitimacy for professional reasons (police believe they have the expertise to optimize policing), practical reasons (more flexibility to respond to new circumstances and lower burdens of compliance measures that consume already limited resources), and even personal reasons (autonomy makes work more fulfilling). Indeed, police support for the various reforms proposed after the murder of Michael Brown differed based on whether individual departments retained decision-making over reform implementation—such as officer training, body-worn cameras, and community initiatives—or became subject to changes imposed by external decision-makers—such as federal oversight, civilian review boards, and independent prosecutors. Like any other organization that values independence, police departments expressed resistance to the latter. Examples of such resistance to federal oversight tend to become apparent in implementation delays, accumulating costs, low morale, and ultimately, mixed effectiveness of new policies implemented at the departmental level (Kelly, Childress, and Rich 2015).

The Policing Machine is thus necessary because police are *legitimacy optimizers*. Police do not maximize legitimacy by, for instance, prioritizing compliance to institutional stakeholders outside the organization (Edelman 1990). Instead, police seek to develop trustworthy relationships with only the subset of the public *needed* to maintain independent decision-making over departmental operations. By cultivating local constituents from the bottom up, empowering them with resources, inducing public endorsements, and deploying enforcement against alternative voices, police can strategically demonstrate that institutional changes are *unwanted* and police services are *in demand*. Demonstrating the demand for police services helps manage the threat of external regulations coerced on them. As in all other aspects of policing, building and leveraging community relations are processes infused with multiple levels of discretion.

One way to think about organizational culture is as a resource that members deploy under institutional constraints, such as intensified public scrutiny (Campeau 2015; Swidler 1986). Public communications on digital platforms, such as Twitter or Facebook, permit police to strategically express information not only to residents broadly but also to their own officers. Thus, as Commissioner Bill Bratton began building the NYPD's social media presence in the mid-2010s, he identified the first goal of his new strategic communications team: "connect with the cops" (NYPD 2016b, 70). Social media, Bratton understood, serves an organizational purpose: "Internally, it means reminding the cops of who they are and why they joined" (70). These digital tools reach the public while also communicating the organizational worldview to police officers themselves by depicting what it means to be an officer, what advances their shared interests, and what is undermining their success. Here, a new technology is layered atop traditional forms of workplace socialization, such as trainings, performance indicators, and documentation requirements—all of which also reveal organizational priorities and establish decision-making incentives (Lipsky 1980; Blau 1963).

Optimizing legitimacy in these ways contributes to the pervasive sense among police that the public does not understand the nature of the job. On the one hand, optimizing legitimacy is a pursuit that involves identifying and building relationships with those willing to defer to police on organizational decisions and practices. At the same time, as police succeed in their pursuit, the pervasive sense of public disconnect becomes rooted in reality. The nature of police discipline epitomizes this disconnect. Police departments express their imperative to optimize legitimacy through staunch resistance to the introduction and successful operation of external forms of oversight, such as civilian review boards (Rocha Beardall 2022). Instead, police lobby for internal disciplinary systems to mete out punishment, which optimizes legitimacy by retaining independent decision-making while still assuring the public there is official quality control in place. These multiple systems of punishment contribute to the public disconnect: the punishments and rewards that matter to individual officers have more to do with shifts, pensions, and promotions (Kohler-Hausmann 2018; Moskos 2008) than with the external boards that their department and union help lobby against.

Conceptualizing police as legitimacy optimizers thus centers two competing organizational priorities: public legitimacy and organizational independence. These priorities can be communicated to officers throughout the organization by using new tools like social media and classic tools like mandatory paperwork. Retaining both priorities shapes the implementation of new initiatives by establishing the baseline incentives influencing the decisions and actions of frontline officers in the course of their work.

Police as Political Mobilizers

The dilemma of how exactly to optimize legitimacy is a problem faced broadly by the powerful and power-seeking leaders across international contexts (Stokes et al. 2013; Schrader 2019). When democratic processes challenge institutional power, the power holders routinely engage in strategic behavior to protect their authority. From electoral politics to illicit empires, patronage relationships are foundational to how people receive resources to survive and how powerful leaders cultivate support to retain control (Gordon 2020; Hicken 2011; Lessing 2021; Smith and Papachristos 2016). For example, Auyero (2000) describes how, in the slums of Conurbano Bonaerense in Argentina, thirty-four-year-old Norma receives and redistributes bread, sausage, and powdered milk from the local government. She also receives a bus from her councilman to bring children to a nearby beach. The more people Norma can mobilize to attend her political party's rallies and vote for her councilman, the more resources she will receive to redistribute, and the more secure her position will be within the party machine. The defining features of such clientelistic relationships are contingent direct exchange, such as material goods for political support; predictability, as regular interactions and local norms instill mutual confidence among the exchange's participants; and monitoring, or oversight by brokers like Norma who confirm that promises are fulfilled (Kitschelt and Wilkinson 2007). Clientelistic relationships are thus voluntary arrangements with reciprocity, but they also are characterized by exploitation and control.

Organizational brokers are key to gaining public support, since they represent collective interests that can be bargained with. For instance, the leaders of a street vending association negotiate on behalf of, distribute resources among, and mobilize the collective to support or oppose particular initiatives (Holland and Palmer-Rubin 2015). Politicians seeking the support of street vendors may simultaneously strike deals with association leaders who promise the political support of their members and demonstrate forbearance in enforcement actions against street vendors (Holland 2016). Legitimizing power is a process that must be cultivated, negotiated, and claimed in an ongoing fashion.

Applying such scholarship on the emergence of clientelism and patronage to the study of American policing challenges us to think about the central role of policing institutions within urban political systems. The Policing Machine provides a framework for understanding police not just as law enforcers or order maintainers but also as *political mobilizers* (Balto 2019; Felker-Kantor 2018). They can gain community legitimacy by exchanging problem-solving (whether actual, promised, or perceived) for public support. Political mobilizers are the local entrepreneurs who seek to cultivate constituents by solving local community issues with their organizational capacity—a term that refers to the attributes and ability to achieve a task which, for community organizations, typically includes material resources, personnel, institutional knowledge about local bureaucratic procedures, and links to other organizations to draw from for help (Barman and MacIndoe 2012; Cress and Snow 1996; Eisinger 2002). Whether political mobilizers promise or actually solve community issues, their goal regardless is to claim the legitimacy conferred when community members turn to them for help. For this reason, police construe local complaints as endorsements of their services (Cheng 2022a; González and Mayka 2023). Thinking of police as political mobilizers pushes scholarship beyond questions about police's enforcement capacity and toward a wider range of tools and strategies police use to fuel the Policing Machine.

Police departments may be apolitical by design; in practice, they're anything but. As political mobilizers, however, I do not refer to police involvement in electoral politics or legislative activity—though they *are* involved (Halpern 1974). Nor am I referring to the politics that individual officers engage in as "street corner politicians" (Muir 1977) or "street level bureaucrats" (Lipsky 1980). Being mindful of police as political mobilizers focuses attention on both the institutionalized and the informal strategies police adopt to advance their organizational interests of legitimacy and independence. It further spotlights their strategic politics of resisting institutional change as a foundational consideration in the operation of urban police departments.

Other political mobilizers working within the same neighborhood spaces as police include both state actors, like elected officials and community boards (Musso et al. 2006), and nonstate actors, like nonprofit organizations and religious institutions (Brunson et al. 2015; Levine 2016; Rodríguez-Muñiz 2017). They, too, aim to assist residents by providing services, thereby cultivating political capital among constituents who can be mobilized to vote, volunteer, donate, attend events, and participate in future campaigns. Mobilizing constituents and demonstrating evidence of effective service provision are important in organizational struggles for state resources (Vargas 2016). For example, in gentrifying neighborhoods in the United States, middle-class African American brokers wield power within "growth machine" politics (Pattillo 2007). They can attract external resources for neighborhood reinvestment while taking a cut for themselves in the form of a "consulting fee, a salary, a program grant, a board appointment, votes, verbal accolades, or, if they are also residents, a share in the benefits that flow from the local investments they have brokered" (121). These political mobilizers have traditionally constituted the "local ecology" of organizations and actors who catalog and aim to solve neighborhood issues (Chaskin 2003; Guest and Oropesa 1986).

Whereas other political mobilizers do exist, the coercive arm of the state is a powerful ally for those wanting local problems solved (Bittner 1990). For one, police exercise a monopoly on crime enforcement data, which enables them to craft narratives to shape public understandings of evolving threats to social order (Vargas et al. 2022). Doing so can help motivate the legal authorization and wider public support needed to produce objects of enforcement: students who are punished in schools (Rios 2011), people who are banished from public parks (Beckett and Herbert 2009), and undocumented arrestees who are deported from the country (Armenta 2017). Such police action is not random but the result of coordinated relationships with the schoolteachers and principals who report criminalized students, business associations demanding enforcement against disorderly people in public spaces, and Latino community members who participate in community policing programs. Police often appear to be the obvious—if not the only—organization to respond to social issues like homelessness, because decades of investment have positioned them to be just that: they have the emergency dispatch system, workforce, vehicles, flashlights, and resulting legitimacy that permit them to respond with force, care, or both (Herring 2019; Stuart 2016).

Police's monopoly on force is even more consequential because cities have concentrated public safety resources into police departments over the past half century. From the 1970s to the 1990s, as cities passed new laws that criminalized drug use and stiffened penalties for the violence surrounding it, police departments have demanded—and won—additional resources to fight crime (Hinton 2016; Kohler-Hausmann 2015; Simon 2007; Vargas and McHarris 2017). As crime decreased (Zimring 2006) and policy approaches softened, police department budgets were never scaled back. Alongside increased spending on education and public welfare institutions, state and local expenditures on police have nearly tripled, from $42 billion in 1977 to $115 billion in 2017 (Auxier 2020). Since the 1970s, the typical city has consistently spent 4 percent of its total expenditures on its police force (Auxier 2020). The high organizational capacity of police departments remains an enduring legacy of the city resources pooled within them during the tough-on-crime era.

An important aspect of police's high organizational capacity is their workforce, which can be repurposed for a range of organizational tasks. In New York City, which has the nation's largest police force, the uniformed head count was 36,342 officers in March 2017—over 10,000 more officers than in 1990, when murders in the city had peaked (Council of the City of New York 2017). The NYPD has the nation's largest police budget ($4.9 billion in 2017) and is among the top in per capita spending, yet the percentage of New York City general fund expenditures allocated to police is actually lower in than most other large American cities—8 percent in New York City, compared with 26 percent in Baltimore and Los Angeles, 35 percent in Houston, and 41 percent in Oakland (Center for Popular Democracy, Law for Black Lives, and Black Youth Project 2017). While Chicago allocated about 20 percent of its budget to its police department in the early 1990s (Skogan and Hartnett 1997), by 2017 policing consumed 38.6 percent of the total (Center for Popular Democracy, Law for Black Lives, and Black Youth Project 2017). These fiscal realities position police to offer to other neighborhood organizations resources like staffing, meeting spaces, and other forms of organizational capacity.

But while the coercive arm of the state may be a powerful ally for solving problems, it will seek recognition in return. To cultivate political capital, police can offer themselves as resources in people's "problem-solving networks" (Auyero 2000; González and Mayka 2023). Police can build these relationships with residents directly, though it can be more efficient and effective to recruit organizational brokers who can conduct such outreach on their behalf. The institutionalization of such relationships can vary, from informal exchanges to formalized positions with police affiliations. As police provide or promise services (or are perceived as doing such), they gather public endorsements for the quality of current policing. Understanding police as political organizations thus emphasizes the relationships built, resources exchanged, and recognition publicized. This is a form of patronage. Such clientelistic policing relationships are more frequently associated with international developing contexts or discounted domestically as isolated cases of corruption, but this book highlights their foundational role in American urban politics.

These understandings of police as both legitimacy optimizers and political mobilizers emphasize that police and community are not separate entities that must be bridged. Instead, police resist institutional change through the strategic relationships they have already cultivated.

THE HISTORICAL FOUNDATION FOR THE POLICING MACHINE

The Policing Machine is not just an analogy derived from classic models of machine politics; it reflects the enduring role of police within the urban political landscape (Balto 2019; Felker-Kantor 2018; Hinton 2021). From the late 1800s to early 1900s, political machines emerged in cities across the United States, including St. Louis, New Orleans, Detroit, Chicago, and New York (Brown and Halaby 1987). In the post–Civil War period and during the world wars, political bosses consolidated power by providing various inducements (money, jobs, and other particularized material rewards) to obtain votes and win elections. Police departments were central cogs in political machines, providing jobs and promotions based on political influence and unequal protection for bribes.

The demise of political machines is often seen as a positive development, yet they also helped integrate poor new immigrants into the US political system and provided valuable services to them (Banfield and Wilson 1963; Scott 1969). Political machines emerged from the rapid social change and widespread poverty during the era, as these conditions shortened people's time horizons and made the resources that machines offered more attractive than lengthy processes such as passing legislation (Scott 1969).

In subsequent decades, police departments shifted their source of legitimacy away from electoral politics and toward their status as professional crime fighters and community-oriented service providers. In the early twentieth century, reformers aimed to professionalize police departments through changes in police management, organization, technology, and tactics (Go 2020; Vollmer 1933). These reforms, ranging from command-control hierarchies to police car radios, increased the distance between police and their previous political influences. However, policy makers believed that police quickly became *too* distant from particular communities. The national movements of the 1960s helped reveal the violent injustices of unequal policing (Hinton 2021). In fact, in 1967 President Lyndon Johnson's Katzenbach Commission published *The Challenge of Crime in a Free Society*. The report recommended that "police departments in all large communities . . . have community-relations *machinery* consisting of a headquarters unit that plans and supervises the department's community-relations programs" (Katzenbach Commission 1967, 100; emphasis added). Furthermore, it emphasized that "such machinery is a matter of the greatest importance in any community that has a substantial minority population" (100–101). In light of escalating social tension and citizen hostility, the commission advised police departments to secure public cooperation through community relations. These relationships should be direct—unmediated by the political influences of past decades.

The police-community initiatives envisioned by the Katzenbach Commission did not gain a nationwide foothold until the late 1900s. Select cities had already begun experimenting with policing practices, like foot patrols, and policing strategies that focused on visible signs of disorder and other specific neighborhood issues through broken windows policing and problem-oriented policing (Goldstein 1979; Kelling and Wilson 1982; Trojanowicz and Bucqueroux 1990). However, the key inflection points in the nationwide adoption of community policing were the televised beating of Rodney King in Los Angeles and the subsequent distribution of federal funds through the Department of Justice's Office of Community Oriented Policing

Services (Felker-Kantor 2018). These turning points transformed the mission statements and organizational practices of police departments to incorporate commitments to the coproduction of public safety through local meetings, collaborations with community organizations, and interagency partnerships (Skogan and Hartnett 1997).

In New York City, the NYPD's investment in community initiatives has been contingent on the visions of particular mayors and commissioners. Under Mayor Edward Koch and Commissioner Benjamin Ward in 1988, the department rolled out its citywide Community Patrol Officer Program. The program included 800 Community Patrol Officers, 75 sergeants, and 75 administrative aides working proactively to prevent and address crime and disorder (Vera Institute of Justice 1988). In 1989, Mayor David Dinkins and Commissioner Lee Patrick Brown expanded the program by lobbying the state for legislative funding to hire 5,000 officers and launch community crime prevention initiatives as part of the Safe Streets, Safe City Program (White 2014). In subsequent decades, under Mayors Rudolph Giuliani and Michael Bloomberg, community initiatives took a backseat to more aggressive forms of quality-of-life policing, including broken windows policing and stop-and-frisk.

The NYPD did not formally adopt a community policing program again until the police murder of Eric Garner in 2014. Then, from 2015 to 2018, it implemented Neighborhood Policing across the city. The new program divided each of the city's seventy-seven precincts into four to five smaller sectors, with two Neighborhood Coordination Officers (NCOs) per sector; assigned "steady sector" officers to respond to 911 calls, freeing NCOs to deal with community issues; and mandated quarterly Build the Block meetings within each sector, allowing police to receive community complaints directly. An independent analysis of Neighborhood Policing found that the program reduced misdemeanor and proactive arrests, but it did not affect the crime rate (Beck, Antonelli, and Piñeros 2022). Nonetheless, nearly a decade later, the NYPD still refers to Neighborhood Policing as the "cornerstone of today's NYPD."[1]

Past analyses of community policing initiatives have likened these programs to classic machine politics, but such comparisons were primarily hyperbolic. Skogan (2006, 174) recounted how, when describing Chicago's community policing initiative to local groups, "I often ask in jest whether CAPS is a 'new political machine.'" The similarities he identified between CAPS (the Chicago Alternative Policing Strategy, which began implementation in 1993) and classic political machines included "assessing resident's needs, delivering services where they are needed, mobilizing the public through marches and rallies, turning them out for mass assemblies, and generating support for the mayor" (174). In this way, Skogan sees community policing as a contemporary version of the very same role that police played in classic machine politics: as a resource to secure political victory for elected officials.

In contrast, the Policing Machine's primary goal is to advance the police's own institutional interests in public legitimacy and organizational independence—not to secure victory at the polls for elected officials who might later threaten oversight over them. As described further in chapter 2, one strategy of the Policing Machine is to establish alternative systems of neighborhood representation composed of constituents police have empowered precisely because elected officials have proved unreliable in advancing police's institutional interests. Strategically representing and raising the demands of constituents as the "legitimate representatives" of the community enable police to exchange services for what they frame as support for (even grassroots demand for) the department and its existing operations.

Rather than classic political machines, I argue that the Policing Machine more closely resembles organizational strategies that may draw from politics but do so in order to advance goals outside political office. For example, modern-day nonprofits trade their constituents as voting blocs to win government contracts (Marwell 2004). These community-based organizations shift the democratic accountability of elected officials away from the general voting public and toward the most prominent of such organizations and their constituents (Marwell 2004). In related research, these groups are theorized as nonelected neighborhood representatives, or the local representatives that funders and other entities prefer to deal with in managing neighborhood issues (Levine 2016). This model emphasizes how accountability is shifted away from elected officials and toward democratically unaccountable resource brokers within communities. Either way, both models highlight how neighborhood organizations empower themselves from the ground up by engaging in the politics of service provision.

THE MECHANICS OF THE POLICING MACHINE

The mechanics of the Policing Machine are attuned to the reality that communities' demands on police are heterogeneous (Bell 2019; Powell and Phelps 2021; Thacher 2001). One way policy makers in general navigate the mass public is by targeting policies that enhance constituents' capacities, interests, and participation (Campbell 2012; Mettler and Soss 2004; Pierson 1996). For instance, the passage of Social Security transformed senior citizens from one of the least to one of the most politically active age groups by empowering them with incentives, resources, and a political identity to mobilize and advance their interests (Campbell 2003). Policies themselves have causal power to create winners and losers as well as new political arenas in which people can vie for policy influence. These feedback processes—wherein policies shape politics and, therefore, subsequent policies—are not passive, particularly in a digital era. Online platforms today empower policy makers of all types to proactively construct "the public opinion" about policy successes (Herbst 2011; McGregor 2020). In pursuit of their own institutional interests, policy makers seek to both empower constituents and retain control over the representation of their public input. Public agencies are instrumental in creating the segment of public audiences with whom they seek to engage.

The Policing Machine brings these insights into the criminal-legal context by explaining how police departments manage heterogeneous community demands on them: by establishing different channels for public input over which police can deploy different strategies of control. As explained below, I conceptualize these channels as department channels, partner channels, and independent channels. Like policy-making more broadly, police can target public resources toward specific channels and the constituents within them. Unlike other policy makers, however, police can also exert different levels of coercive force and regulatory leniency to further advance their interests as political entities. The particulars may vary by community, but the rules of the regime are as follows.

*First, police prefer to direct all community complaints toward **department channels**, where they exercise asymmetrical control over the recording and representation of public input.* For example, Neighborhood Policing meetings (called Build the Blocks in New York City) are run by police officers. These meetings are presented as opportunities for residents to express any issues or concerns that they have to the officers assigned to their neighborhoods. Because these meetings are offered by the police department, officers have full control over where meetings are held and whether and how complaints are recorded in organizational records and represented to the public (see chapter 1; see also Cheng 2022a). Digital platforms like Twitter are particularly valuable for advancing claims about organizational performance and public support (Cheng 2021). Furthermore, while public agencies of all types are organized around managers, metrics, and evaluations (Lipsky 1980), policing is particularly hierarchical and performance driven (Weisburd et al. 2003). To impress supervisors and receive recommendations for promotion, local officers operating community initiatives must demonstrate that the program is working the way supervisors envision. Departmental trainings, documentation requirements, and other agency dynamics simultaneously constrain officer discretion and guide it toward organizational priorities. Consequently, individual officers hosting community meetings will foreseeably prioritize symbiotic relationships with those individuals and organizations wanting to use the services police have been trained to provide.

Outside department channels, however, police cannot exert the same level of control to curate community complaints arising externally. Instead, police must manage such grievances by shaping the capacity of neighborhood groups to organize them. Rather than curating content at the complaint level, police's strategies toward nondepartment channels thus operate at the organizational level. These strategies are central to the Policing Machine, because police distribute public resources in ways that ease burdens for some organizations (which can grow reliant on police assistance) but confront others with regulatory enforcement. Indeed, regulatory leniency is fundamental to the Policing Machine, because police have the discretion to selectively tolerate the breaking of ordinances, policies, and rules that they are supposed to enforce. These practices enable police to take advantage of the variation in community preferences regarding them—empowering police to align themselves with selected complaints, constituents, and channels for public input.

*Second, police target resource distribution and regulatory leniency to amplify the demands for police services emerging within **partner channels**.* Partner channels are organized by cooperating neighborhood organizations. While police's strategies across partner channels differ depending on the neighborhood entity's organizational capacity (see chapter 3), their goal is the same nonetheless: to cultivate political capital through strategic relationship-building with constituents. Specifically, police can cast certain constituents as the legitimate representatives of the community and frame the public input emerging through partner channels as accurately reflecting community sentiments on the ground. By exerting influence over partner channels, police can induce public endorsements of police practices by amplifying those community complaints demanding greater police presence; coordinating the distribution of community awards to police officers as local recognition of quality police work; and arranging for other political mobilizers to introduce, endorse, and validate police to their audience networks. Partner channels thus become an important source of political capital, their value vested in their utility for mediating public pressures for institutional reforms.

*Third, police exert coercive force to contain the demands for institutional change emerging within **independent channels**.* As grievances remain unanswered through department and partner channels, residents mobilize and form community organizations demanding police transformation. Such demands include launching initiatives like data collection and reporting requirements to increase police transparency; ending qualified immunity to increase police accountability; and restructuring city budgets to prioritize social services and reduce the footprint of police in neighborhoods (Bell 2017). As with partner channels, independent channels often feature community nonprofits aimed at reducing violence and strengthening neighborhoods. However, rather than organizing community complaints that seek more police services, independent channels serve as stages for complaints pointing to police as sources of community harm. Rather than endorsing the quality of current policing, independent channels organize complaints seeking to strengthen community vitality, whether through reduced police presence or increased accountability (Phelps, Ward, and Frazier 2021). Despite the variety of demands to transform policing, independent channels are united by their shared premise that police lack public legitimacy and require more oversight than independence—the exact sort of demands the Policing Machine has sought to minimize.

Police strategies across department, partner, and independent channels unfold simultaneously and must be understood relationally. For instance, as police pursue regulatory enforcement against independent channels, they demonstrate leniency toward partner channels and the events they operate to mobilize public input. Similarly, as police provide resources to build the capacity of partner channels, they withhold resources from community nonprofits organizing independent channels. Even if the activists organizing independent channels would have rejected police resources, the point is that the unequal distribution of material resources is both consequential and underwritten by the police as state actors. These complementary strategies toward partner and independent channels, plus police's control over department channels, comprise all the options that people have to express community grievances. The takeaway is not that police should be reflexively incorporating the demands of each and every community member, an impractical task. Rather, it is that police are able to eschew the fundamental point of community initiatives in the first place—deliberative exchange, representative input, shared decision-making (Thacher 2001)—in pursuit of political capital valuable in securing legitimacy and independence.

Analyzing the mechanics of the Policing Machine provides important lessons for even *non*policing scholars. Most important, it directs scholars to consider how organizations navigate public crises, not by acceding to established modes of governance, but by resisting those modes and establishing new lines of accountability. The Policing Machine highlights the generative potential of thinking about actors and agencies operating simultaneously within different systems, pursuing goals like legitimacy and independence through unwritten practices nonetheless understood as organizational imperatives.

Organizations of all types identify endorsements that are meaningful to them and foreseeably pursue strategies to cultivate and showcase them as indicators of organizational success. The Policing Machine shows how the organizational politics of public services can entrench inequalities in their provision, with the coercive consequences and oftentimes violent realities that distinguish American policing.

STUDYING THE POLICING MACHINE

This book examines the political machinery of police-community relations by focusing on the largest police department in the United States: the NYPD. In absolute terms, the NYPD's thirty-six thousand sworn officers and nineteen thousand civilian employees oversee a population larger than that of Denmark. Besides this baseline threshold of significance, the NYPD is a particularly insightful case study because what it lacks in representativeness it makes up for in influence. Its past initiatives, from broken windows policing (Harcourt 2001) to CompStat[2] (Weisburd et al. 2003), have diffused to police departments across the nation. Indeed, its Neighborhood Policing program has already diffused to the Chicago Police Department, where it is known as the Neighborhood Policing Initiative. Commissioner James O'Neill has described Neighborhood Policing as "the largest change to the NYPD since CompStat in 1994" (NYPD 2018).

I began this project to learn how the NYPD was incorporating public input on policing. Despite my focus on the department, I consider this not a study of police per se but rather a study of police *through* community, because the NYPD never granted me formal access. While "hard-to-reach populations" are hard to reach for multiple reasons (Ellis 2021), the label is still typically reserved for marginalized populations. Yet institutional actors can also be hard to reach—though with different power dynamics and ethical stakes. In this study, I did not officially interview a single officer. Over the course of eight months, the NYPD Office of the Deputy Commissioner, Public Information repeatedly denied my requests for interviews, either explicitly through email denials or implicitly through silence. My requests expressed my openness to discussing Neighborhood Policing with the NCOs I had built relationships with (who needed permission before they could agree to formal interviews), the NCO coordinators, the precinct commanders, the deputy commissioner of collaborative policing, or *anyone* else in the NYPD with knowledge of the program. The replies I did receive were short: "Thank you for your interest in the New York City Police Department. Unfortunately we are unable to accommodate your request no one is available for an interview."

The challenge of being blocked from formal access, however, generated my collection of an unconventional array of primarily public data sources. Together, these provide a composite of public input on policing in New York City. Because institutional immersion was not possible, I approached interviews with residents and opportunities for participant observation of public spaces as leads; these helped me identify innovative data sources for analysis, such as the types of documents to request via New York's Freedom of Information Law or online posts to monitor on Twitter. Being positioned external to the object of study, rather than embedded within it, had its advantages and disadvantages. For instance, while incentives can at times be inferred, the data from this study are more suited for uncovering processes and consequences at the organizational level rather than the individual-level intentions among specific officers. Furthermore, this approach may be less equipped to give voice to the hard-to-reach perspectives of police, yet it facilitated a level of critical independence that might otherwise be dulled through immersion.

Table 0.1 provides a descriptive overview of my fieldwork. For eighteen months, between March 2018 and September 2019, I conducted fieldwork in two pseudonymous precincts in New York City: the Fifty-Fifth and the Eightieth. Given the contemporary stakes of policing, I use pseudonyms to protect the identity of the residents who participated in this study. Apart from the community meetings hosted by the NYPD, the study focused on police interactions with three different types of organizations: community councils, clergy councils, and the group that I call RALLY, which hosted the Excuse to Dance fundraiser that opened this chapter.

TABLE 0.1. Data sources from fieldwork

Organization	Type of public input channel	Examples of events attended	Number of events	Number of interviews
NYPD	Department	Quarterly meetings	40	0
Community council	Partner	Monthly meetings, various public events	48	20
Clergy council	Partner	Monthly meetings, shooting responses	18	14
RALLY	Independent	Marches, vigils, rallies	17	15
Total			123	49

Community councils were emphasized by the NYPD's website, indicating they are key to how police operationalize police-community relations. Since 1944, every precinct in New York City has operated its own independent community council, run by an elected board of volunteer residents, which hosts monthly public meetings between precinct leadership, officers, and residents. Everyone is invited to attend community council meetings and events, which aim to improve the community by fostering open lines of communication between the police and the public. The NYPD has referred to these councils as the "oldest and most successful expression of 'community policing.'"[3]

I decided to focus on Brooklyn, because it is New York City's densest borough and one of its most diverse. For theory building, I drew a random sample representing a quarter of Brooklyn's precincts to begin attending community council meetings. Although I continued to triangulate my findings across these precincts, after two months I decided to focus specifically on the Fifty-Fifth and Eightieth Precincts, because they had consistently high meeting attendance. This decision also reflects the practical trade-offs of qualitative research: meeting and event times across the six precincts began overlapping, and focusing on two precincts would permit the in-depth analyses that facilitate novel data sources and findings. As I attended community council meetings, officers promoted Build the Block meetings as more intimate settings where residents could submit complaints to the officers designated to their neighborhoods. In following up, I learned about Build the Block dates, times, and locations through the NYPD's social media page and began attending them in the Fifty-Fifth and Eightieth Precincts. If I was going to learn what "successful" police-community relations looked like, it was going to be in these two precincts.

Over the course of my fieldwork, I learned that the Fifty-Fifth and Eightieth Precincts have more similarities than differences. Table 0.2 provides a basic overview of their demographic and crime data. Historically, both precincts have had high crime rates and high police presence relative to other parts of New York City—though less so in recent years, as crime across the city has leveled. Both have high percentages of Black and foreign-born populations, with the Eightieth Precinct less so because of its faster gentrification from being closer to Manhattan. With their large Afro-Caribbean populations, cultural

TABLE O.2. Selective demographic and crime data for the Fifty-Fifth and Eightieth Precincts

	Population	% Black	% Foreign Born	2018		2019	
				Major felonies rate	Murder rate	Major felonies rate	Murder rate
55th Precinct	150,000	87	50	1,150	4	1,050	5
80th Precinct	90,500	58	30	1,250	2	1,130	15
Brooklyn	2,560,000	34	37	1,071	4	1,093	4
NYC	8,300,000	26	37	1,150	3.5	1,147	3.6

Note: Data are presented as approximations to preserve the identities of the precincts. Major felonies and murders are presented as rates per 100,000 residents.

Sources: US Census; New York Police Department.

events like J'Ouvert touch parts of both precincts. Many people work in one of the precincts and reside in the other, or they have relatives that span both.

As I attended community council meetings and conducted interviews with their leaders and attendees, I realized something surprising: for all the vagueness around the term *community* and the boundaries and composition it implies (Levine 2017; Herbert 2006, 2008), police had a clear sense of who was included. At community council meetings, police would thank the community for listening, present Cop-of-the-Month awards to officers on behalf of the community, and announce police-community events organized by the precinct and the community council. For police, the community council— especially its president—*is* the community.

Community councils operate as nonprofit organizations. While the Eightieth Precinct Community Council currently has 501(c)(3) nonprofit status, its counterpart in the Fifty-Fifth Precinct lost that status in 2010 for failure to submit the proper paperwork. Overall, of the 80 community councils that exist across New York City today, 31 (40 percent) have had 501(c)(3) nonprofit status at some point. In fact, during Sharkey, Torrats-Espinosa, and Takyar's (2017) study from 1990 to 2013, all these councils were functionally active in New York City, 18 possessed active 501(c)(3) nonprofit status during that time, and 6 fit the study's specific National Taxonomy of Exempt

Entities codes. But while the study would classify these 6 community councils as nonprofits that are organizationally distinct alternatives to police, the evidence in this book describes how police integrated themselves into informal social controls like community councils.

One month into my fieldwork, the NYPD fatally shot a thirty-four-year-old African American male named Saheed Vassell in Crown Heights, Brooklyn. The killing followed an increasingly familiar pattern: Vassell was an unarmed Black man holding a small metal object; four officers fired ten shots and killed him (New York State Office of the Attorney General 2019). Despite being locally known as a friendly father who suffered from bipolarism, 911 calls suggested that Vassell was pointing the metal object at pedestrians—prompting officers to shoot on sight. The New York Attorney General's Office, who has jurisdiction to investigate civilian deaths by law enforcement agents, determined that the killing was justified.

This shooting occurred in the Seventy-First Precinct; although it was not one of my focal precincts, I decided to attend its upcoming community council meeting, scheduled just one week after Vassell's death. That meeting was unlike the others I had attended: more people in attendance, especially young adults; more criticisms and rebuttals interrupting speakers; and more demands for police accountability. I learned afterward that the individuals speaking out were organizers from various community groups that comprised the collective called RALLY: Reforms Advancing Long Lives for our Youth. RALLY represents the main activist network in New York City mobilized for demanding police accountability and justice for victims of police violence. Although RALLY represents a coalition of about two hundred member organizations from across all five boroughs, the organizers I met were most active around Central Brooklyn.

Formally, RALLY is an entity with 501(c)(4) nonprofit status. While its member organizations all operate as nonprofits in practice, some have decided not to obtain formal nonprofit status, because they fear that doing so would limit their strategies and messages. To complement and contrast my observation of community councils, I began attending events held by RALLY organizational members, especially those in the Fifty-Fifth and Eightieth Precincts.

Besides community councils and RALLY events, I began observing a third collective after repeatedly encountering its members across my fieldwork: clergy councils. Though I could have studied other groups and institutions with whom police were pursuing relationships, such as schoolteachers or block associations, I chose the clergy council because it appeared to have a prominent role in police-community relations, given the frequency of meetings held within places of worship (see chapter 2). Like community councils, clergy councils are present in every precinct, though at varying levels of activity. I studied the Fifty-Fifth Precinct Clergy Council (currently has 501[c][3] nonprofit status) and the Eightieth's (never had nonprofit status). As networks of religious leaders within precincts, clergy councils exist in cities across the United States (e.g., Braga, Hurcau, and Winship 2008; Brunson et al. 2015; Meares 2002). The NYPD's Community Affairs Bureau describes its Clergy Liaison program as a "partnership" by which "participants [sic] close connections to the community place them in a unique position to identify and intervene in community issues early on, acting as a link between the department and the people they serve."[4] The most active members of clergy councils are oftentimes appointed NYPD Clergy Liaisons; their role requires a nomination from the precinct and approval from NYPD headquarters.

By focusing on police interactions across these three organizational types, my fieldwork provides a composite picture of how police differentially influence public input and the neighborhood organizations that coordinate it. I attended meetings, vigils, cookouts, trainings, and other public events; met people for interviews in their homes and at coffee shops; and tried to maximize variation (rather than representativeness per se) in the people I spoke with and the events I attended. As an Asian American male, I believe I navigated these spaces with more third-party neutrality than I would have with most other demographic combinations. In addition, I was always explicit about my status as a student at the time, and I communicated that implicitly by always carrying a bookbag. I answered all the questions I received honestly. Most commonly, I was asked by residents and officers where I lived, why I was attending meetings, and how their neighborhood issues and meeting attendance compared to others I was observing. Over time, both officers and residents expressed their appreciation for my consistent attendance at neighborhood events. Since these events were public, I audio-recorded discussions for later transcription while also jotting notes into my cellphone. I unpacked my scratches into full field notes as soon as possible after an event ended. For these notes in the pages that follow, my use of quotation marks indicates either audio-recorded statements or those transcribed verbatim.[5]

Throughout my fieldwork, I collected additional data sources to triangulate findings: submitting and appealing Freedom of Information Law requests, scraping NYPD tweets, photographing meeting complaint boards, and requesting access to internal and historical documents from the neighborhood organizations I studied. Given the diversity of data that inform this study, I will continue to discuss my data sources and analytic decisions throughout the text rather than silo them into a formal methodological appendix. Virtually all names and locations used in this study are pseudonyms, with the exception of public officials like the mayor and the NYPD commissioner.

PLAN FOR THE BOOK

The five chapters that follow align with the stages of the Policing Machine. These stages are presented separately for analytic purposes, but the processes actually unfold simultaneously as officers across the city coordinate activities with various neighborhood individuals and groups.

I begin by more fully unpacking the necessity of the Policing Machine—how police seek to direct heterogeneous community demands toward department channels like the Build the Block meetings offered through the Neighborhood Policing program. Department channels for public input are necessary because of—not despite—polarized preferences within the community for ascribing neighborhood problems and, therefore, what police should prioritize: police administration, requiring investments in service provision, or police accountability, requiring the redistribution of state power. By exercising asymmetrical control over the documentation of complaints raised within department channels, police can begin coalescing power around the public value of police's core functions.

Yet the mere introduction of department channels does not guarantee attendance and participation by target audiences. Nor does it help police respond to the increasingly vocal and visible contestation outside meeting venues emerging from unsatisfied residents. In chapter 2, I dig into how police cultivate constituencies as the bottom-up bases of support to which they prefer to hold themselves accountable. This chapter identifies two strategies: establishing an alternative system of neighborhood representation, embodied by community councils, and coordinating access to established audiences, such as through clergy councils.

Constituents scale with power and privilege. In chapter 3, the third stage of the Policing Machine, I detail how police selectively distribute such power and privilege through public resources, regulatory leniency, and coercive enforcement. These are the carrots and sticks the NYPD uses to control and consolidate its constituencies—and quell critics—strategies so key to optimizing their public legitimacy with organizational independence. These decisions reflect just how intimately police shape the landscape of voices, events, and organizations mobilizing around policing in the city.

With empowered constituents, police can now earn and extract the payoff from the Policing Machine. Chapter 4 analyzes how police mobilize the political capital earned (described throughout the previous chapters) to resist institutional change. I emphasize the importance of social media platforms, and what police strategically present in and omit from them, in claiming various kinds of public endorsements. The fifth chapter sees the public push back with ground-level resistance through a series of strategies attending to the complicated realities that complete disengagement with the Policing Machine is risky (since police will continue pursuing it regardless) and that the Policing Machine can still provide valuable public services. I close with the consequences of the Policing Machine, insights into its evolution onto the national stage and, taking the previous chapters as an evidentiary base, starting points toward its de-monopolization.

Together, these chapters offer the vocabulary and the evidence for how police cultivate political power through the machinery of police-community relations—enabling readers to analyze the police department in their own city through the Policing Machine framework.

1

Channeling Heterogeneous Demands

"Tonight, our precinct is really being honored." The March 2019 meeting of the Eightieth Precinct Community Council featured a special guest speaker. The larger than usual audience applauded as the council president announced, "At this time, I give you the patrol chief of the largest police force in the world: Chief Terrence Robinson."

Chief Robinson began with a story. On a Saturday not so long ago, he said, his new neighbors two houses down began playing loud music. "I'm all for playing your music and having a good time and partying, and this, that, and the other. But it was kinda like twelve o'clock in the afternoon, which wasn't necessarily a big deal, but the music was blasting loud enough where the frames on my wall were shaking." Soon, it passed one o'clock. Then two o'clock. And then four and six o'clock. After six hours of the wall-shaking music, Chief Robinson was caught in a bind. Though he could exercise his police authority, new ordinances circumscribed the occasions when officers can order people to turn down their music. He debated dialing 311, the phone number to request nonemergency municipal services, but he wanted to be understanding. But when eight o'clock rolled around, the chief called 911. However, the emergency operators explained there was nothing they could do. The situation ended only when the neighbors turned off their stereo at one o'clock in the morning.

"I share this story with you because—ladies and gentlemen—that should not happen. Somebody here has had a quality-of-life concern or issue that you needed resolved," Chief Robinson said, looking around the room. "Maybe people speeding down a block, maybe somebody walking a pit bull off a leash, maybe somebody smoking marijuana—if you don't like that smell." The chief then simultaneously empathized and solicited empathy: "There's nothing worse in the world than not being able to call somebody. Not being able to get that assistance. Not being able to get that help. I'm gonna be honest with you, that day I felt helpless."

What was the NYPD's solution? Neighborhood Policing. The chief explained that under this initiative, every person in the city has a Neighborhood Coordination Officer (NCO) to call on. He emphasized that those who did not know their NCO's contact information were doing themselves a "major disservice." Neighborhood Policing instituted additional changes: it divided police precincts into four to five smaller sectors; organized quarterly Build the Block meetings run by the NCOs within each sector; and delegated "steady sector" officers to respond to 911 calls, thus freeing up NCOs to deal with community issues.

As the NYPD began rolling out Neighborhood Policing in the years following the murder of Eric Garner, the department's leaders took every opportunity to encourage residents to contact their NCOs and attend Build the Block meetings. For example, the New York City Police Foundation, the department's nonprofit arm, used $200,000 to hire filmmaker Spike Lee's advertising firm to shoot videos for its public engagement campaign on Neighborhood Policing (Kanno-Youngs 2018). On the ground, leaders like Chief Robinson spoke at community events to drum up neighborhood participation. In fact, one of the most striking things about his speech was that he stood before the crowd at a police-community meeting and urged attendees to attend a *different* one: a Build the Block meeting. "We have community council meetings—which is what's going on tonight—but guess what? You may have something in your own area that you might want a cop to handle, be it something small or something big," he noted. "And it's very important that you go to these Build the Block meetings, find out where they are, and share your concerns with that Neighborhood Coordination Officer that's running the meeting" (Eightieth Precinct Community Council, March 2019). Chief Robinson debated calling on audience members to test their knowledge of their NCO's contact information, but he settled on encouraging them to introduce themselves to their NCOs after the meeting to begin building personal relationships. Otherwise, he warned, "you're gonna wait for the crisis to happen and then try to develop that relationship. And that's the wrong way of going about it. . . . Don't call when you need them. Call them now."

This speech reveals how police understand neighborhood problems. First, it showed that substantive law classifying an activity as legal is still insufficient in deterring police action against neighborhood issues that residents identify as problematic. The chief's neighbor did nothing illegal by playing loud music. The chief knew about a recent ordinance that circumscribed police authority in such situations and even confirmed the limited legal authorization when he called 911. Other examples he listed, like walking a dog off leash or smoking marijuana in public, may or may not be illegal activities, depending on the circumstances. But those circumstances, delineated by law, were irrelevant to his purposes here. His point was that any issues perceived by residents as problematic required intervention.

And who should intervene in neighborhood problems? The police, the chief suggested, were a better choice to handle the situation than the resident alone. He recounted how he had considered his options when it came to dealing with his loud neighbors: intervening as a police officer, calling 311, or dialing 911. However, he omitted another, arguably more direct option: simply asking for the music to be lowered in his capacity as a neighbor. He had instead sought state intervention over personal intervention, and instructed audience members to do the same—to contact police as their primary source of help (see Carr 2005). These complaints, he implied, should not wait for the next community council meeting or occupy the scarce resources of emergency service lines. Rather, they should be submitted directly to the NCOs designated for the provision of tailored police services.

—

What I call the Policing Machine unfolds in stages, and this chapter details the first: channeling heterogeneous (that is, multiple kinds of) demands into department channels. Department channels refer to programs and initiatives that invite public input but are fully operated by police departments. Police prefer to direct all community complaints toward department channels because they exercise asymmetrical control over how the neighborhood problems raised within those channels are documented and represented. This intervention is neither passive nor neutral. It is an act of political mobilization that serves to coalesce power as police curate and transform community demands into opportunities to demonstrate the value of police's core functions. In this way, complaints *about* policing can be reframed as community, even grassroots demands for *more* policing.

This chapter offers three key takeaways that are organized around its three main sections. First, it shows polarized preferences among community members regarding what they envision as the institutional priority of police: addressing issues related to either the administration of policing or the accountability of police. A problem's ascription shapes the applicable solutions: issues of police administration foreground investments in service provision, while issues of police accountability implicate the redistribution of state power. Examining how community members ascribe neighborhood problems helps reveal the sources to which they attribute their specific issues, and that necessarily frames the appropriate solution. But although framing the problem is framing the solution, not everyone agrees how problems should be framed. This diverse ideological landscape fuels the Policing Machine.

Second, I will demonstrate that police are not bystanders within this landscape of polarized preferences in police priorities. The heterogeneity of neighborhood issues and the disagreement over how to ascribe them is precisely what motivates police to establish department channels for public input. Department channels, often introduced in response to controversial incidents, are generative for police as a political space for building consensus and coalescing power around the particular ways *they* ascribe neighborhood problems. My analysis of how officers recorded and represented complaints raised in Neighborhood Policing meetings demonstrates how they transformed complaints into the most organizationally salient ascription: whatever the issue, it seemed, it could be viewed as one rooted in police administration and thus solvable through service provision. Police may be willing to share state power, but only with those uninterested in redistributing it away from police.

The third takeaway in this chapter is that the exclusion from department channels of community members who ascribe neighborhood problems in alternative ways (particularly as police accountability issues) motivates the initiation of independent channels. Whereas police exercise asymmetrical control over department channels, independent channels involve challenges to the police. These initiatives range from city hall rallies around particular cases of police violence to digital strategies that directly undermine department channels. At the very first stage of the Policing Machine, strategic resistance from dissenting voices is already emerging.

THE LANDSCAPE OF COMMUNITY DEMANDS

To get a sense of what residents across my study believe police should prioritize, I asked interviewees to complete a "circle exercise." First, I asked them to list all the community organizations they know that deal with policing in any capacity. Next, I asked them to identify what should be the NYPD's "number one priority today." I then handed them a sheet with three circles, the innermost providing space for them to write their answer. Finally, I repeated their list of community organizations back to them, asking them to write each organization in one of the three circles, depending on how well the organization's goals aligned with the NYPD priority they identified.

Since the circle exercise was embedded within the interviews I conducted, I approached it with a logic of "sequential interviewing" (Small 2009). By treating each interview as a case unto itself, I was guided by variation, not representativeness. I aimed to learn about the landscape of community perspectives on police from stakeholders active in policing issues, and so I spoke with people present at meetings, protests, and policing events I attended—those residents who were in the ears or faces of police officers each day. The voices below reflect not a random sample of individuals or households but a sample of engaged individuals interacting with police through official and unofficial channels. This exercise was important in identifying the distribution of people's perspectives within and across the particular spaces I was studying.

The circle exercise showed me that residents were divided on their preferred police priorities and on which organizations advanced their particular interests. Those who spoke about issues like practicing sufficient trust and ensuring that police were optimally deployed to reduce crime were talking about the administration of policing. Their counterparts, who could be found in separate meeting spaces, focused instead on issues of police accountability, ranging from holding individual officers responsible for violence to institutional transformations to decrease police's role in neighborhoods. These frameworks, as mentioned above, matter because they imply a different set of solutions: whereas expanded service provision may alleviate some issues of police administration, police accountability requires examining the distribution of state power.

Some community members used their diagram to prioritize increased investment in initiatives to improve police-community relations. For example, Barbara is an African American resident in the Fifty-Fifth Precinct who is a social worker by training (Barbara, interview, July 9, 2019). Since she was young, she had wanted to become a law enforcement officer, but she was unable to join in the 1970s because of her height and need for eyeglasses. In retirement, however, she decided to sign up as an NYPD auxiliary officer. Auxiliary officers are citizen volunteers who lack arresting power and do not carry firearms, but their uniforms are virtually indistinguishable from those of sworn officers. Only the observant would notice the word *auxiliary* inscribed at the top of their NYPD badges. Though Barbara held this role, she had no priority access to the precinct; I met her at a police-community meeting she attended to raise complaints about her blocked driveway. As she told me, "A lot of officers really don't like auxiliary, they think that they're fools for taking on a job that has no pay and is dangerous."

Barbara's number-one priority for the NYPD is, in her words, "public safety and good community relations" (see fig. 1.1, left). When I asked her to rank community organizations in terms of their alignment with that priority, she placed the Fifty-Fifth Precinct Community Council in the inner circle, the precinct's clergy council in

FIGURE 1.1 Example "circle exercises" from two residents.
Note: Blurred areas refer to specific organizations or precincts. On the left, the blurred portion refers to the Fifty-Fifth Precinct. On the right, the blurred portion lists RALLY.
Source: Constructed by author.

the middle circle, and the Boys and Girls Clubs in the outer circle. In justifying the central placement of the community council, Barbara explained, "Certainly, I believe that issues brought up in the meetings are brought to the [precinct] commanding officer's attention, and if enough people are concerned about it and bringing it up enough, it will be addressed." She also referenced the council president by name and said that given the length of her tenure, the president "knows people and knows how to make things move." Of the outer circle, she noted that the Boys and Girls Clubs were involved in safety, but "it's about recreation more so." Despite being less familiar with the Fifty-Fifth Precinct Clergy Council, she explained that she entered it in the middle circle because "people in the church should be caring for the community, and to have the police in communication with that should be good."

Those affiliated with community councils and clergy councils completed the circle exercise in similar ways. Mr. Holloway is the president of the Eightieth Precinct Community Council. When I asked him to identify community organizations that deal with police, he named only three different precincts' community councils. He suggested that the NYPD's number-one priority should be "funding for community councils," and then he wrote all three community councils in the inner circle (Holloway, interview, July 10, 2018). When I gave him the chance to add organizations, he declined, reiterating that the councils he'd already included represented the best examples of organizations improving policing in New York City.

Mr. Holloway's vice president on the Eightieth Precinct Community Council, Laurette Simmonds, believes that the NYPD's number-one priority should be to "continue respecting each other" (Laurette Simmonds, interview, September 21, 2018). In her view, officers and civilians could be "not nice" to one another, though respect was important to maintaining relations. When asked to include in the diagram the three community organizations she noted—community councils, Youth Explorers (an NYPD youth program), and Save Our Streets (a violence interruption program)—she put all of them in the inner circle. The first two, she commented, did not require explanations, and the third was included because "they work closely with the precinct." I asked whether there were any organizations that she would place in the outer circles, and she reluctantly replied, "I guess probably the gangs, but I don't want to put that." Another participant,

Pastor Campbell, was a member of the Eightieth Precinct Clergy Council. He identified the NYPD's top priority as "remodel[ing] precincts to make people feel welcomed and improv[ing] services" (Campbell, interview, September 17, 2018). Like Barbara, Mr. Holloway, and Laurette, Pastor Campbell identified clergy councils, community councils, Save Our Streets, and other partnering organizations as being the most aligned with advancing that priority.

In contrast to those who focused on investments in improving the administration of policing, other community members focused on police accountability and the need to redistribute state power. For example, June is the codirector of Justice Now—a social justice organization under the umbrella of Reforms Advancing Long Lives for our Youth (RALLY) that specifically organizes events and campaigns aiding the family members of NYPD victims. When I explained to her that I was interested in "studying police-community relations in New York City," she immediately corrected me: "That's the wrong question. The question about bettering police-community relations is actually a rhetorical tool that's used by the NYPD and the [mayoral] administration to distract from the real issues" (June, interview, August 4, 2018). The real issues, she said, were the "abusive power, race-based policing, and policing based on other forms of profiling, and the systemic lack of accountability for officers that brutalize people [and] commit misconduct." Investments in improving police-community relations, June thinks, both detracted and distracted from the pursuit of police accountability by displacing systemic reforms in favor of "minor tweaks"—and minor tweaks were not enough to prevent the next police shooting (or the one after that).

In the circle exercise, June articulated what should be the NYPD's priority as "hold[ing] cops who commit misconduct/brutality/crimes/etc. accountable" and "decreas[ing] its role in our communities" (see fig. 1.1, right). The only priority-aligned organization June identified was RALLY, because "depending on how you count it, it's like a hundred organizations." As a member of the RALLY steering committee, she emphasized that her priorities are the "ideas that our organizations have unified around, so there's great alignment." When I prompted her to think of any other organizations working on her priorities, she demurred, "Obviously, organizations on the other side of the political spectrum," then specified the Police Union and the Police Foundation, both of which she decided to write on the corner of the sheet, deviating from my instructions by recording them outside all three circles. When I asked her about community councils, June explained that everyone agrees that officers should be disciplined if they are doing "bad things and committing crimes." However, "the understanding of what is 'doing bad things' and what is 'committing crimes' is different." I asked June to add community councils to the diagram; again, the councils were relegated to the corner of the sheet, outside the circles. Twice, she chose an option I hadn't presented.

Other policing activists completed the circle diagram similarly. For example, a twenty-seven-year-old Brooklyn native named Phil had been actively engaged in policing issues since attending college at a historically Black institution. At first, he identified the NYPD's top priority as "reform," but then he remembered how a professor once explained to him that "reform might just end up being the next evolution of oppression" (Phil, interview, July 20, 2018). He crossed out that word and wrote "transform," telling me that such action "ensures that you cut that shit down by the knees and you're actually working to fix the problem." He elaborated on transform by writing "moving from a crime fighting organization to a community protection organization." When I asked Phil to begin ranking organizations across the three circles, he clarified: "Three is the furthest, correct? Well, you already know where I'm gonna put this one. Let's just get this one out the way." The community council went in the third, outermost circle. Then came the National Lawyers Guild in the middle circle and RALLY-affiliated organizations in the inner circle.

I was taken by the fact that other policing activists did not even think of listing community councils as a community organization centered on policing. When I raised community councils as an option, several recorded these outside the three circles—again, an option I did not present. These respondents seemed to agree that improving police-community relations would only come as a by-product of greater police accountability. For example, Bill is the founder of a Manhattan-based community nonprofit that focuses on police transformation. He described the importance of properly framing the problem: "The way to characterize the problem is, we have a problem with abusive and discriminatory policing, and that's inflicted upon vulnerable communities—Black and Brown communities in our city" (Bill, interview, July 30, 2018). He understood that defining the problem as abusive policing rather than poor community relations changed the policy solution: "So the way to address the problem is not to have more dialogue or to have more neighborhood policing... the way to fix the problem is to end these bad practices." Doing so would, he said, naturally improve the trust that the police sought from the public.

Following the circle exercise, I further surveyed community stakeholders by asking, "Do you think police-community relations in your community have significantly worsened, slightly worsened, stayed the same, slightly improved, or significantly improved?" Following the pattern seen above, respondents focused on the administration of policing shared a similar view. Mr. Holloway responded that police-community relations have "significantly improved" (Holloway, interview, July 10, 2018). He explained, "I know when I took over [as president of the community council], we ain't have no voice. Now we have a big voice." Alisha Grey, leader of the Brooklyn Gardens Tenant Association and the newest member of the Fifty-Fifth Precinct Community Council, responded more cautiously: "They've improved. I'll say 'significant.' I can say that" (Alisha Grey, interview, March 9, 2019). But Reverend Powell, a member of the Fifty-Fifth Precinct Clergy Council, had no hesitation: "Significantly improved—a lot" (Powell, interview, August 29, 2018). He cited several programs—Neighborhood Policing, civilian observation patrol, and youth programs—as examples of how "that blue wall [of silence] has come down."

In contrast, the most common response among police accountability activists was "stayed the same"—they believe there are no police-community relations, and that hasn't changed. In other words, most of them disputed the underlying implication of my question: Bill and June quickly responded, "That's the wrong question," because the focus should be on police accountability (Bill, interview, July 30, 2018; June, interview, August 4, 2018); Linda, that the question "is based on the premise that they were ever good" (Linda, interview, August 8, 2018); and Nasir, the founding director of a RALLY-affiliated organization, that the idea of police-community relations "doesn't make any sense to me," given police's long history of abusive enforcement (Nasir, interview, July 6, 2018).

Amid such fundamental divergences in community views about police priorities, the police department is anything but a neutral actor. In order to maintain legitimacy and independence, police need to build community consensus on the particular ways *they* ascribe neighborhood problems. Therefore, as described next, Neighborhood Policing was designed to fit with the police administration framework—funneling local demands through a department channel to offer increased service provision and improved execution of policing.

ASYMMETRICAL CONTROL OVER DEPARTMENT CHANNELS

To analyze the implementation of Neighborhood Policing, I attended forty Build the Block meetings, where I heard residents voice 294 complaints between April 2018 and September 2019. Because these meetings were public, I audio-recorded and later transcribed the complaints; my efforts should have simply duplicated the NCOs', as they were supposed to record every complaint on a whiteboard. (That only happened at twenty-six of the forty meetings I attended.) The whiteboards offered me, as a researcher, a rare opportunity to see police discretion unfold in real time. I photographed the "board-recorded" complaints for later comparison with the actual language of residents' complaints based on the audio recordings. NCOs were further required to submit all the complaints made at the meetings to their supervisors via organizational records. Then, in what normally became the only public record of each Build the Block meeting, the precinct would summarize the meeting discussions on Twitter. Using these sources, I tracked meeting complaints, from the resident's mouth, to meeting whiteboards, to organizational records, and finally onto Twitter.

These records show one reason why police accountability is so elusive: police fundamentally disagree that they have done anything wrong in the first place. Organizational sociologists describe how the policies and practices of a given institutional environment can act as powerful "myths," the incorporation of which provides "an account of activities that protects the organization from having its conduct questioned" (Meyer and Rowan 1977, 349). From writing issues on whiteboards to engaging the public on social media, Neighborhood Policing purportedly features some of the best practices in community policing. In practice, however, its implementation is no less political

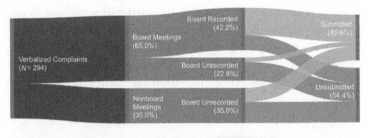

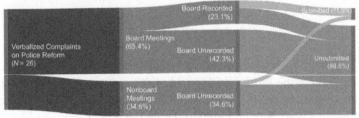

FIGURE 1.2 Flow of total complaints (*top*) and police accountability complaints
(*bottom*), from verbalization to submission.
Note: Thickness of lines is proportional to the percentage of complaints.
Source: Constructed by author.

than its organizers: the goal is to mobilize stakeholders' support for
police's particular understanding of whose actions were right, wrong,
and/or justified. Institutional mythmaking by the armed representatives of the state can have violent consequences.

Figure 1.2 illustrates the flow of total complaints, from verbalization by resident to submission by officer. At "board meetings," those
in which NCOs used a whiteboard to record grievances, some but
not all complaints were recorded on the board, and some but not all
were submitted into organizational records. At "nonboard meetings,"
where NCOs did not use a whiteboard, all complaints went unrecorded on the board, though some were still submitted into organizational records. Of the 294 complaints I heard residents verbalize
at meetings, NCOs submitted just 45.6 percent into organizational
records (fig. 1.2, top). More than half the community complaints were
omitted—never seen or heard by police supervisors or the wider
public. More pointedly, over the year and a half's worth of police-
community meetings I observed, the odds of a resident's complaint
being submitted into organizational records was about the same as a
coin toss.

Notably, the unsubmitted complaints were not completely random. Within the meetings I attended, 88.5 percent of the complaints demanding institutional police reforms were never submitted into organizational records (fig. 1.2, bottom).[1] In other words, no trace of these community demands for police reform now exists within the police department: supervisors never saw them, the residents who voiced them may not follow up, and researchers relying on administrative data would draw inaccurate conclusions about what engaged residents want from their police.

These patterns put numbers to the experiences of many who never returned to Build the Block meetings. As a department channel, these meetings empower police officers with asymmetrical control over citizen complaints. Officers are not passively receiving and recording the complaints that emerge within Build the Block meetings; they are actively curating *which* complaints get documented and internalized within the police department.

How Neighborhood Policing Ascribes Neighborhood Problems

The NYPD's ascription of neighborhood problems to issues of police administration rather than police accountability is actually encoded into a departmental form—one that all NCOs are required to complete to document community complaints and that I obtained via a Freedom of Information Law request. Figure 1.3 shows the options presented on the form. The form's first prompt, "Crime Condition," reveals departmental priorities in identifying and tracking only the subset of community complaints that utilizes police services. The options presented include "Homeless Issues (Encampments/Shelters/Panhandling)," "BBQs" (e.g., parties on sidewalks), and "Larcenies" (often package thefts). At best, issues about overpolicing would have to fit into catch-all categories of "Other Quality of Life" or perhaps "Other Crime." *Nowhere* on this list is there anything that points to the police department itself—its policies, practices, or officers—as possible sources of community complaints. As a reflection of organizational intent, the drop-down menu of crime type options ensures that even the most committed NCO who wants to document complaints that are actually representative of public input cannot do so effectively. Mandatory organizational documents also communicate

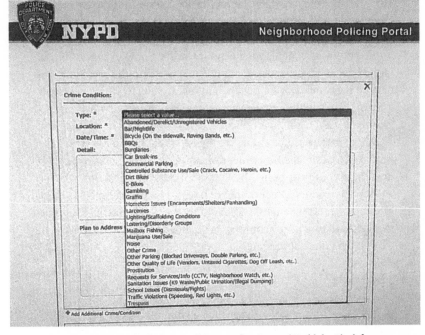

FIGURE 1.3 Options for "crime condition type" on internal Build the Block forms.
Source: Freedom of Information Law request.

priorities to NCOs about what they should be recording—complaints
that consume, rather than critique, police services.

In following the form, NCOs transform complaints into organizationally meaningful tasks by applying an enforcement framework to
the community grievances they *heard* at Build the Block meetings,
not necessarily what the residents *said*. A routine 80C[2] meeting shows
how. The NCO sergeant in charge of Neighborhood Policing for the
entire Eightieth Precinct opened that meeting: "These meetings are
for you. You guys came here because you care. You live here, you work
here, or maybe you just go through the neighborhood" (Sector 80C,
March 2019). The sergeant, like Chief Robinson in the opening of this
chapter, told residents that their NCOs should be seen as "your go-to
people," given that 911 is reserved for emergencies and 311 is "flawed."
The relationship worked like this: "Everything that you guys give us,
we write a transcript on this board and we take notes, and we go back
and do our little report, and we kind of pay attention to these con-

cerns rather heavily, because they're coming from you. You took the time to come here and give us that information, so we want to address them." He primed the audience with examples of relevant complaints, including "people outside drinking" and "there's homeless guys on my corner." Before turning the mic back over to the NCOs, the sergeant emphasized, "We like people to be nosy neighbors. It helps us do our job."

Two complaints were raised at this meeting. The first was made by a resident who began, "Well, we've had some concerns in our building because recently, we had some people come in and take boxes out." The day before, the resident reported, the building superintendent had showed them surveillance footage of a woman entering the building with a shopping cart, filling it with packages, taking the elevator up and down to open them, and then leaving with only the items she wanted. The NCOs recorded the issue as "package" on the whiteboard and documented it as "Larcenies" in the formal organizational write-up (fig. 1.4a).

The second complaint came from a resident who stated that "the corner of Webster and Grand Avenue needs to be paid attention to, especially as the weather gets warm." The NCO sergeant asked whether the resident had noticed anything in particular, but the resident was hesitant. "I mean, if you tell us to look at the corner," the sergeant prodded, "we'll look at the corner. But if there's something that you can say that you have seen at some point or maybe a particular time of day that we need to be paying better attention over there—is there illegal activity occurring over there? Maybe in the evenings or mornings? Drugs? Cars flying through stop signs?" Still tentative, the resident revealed haltingly, "Well, it was mentioned to me last year, somebody said, people saying drugs." The NCOs recorded this issue on the whiteboard as "Narco," and they submitted it in their formal write-up as "Controlled Substance Use/Sale (Crack, Cocaine, Heroin, etc.)" (fig. 1.4b). From a meeting at which residents raised concerns about package thefts and were pressed into specifying unsubstantiated drug activity, the NYPD now has documented community complaints of larcenies and narcotics. For a police supervisor reviewing these records and making policy decisions, seeing a cluster of larcenies and narcotics complaints would require a qualitatively different law enforcement response than that to package thefts. As explained

Neighborhood Policing Meeting Reviewed
Meeting ID:

Crime Type : Larcenies
Location : ▓▓▓▓▓▓▓▓▓▓
Date/Time : ▓▓▓▓▓▓

Detail :
A unknown female did remove a package from the lobby of above listed location.

Plan to address Crime/Condition :
NCO will keep in contact with complainant and attempt to obtain footage from the building super. As well as conduct directed patrols and interiors inside of above listed location.

Crime Condition :

Crime Type : Controlled Substance Use/Sale (Crack, Cocaine, Heroin, etc.)
Location : ▓▓▓▓▓▓▓▓▓▓
Date/Time : ▓▓▓▓▓▓

Detail :
People selling drugs on the corner of ▓▓▓▓▓▓ and ▓▓▓▓▓ during the summer time

Plan to address Crime/Condition :
NCO will keep in contact with complainent and conduct directed patrols around the area.

FIGURES 1.4A AND 1.4B Two examples of organizational
records of Build the Block complaints.
Note: Parts of the records are blurred to anonymize the identities of the precincts studied.
Source: Freedom of Information Law request.

more below, documenting complaints in this way authorizes NCOs to conduct patrols both inside and around buildings to mitigate such "community complaints."

NCOs responded to complaints about community violence, especially recent incidents within the precinct, as opportunities to mobilize attendees—not just as police's eyes and ears but as their voices. In an 80B meeting, a resident said she had read a news article describing a tense relationship between the police department and the Brooklyn district attorney following a series of recent shootings (Sector 80B, August 2019). An NCO complained in response that the suspects they arrest are "back on the street before our paperwork is done." Another officer agreed: "There are plenty of people with double-digit gun charges walking around, arrested all the time with guns, whether they were involved in a shooting or not, maybe they were picked up, but it happens way too much." The resident, now oriented away from their worry over a poor relationship between the DA and the NYPD, asked whether there was anything they could do to assist. The NCO retorted that all police could do was "make the arrest, fill out the paperwork," and that the responsibility ultimately lies with the DA's office. "You can contact them [the DA's office] about things at the community level and ask them why is this happening," he suggested. The NCO actively encouraged meeting attendees to take political action by contacting their district attorney, apparently to motivate greater deference by the DA to the police.

NCOs in a different precinct made an identical request, seeking to mobilize meeting attendees to exercise their political voices in ways that advanced the Policing Machine. In 55C, the NCOs encouraged residents to "write a letter to the local district attorney or write a letter to your city council member" to communicate that issues like the nonprosecution of marijuana constitute a "community problem" that residents want solved (Sector 55C, February 2019). In fact, in the following quarter these NCOs went a step further and stated that they would facilitate the delivery of such letters to the DA: "You guys, if you wanna address that problem and help us, everybody on the block, get together, we'll write up a letter, I'll stamp it, mail it with you over to the DA's office—asking 'please prosecute more weed arrests, especially in the area.' They do listen, you're voting citizens" (Sector 55C, May 2019). Significantly, NCOs are not mobilizing residents to contact elected officials or district attorneys to secure police accountability. Instead, these direct, political mobilization efforts are invoked only for issues the NCOs themselves interpret as ways to expand the consequences of their enforcement practices.

When residents did raise issues of police accountability, NCO responses reveal how the Neighborhood Policing program was premised on the sufficiency of existing legal remedies. NCOs understand complaints about police violence as issues of *trust*, which Neighborhood Policing was created to resolve. For example, at a 55A meeting, a resident complained, "You call the police, 'Oh, your son is having a problem, your daughter is having a problem,' then next thing they coming, boom, boom, boom, they shot your kid down" (Sector 55A, September 2019). Then the resident voiced a lament: "And I don't understand why this is happening. Why can't they just talk? The minute they turn their back, they get shot." The NCO responded, "So, that's what this is about. The department is going in a different direction now. We're trying to reach out and build a stronger relationship and build that trust." By interpreting the complaint as an issue of trust rather than one of unjustified force or insufficient police accountability, the NCO pivots, pointing to their very position as an NCO as evidence that the department is already addressing this issue through Neighborhood Policing. Unsurprisingly, Freedom of Information Law records show that this complaint went unrecorded in the meeting's formal write-up.

For quality-of-life issues, NCOs express a similar confidence in existing police accountability and legal remedies. At an 80B meeting, a middle-aged African American resident named Marcus asked the meeting's first question: "What's the purpose for unmarked cars riding around in Brooklyn? . . . These unmarked cars, Fords, young guys, stopping random cars—for no reason" (Sector 80B, May 2019). Marcus said he'd recently been stopped, though the plainclothes officers said it was a mistake and did not detain him. NCO Geller responded that "there could've been a crime going on with your car as a description and that's why they stopped it. And once they realized that it wasn't you, they went on their way." Marcus rebutted by noting that these stops were clearly patterned, and most seemed "frivolous"—as if the officers were simply "joyriding."

Officer Geller defended the unnamed officers: "Their purpose is to prevent crime, just like the regular marked cars." In fact, Geller insisted, "there's always a reason for a stop. . . . Maybe you don't know it, maybe it's not explained to you every single time, but the police do what they do for a reason." Citing his personal experiences and those of his friends, Marcus continued to press Geller, saying how "it's like a big joke," because officers rarely even identified themselves in these stops. Geller redirected focus to the officers' positive contributions and public service: "Those are the same guys who are getting the guns off the street, who are going on those major calls of robberies, shots fired, people getting shot, those are those guys." NCO Mora concluded the conversation by moving on: "Anybody else has questions?"

Later in the meeting, Marcus raised another question: "What about the excessive ticketing in our community?" In his twenty years in the neighborhood, he said, he'd never received a ticket. But since the onset of gentrification, he and his friends had received many tickets—implying that the correlation is not coincidental. NCO Mora asked Marcus what the stated violation was on the ticket—no signaling—and then recommended he pursue existing legal remedies: "Okay. What happens when you receive a ticket with the NYPD, you can fight it in court." Marcus clarified that his grievance was not about his *personal* ticket but rather that police policies and gentrification were communitywide policy issues: "I'm saying it's the community at large feeling pressure from the increase in cops in this community, that they have been targeted, and I didn't believe it until it started happening to me. So I'm saying that there's a problem with that—there's a problem with the influx of cops . . . that they're targeting Black folks." At this, Officer Mora doubled down on her earlier response: "If you receive a summons for any violation, if you feel like you unjustly— doesn't matter if you're Black, white, Hispanic, Asian, whatever it is— if you received a summons and you feel like you didn't deserve it, you fight it in court." Like Marcus's first complaint, this issue was omitted from organizational records summarizing the meeting. I never saw Marcus at another Build the Block meeting.

Drawing these connections between mandatory paperwork and NCO practices provides evidence of how the NYPD as an organization wants its NCOs to manage neighborhood problems. Across the precincts I studied, these officers applied an enforcement framework to transform and record complaints in organizationally salient ways. Doing so either omitted or repackaged complaints about police accountability into ones about improving the administration of policing, setting the possible options for how to resolve them.

How Neighborhood Policing "Solves" Neighborhood Problems

The manner in which Neighborhood Policing ascribes neighborhood problems necessitates the expansion of police services. Many complaints raised at Build the Block meetings featured residents demanding both expanded police services and increased police accountability. However, Neighborhood Coordination Officers often focused on the authorization of police action without accountability for the various social and interpersonal factors that residents wanted NCOs to consider. For instance, at a 55C meeting the residents in attendance primarily sought police help with motorcycle crews riding throughout the neighborhood (Sector 55C, May 2019). They complained that the bikers rode so fast and had such loud motorcycles that walls shook, sleep was disrupted, and crosswalks became uncrossable. NCO Malone responded by citing NYPD policies prohibiting the chasing of motorcycles, on the basis that such high-speed pursuits pose additional community dangers. A resident named Devin agreed that chasing added to the dangers but asked about an option before needing to engage in a chase: "Can you not speak to people?" NCO Brannigan responded, "We know who these guys are, [the] Auto-Larceny [Unit] is arresting them, we've summoned and arrested them." Devin contested that he did not support "people getting arrested. I'm not for that, I'm not for that."

Officer Malone clarified: "It's not a matter of people getting arrested. There has to be consequences to actions. Somebody can tell somebody until they're blue in the face, and they're not going to care." Following a common rhetorical strategy police use to stigmatize (Fassin 2013; Thai 2022), Officer Brannigan asserted a categorical difference between Devin's character and that of the motorcyclists: "You're a normal, decent, god-loving man. If I come to you, 'Hey, sir, do me a favor, just don't ride your motorcycle on the street for me?' You're gonna do exactly that—you're gonna go, 'No problem. I'm gonna move it off the sidewalk and I'm gonna do what I can.' . . . Unfortunately, just by their behavior in general, a lot of times [the motorcyclists] ignore me. They just straight ignore me." As if to ask what else he was supposed to do, Brannigan mentioned his obligation at that point to take direct action: "Unfortunately, I am still the law. It sucks. I don't want to do it. I don't want to put my hands on anybody." While Devin continued to raise alternatives, such as confiscating the motorcycles, the NCOs insisted that they already had a plan in place. For weeks, they said, the NCOs had been organizing a coordinated effort with the NYPD Vice Squad, the Department of Buildings, the Fire Department, and fire marshals to conduct a MARCH operation (multiagency response to community hot spots) targeting the building where the motorcyclists congregated—a spot the NYPD also believed to be an illegal nightclub. Rather than "burden shuffling" the complaint to another agency (Herring 2019), the police department had organized a collaborative enforcement plan that was not going to be overturned by grievances residents raised during the Build the Block meeting.

At this, a motorcyclist and resident named Luke stood to raise his concerns about police sweeps and false positives—which he thought would be exacerbated by the "enhanced enforcement action" of this joint effort. Once before, he said, when walking home from the corner store, he'd been stopped by police officers, instructed to go up against a nearby wall, and booked for two nights in jail. There were two bags of weed on the ground—neither were Luke's. NCO Malone called it "really bad luck." Luke responded that because he rides a motorcycle and is often outside working on it, he feared he'd be "caught up again" in the enhanced enforcement action. NCO Brannigan stepped in to recommend that Luke and all the other residents proactively cooperate with police: "I gotta identify who's the problem, which is why I said email me plate numbers, description of bikes, send me pictures off your security footage—because now I know exactly who I'm dealing with." If citizens shared such "evidence" with Brannigan, then he could forward it to fellow officers and say, "That's the guy you want to get, because he's causing the community problem." According to the NCOs, Luke's best bet for avoiding a false arrest was to *join* the police's enforcement project. That way, Brannigan assured Luke, police would focus on these targets and "leave you alone."

Luke's case exemplifies NCOs' propensity to accept the community's complaint but not its proposed solutions. The 55C NCOs recorded this issue in their organizational write-up as "Reckless Motorcycles—All Times." Despite attendees' concerns about overenforcement and explicit preferences for alternatives to enforcement, the proposed plan of action that NCOs submitted was for "additional traffic enforcement," "further enforcement on a possible motorcycle/bottle club," a request for "an all out post [to] be placed near this location for omnipresence," and "daily directed patrols to monitor these conditions." No matter what concerns residents raised, the solution both before and after the meeting was to conduct more enforcement. And the only way for neighbors to protect themselves from the increased enforcement was to help police better target those deemed deserving of enforcement.

The exchange just described is not unique: organizational records reveal a pattern of NCOs' preferences for solutions centered on enforcement services. Table 1.1 shows the types of solutions that NCOs proposed in their write-ups for Build the Block meetings I

TABLE 1.1. Frequency of NCOs' proposed solutions in formal write-ups

Proposed solution	Example	N (%)
Increase police presence	"NCO Eddie will conduct directed patrol within the vicinity of the church and schools" (Sector 55E, December 2018)	72 (27.2)
Interagency/Dept. forwarding	"Will forward complaint to DOT [Department of Transportation]" (Sector 55B, September 2018)	68 (25.7)
Enforcement action	"Conferral with S.O.L [Special Operations Lieutenant] to conduct S.N.E.U Op [Street Narcotics Enforcement Unit Operation] at the location" (Sector 80A, July 2019)	65 (24.5)
Mediation/ Nonagency outreach	"Will speak to other residents at location and advise them about illegal dumping and come up with a solution amongst the residents" (Sector 55D, September 2019)	33 (12.5)
Provide literature	"NCOs provided attending community members with literature containing strategies to protect against identity theft. NCOs also discussed monitoring credit reports and bank accounts" (Sector 55C, February 2019)	13 (4.9)
Contact NCOs/311/911	"Gave contact info to complainant, asked him to reach out to NCO while noise is happening for quicker response" (Sector 80B, November 2018)	9 (3.4)
Follow up	"NCO will keep in contact with complainant and attempt to obtain footage from the building super" (Sector 80C, March 2019)	5 (1.9)
Total		265

Note: Complaints could involve multiple proposed solutions.

attended. The most common solution was to increase police presence via conducting additional directed patrols, making an appearance at a location to deter unwanted activity, and so on. Despite NCOs explicitly proposing enforcement action in only a quarter of the written complaints, officers often stated in meetings that they may be NCOs, but "at the end of the day, we're cops" who must enforce the law (Sector 55D, June 2018). In other words, the threat of enforcement underpinned every NCO interaction, reflecting the coercive foundation of policing—even for interactions initiated in nonenforcement contexts.

Neighborhood Policing features the inevitable expansion of police services because NCOs exercise their discretion to propose police interventions, even when residents demand police accountability, explicitly suggest nonpolice interventions, or help legalize an activity and render it perfectly legal. Exemplifying the first condition, a man named Mr. Herring came to the Sector 80A meeting because his son had received a ticket for riding a bicycle in Jackson Park, where it was not allowed, but many others had done so without penalty. As evidence, Mr. Herring brought cell phone photographs of others freely riding their bicycles and even walking their dogs, another prohibited use of the park (Sector 80A, July 2019). Further, he explained, after his teenage son received the ticket, a patrol car followed the boy out of the park and back to his home. NCO Musa explained that he was not there and did not know the son's "situation," but "it's all up to the discretion of the officer what he's gonna write a summons for and what he's not gonna write a summons [for]." Mr. Herring suggested that the discretion was biased and unfairly targeted his son.

NCO Petroni grew agitated and intervened: "You can say that, that's fine, double standard, whatever you want to call it. You know there were shots fired, right? Washington Place shots fired, shots fired at Jones and Mott." Officer Petroni explained how Mr. Herring's building "is a gang-prone location"; claimed the son was "associated with known gang members"; and, given the recent shootings near the park, "there's zero discretion within the confines of the park—zero discretion for gang members and their associates." Mrs. Herring now refuted his statement: "My son is not a gang member." But Petroni denied he ever implied that: "I didn't say that. . . . Your son was *associated* with known gang members."

Officer Musa cited the community's demand for police enforcement: "The neighborhood has spoken, they need the New York City Police Department to get known gang members out of these parks so nobody gets shot." The discussion remained heated until Mr. Herring exited the auditorium. At his departure, this complex discussion about gang enforcement, discretionary policing, and double standards was translated onto the whiteboard as "Dog Walking—Jackson Park." This translation carried over to the formal write-up, where NCOs documented the issue as "dogs off leash in the early morning and late evenings." These officers proposed that they "will speak with dog owners and advise them of the leash law and issue summonses when necessary." Whereas Mr. Herring wanted his complaint about unequal policing resolved by reducing the overpolicing of his son and his son's friends, the NCOs recorded the complaint as a request for increased enforcement of certain park rules. Whether Mr. Herring's son is genuinely gang affiliated or not is beside the point of how NCOs deployed the unaccountable classification to justify both unequal and greater enforcement action.

The second variation on NCO discretion took the form of write-ups that proposed police interventions even when residents had explicitly suggested nonpolice solutions. To begin an 80C meeting, NCOs raised a pattern of robberies and after-school bullying in a centrally located park surrounded by multiple middle schools (Sector 80C, June 2019). An older African American resident named Jim Washington recalled how "it was happening when I was a pre-teen." The NCOs welcomed the confirmation: "Okay, so it hasn't stopped." Washington affirmed that, but then he suggested one effective solution the community had tried in the past: coordinate with parents of current and past students and "get them to stand outside on the street and basically talk to all the children and watch people coming and going. They know who the kids are." While the robbing and bullying issue was raised initially by the NCOs rather than a resident, it was nonetheless recorded on a whiteboard with keywords from the discussion: "Tenant patrols with parents/Kids—travelling—to school and home—safe zones—safety zones for kids—next year plan." The content of the board recording seemingly reflected NCO awareness that the proposal was for a nonpolice intervention. Nonetheless, the issue was entered in organizational documents as "School Issues (Dismissals/Fights)." For the plan of action, NCOs wrote that they would "conduct directed patrols in and around the park during school dismissals to deter crimes around school dismissal time." Washington's proposal for parent patrols was organizationally converted into a request for police patrols.

In the third instance, NCOs proposed enforcement action even when legalization had rendered an activity perfectly legal. At a Sector 55C meeting, NCO Shea responded to a request for an update on marijuana laws by explaining how smoking marijuana outside is "gonna be legal soon" and how "the culture of the country is going that direction—and the culture of New York City—where marijuana is becoming far more acceptable, just like drinking is" (Sector 55C, February 2019). Then Officer Shea asked the resident: "Are you having a problem with that right now in your building, or in the area, just outside? I mean, anywhere specific? Even if all I can do is drop by a few times a week, turn on my lights, and crank my radio up, makes people uncomfortable." The NCO plainly recognized the growing legal and cultural acceptance of marijuana use, yet he suggested workarounds to get the police involved by addressing the "ancillary problems that come from it [marijuana]."

When the resident added that they had seen someone smoking inside a vacant house next door, Officer Shea grew excited: "Oh, vacant house, that's a whole 'nother issue." He instructed the resident to call or email him the address, and he promised to "come up with some sort of solution—it might not be arresting them for the marijuana, but if it's a vacant house, they're trespassing, even if it's something small like every time I drive by, I jump out of the car and make sure they're not there. Then all of a sudden they're nervous and they don't want to go back there, and they never come back—hopefully, ideally." After the meeting, the Fifty-Fifth Precinct tweeted about how the NCOs received "community complaints about . . . marijuana" and were working to address them. Publicly representing Build the Block meetings by taking such angles communicates what goes on there in a way that foreseeably encourages the subset of residents with similar complaints to attend future meetings.

In a meeting within Sector 55D, the NCOs had a similar lament: "Basically, anything that has to do with marijuana now, nobody cares" (Sector 55D, November 2018). Like the officers in the other sectors discussed above, these NCOs explained that as quickly as they would arrest someone for marijuana, the Brooklyn District Attorney's Office would drop the charges. They suggested two strategies. First, they could "have one set form or like a letter that everybody goes to pick up, sign their name to, send to the DA's office." They sought to mobilize audience members in the same way that NCOs I observed at other Build the Block meetings had—by encouraging them to submit complaints directly to the DA's office, explaining how its policies were "making my life a living hell."

Second, the NCOs explained that they had been coordinating with narcotics officers to "figure out what we can do," since it was still illegal to smoke marijuana in building hallways, for instance. The officers were confident that they could figure out a creative enforcement solution—since this was actually not the first time that legal and policy changes had "handicapped" them. In the past, for example, they could charge someone with the misdemeanor of criminal trespass if that individual had entered a building or fenced area to smoke marijuana. If the person did not live in the building, police could upgrade the charge to burglary or criminal trespass with the intent to commit a crime, the crime being doing drugs. However, the Brooklyn District Attorney's Office "did away with the whole burglary thing, then they did away with marijuana, then they did away with trespass." The NCOs concluded, "They just, for us, made it a little more difficult to enforce."

Police did not view the legalization of marijuana, despite its having been democratically enacted, as a restraint on state power or as a reason to stop enforcement. Instead, it was a reason to *adapt* enforcement and draw from a new set of laws, levers, and other tactics to solve the persistent neighborhood problem. At an Eightieth Precinct Community Council meeting, the precinct's commanding officer even dismissed a series of elected officials who had spoken before him about marijuana's legalization: "We heard marijuana and how marijuana is gonna be legalized, or whatever it is. But, that's what the politicians do. I want to just tell you, it's still illegal" (Eightieth Precinct Community Council, September 2018). Legalization does not restrain officer discretion when police are empowered with a multitude of alternate pathways for obtaining legal authorization to intervene. As with the other circumstances identified in this chapter, police power finds a way to overcome challenges to its application.

INITIATING INDEPENDENT CHANNELS

The exclusionary nature of department channels prompts community members with alternative ascriptions of neighborhood problems to initiate independent channels to amplify their grievances. As founding director of a RALLY-affiliated organization, Nasir parroted the procedural response from Neighborhood Coordination Officers (NCOs): "Did you call the NCO, did you call the NCO?" (Nasir, interview, July 6, 2018). But, he continued, "to do what? The NCO can't help with tenant organizing" to press local issues like evictions. Instead, Nasir said, it is typically the "landlords [who] call the police." In these landlord-tenant disputes, police interventions prioritize facilitating a smooth eviction—not educating tenants of their rights, not advocating for a tenant association, and ultimately, not strengthening the community. To Nasir, the kinds of help NCOs brought seemed to harm the community.

Rather than attending Build the Block meetings to obtain police services, police accountability activists seek to strengthen community by redistributing state power away from police. On the ground, redistributive practices are dictated by the victims of police violence and their family members, the most directly impacted community stakeholders. After a woman named Jawhara won a civil lawsuit against the NYPD in the fatal shooting of her son, the city filed an appeal to overturn the verdict. I attended the Drop the Appeal rally at the city hall steps. June, whose organization was the primary coordinator of the event, explained how the group had been helping Jawhara throughout the trial. When the appeal was submitted, "Ms. Jawhara was like, 'I want to do the press conference, I want to do a rally at city hall. We need to go do this now. Let's go do it.' So we helped her" (June, interview, August 4, 2018). And so about forty community activists, religious leaders, elected officials, and other supporters held a press conference demanding that the mayor drop the appeal so that Jawhara and her family might gain closure (field notes, September 2018).

Andre, a thirty-two-year-old African American, became a community organizer two years prior after his brother was killed by police in Brooklyn. Now he is part of an organization representing over one hundred family members of victims of police violence in the Tri-State area of New York, New Jersey, and Connecticut. Andre's activism is about "work[ing] with the families and see[ing] what demands they might have, and uplift[ing] those demands" (Andre, interview, July 19, 2018). Having personally experienced the aftermath of a loved one's police-related death, he emphasized his uplift strategy: never show "the first sign of [we're] just gonna let it go or no one cares, [because] then [the media and public] don't care." Instead, his aim is to space out events so that media attention remains high and reporters don't "get bored with coming out and hearing the same thing." Movement leaders are family members like Jawhara and Andre, who have the final say over how justice is pursued in their case and therefore the precedent it sets for police transformation in the city.

At the same time, not all surviving family members seek to, or can, get involved in the same ways. Andre noted that families grieve differently, with some declining to rally and others physically unable to participate: "We have families where parents are losing weight at a huge rate, and they're literally killing themselves because they can't eat, they can't drink, they can't exercise, they can't do anything because they're still grieving—years later." As an organization filled with individuals who have navigated the public and legal aftermaths of their family member's shooting, these activists understand that everyone is not immediately ready to become the face of high-profile justice and reform efforts. Many family members are unprepared for the spotlight: "We're doing interviews, we're rallying, we're protesting, we're marching. And these are things that a lot of us were not accustomed to until we got thrown into it." In these cases, Andre and other organizers provide support and encouragement: "We are here for you, no matter what it is that you need."

Importantly, while these strategies are centered on victims and surviving families, the success of independent channels for police complaints is contingent on the support of the wider community. From the very beginning, family members have to "stay in front of what the police may potentially say to criminalize our loved ones," helping the public understand the injustice perpetrated (Andre, interview, July 19, 2018). Monica, a seasoned copwatcher[3] in her thirties residing in Brooklyn, explained how the language the public uses to remember police violence can either reinforce police's responsibility *or* expedite its erasure. It is, she pointed out, the difference between remembering Eric Garner as someone who "couldn't withstand the chokehold" versus "[Officer] Daniel Pantaleo killed him using a chokehold" (Monica, interview, November 9, 2018). Controlling messages is hard work, but to Andre, advancing the cause cannot be limited to the affected families; the whole community needs to hear the messages and take them up too. "You *expect* us [the victims' families] to be heard, you *expect* us to be outraged and livid about things. But now, when we have the support of a full community—we're talking about two thousand to three thousand people at a time, that's always the goal—then you *have* to listen to us" (Andre, interview, July 19, 2018). Mobilizing community members to help amplify the demands of affected family members is critical to winning wider support for police accountability.

Corey exemplifies a valuable ally. "As a white resident moving to a predominantly Black, Caribbean neighborhood, I was just very aware of my responsibility to stay informed," he told me of his move from Manhattan to Central Brooklyn four years prior (Corey, interview, August 31, 2018). An elementary schoolteacher in his thirties, Corey decided right away to get involved in a grassroots organization focused on affordable housing and police accountability. In addition to his involvement's being a way to keep abreast of community needs, he wanted to contribute to "the fight against gentrification, 'cause, like, as a white person moving into a neighborhood like that, I am participating in gentrification in a certain way. And so yeah, it started as a sense of personal responsibility." Soon, though, it became "clear how many fronts some of that work has to be fought on." Thus, Corey's activism began with protecting local small businesses through efforts like street campaigning, flyering, and organizing calls and letters to landlords, but it soon involved participating in actions of solidarity with those affected by police violence.

To Corey, his attendance at rallies and other actions is important to communicate to police the solidarity of people like him with the affected families' demands for justice: "To me, it's not necessarily coming from a place of thinking that the police will listen, because they often don't. But showing up with families is important because the police do need to see that." Corey's engagement exemplified the importance and value of independent channels incorporating nonvictims of police violence, including white newcomers, into their efforts (Doering 2020).

Organizers of independent channels also play offense, which includes mobilizing support and educating the public about the harms of department channels. Linda is a tech worker in her forties who had been laid off the Friday before we conducted the interview. A mixed-race Latina and white woman, she told me she was always politically active growing up in Tennessee. From writing letters to council members as a youth to helping coordinate the social media campaigns of #OccupyWallStreet, she prides herself on her history of social activism. Eight months earlier, she continued, when she moved from Eastern Brooklyn to Central Brooklyn, she immediately noticed the light pollution caused by the flashing lights of parked police cruisers and the overbearing light towers the NYPD had erected as crime deterrents. That led Linda to connect with local activists in the neighborhood through her #OccupyWallStreet network. Taking action is important, she noted, because "if we're all living together in this neighborhood, we should all try to make it better for each other, right?" (Linda, interview, August 8, 2018).

After breaking her arm, Linda decided to focus on less physically demanding actions—attending police-community meetings rather than direct actions on the street. Although she moved from an independent to a department channel, her goal remained to voice concerns about police. Recognizing that abusive policing facilitates neighborhood gentrification, Linda tried to recruit her friends to attend meetings too. "I was trying to convince other people who lived here, who are obviously new residents to the neighborhood—not Black—to go to these meetings and basically say the same thing: 'You need to stop overpolicing us. This is bullshit.'" Though others wouldn't join her, she nonetheless attended the meetings and distributed information about overpolicing.

To educate the broader public, Linda spearheaded a social media campaign in her RALLY-affiliated organization under the hashtag #NCO—a play on Neighborhood Coordination Officers, with the acronym repurposed to mean #NoCommunityOverpolicing. The campaign asked New Yorkers to post photos and videos showing examples of overpolicing, tagging them and adding the location. It's a strategy that had been used successfully before; policing activists in New York City, for instance, organized to post photos of police violence when the NYPD, in an effort to show its improved public relations, asked the public to post about the police using the hashtag #MyNYPD (Jackson and Foucault Welles 2015).

Linda brought me on a walk around her neighborhood to show me how she had been building the new campaign. As we went, she snapped photos and created GIFs of police cars, their license plates, and the street signs marking the intersections where they were parked. By documenting particular blocks that had high police presence, she had a multifaceted aim: to provide the wider public with a sense of daily life in overpoliced areas; to identify the neighborhoods where police were focusing their attention; and to collect data for copwatchers so they could better target their patrols. In redefining the hashtag #NCO, the campaign also signaled to the public the risks and consequences of participating in department channels with neighborhood officers—that working with the NCOs leads to more intense policing and harmful community consequences. At the same time, such contestation of department channels through the initiation of independent channels reflects a foundational sorting process that positions police to tailor their strategies of social control, as I will show in subsequent chapters.

—

This chapter has detailed how the NYPD as an organization has sought to build consensus on and coalesce power around the particular ways it ascribes neighborhood problems. Why? Because how neighborhood problems are ascribed determines which responses are appropriate and which are inapt. Consensus building is necessary, precisely because divergence exists within the community on whether neighborhood problems should be attributed to issues of police administration or those of police accountability. The NYPD introduced Neighborhood Policing as a department channel for public input that was fit for the former. Yet by analyzing the complaints that residents vocalized against those that NCOs documented, I showed how Neighborhood Policing operates on the principle of sharing state power, but with only those uninterested in redistributing it. Those who seek to redistribute power away from police initiate independent channels for public input to amplify their complaints as issues of police accountability, not police administration.

The dynamics between department channels and independent channels, however, present several challenges for police. First, the mere introduction of a department channel does not guarantee attendees—police must still consistently recruit a steady stream of cooperative residents to attend, fill, and return to Build the Block meetings. Second, police need community members to become police advocates, not just within department channels, but outside them as well. If independent channels are amplifying grievances about police accountability on city streets and social media, then police must invest in relationship-building with community entities that can vouch for the quality of police services in similarly broad venues. Next, it's time to step outside Build the Block meetings to uncover the complementary set of police tools, decisions, and strategies that together advance the Policing Machine. The following chapter details the second stage of the Policing Machine, when police work to cultivate *residents* into *constituents*.

Cultivating Local Constituents

In major cities across the United States, their mayors appoint their police chiefs. In other words, public accountability of the police department is typically formalized through democratic means: citizens elect the mayor, the mayor appoints a police chief, and if the people are dissatisfied with the chief's performance, then the threat of voting the mayor out of office and other forms of political mobilization improve alignment between the public, the mayor, and the police department. We often see these lines of accountability reestablish themselves in the aftermath of controversial law enforcement incidents, when public pressure for police reform motivates elected officials to introduce legislation that enhances various forms of police oversight.

Such traditional lines of accountability are problematic for police departments. The Policing Machine works to rearrange them: rather than deal with elected officials who constantly threaten the independence and capacity of police departments, police prefer to cultivate their own constituents, whom they can empower and amplify as the authentic representatives of neighborhoods. Police can mobilize these local representatives to help affirm community demand for police services and contest the necessity of institutional reforms and external oversight. In other words, in facing top-down pressures from elected officials, police seek to root their accountability in the constituents they have cultivated from the bottom up.

When we met, Dina Lyons was a former three-term New York City Council member and current district leader. In May 2019, she attended the Eightieth Precinct Community Council meeting in her political capacity—like other local officials—to provide updates about upcoming events, hear complaints, and demonstrate her engagement within the community. Recall that since the 1940s, each precinct in New York City has operated its own community council, run by an elected board of residents who hold monthly public meetings to improve police-community relationships. The precinct commanding officer's report is the centerpiece of community council meetings, which is reflected in the fact that meeting agendas are commonly reorganized at the last minute to accommodate that officer's schedule. During the May 2019 meeting, once the commanding officer for the Eightieth Precinct gave his report, featuring, as always, crime statistics and major incidents, he asked whether anyone in the audience had questions. Lyons, who had spoken in her official capacity earlier in the meeting, raised her hand and stood up.

"On Friday, in front of my office, it's right by in front of the McDonald's . . . there's a lot of mental illness there" (Eightieth Precinct Community Council, May 2019). She continued, saying that every time she leaves her office, she feels she has to look left and right; she wanted to discuss how to "deter" the presence of mentally ill loiterers around her workplace. Lyons shared that she believed that most of these individuals were coming from the nearby men's homeless shelter, so "maybe we need to go talk to the shelter and see what they are doing—they're just letting them loose and go so far."

The commanding officer—CO Marino—responded with his expert take: "With mental illness, there's a couple of things." For one, he noted, the location of Lyons's office is near a terminal point for the subway. Crowds will naturally gather there. Second, people try to use McDonald's free Wi-Fi—another inducement to loiter. Officer Marino emphasized that the precinct was working with a nonprofit organization to help manage "that problem." Then he assured Lyons: "If there's something going on, we'll respond to it and of course, if there's an ongoing issue, we'll up our patrol in the location. The last thing I want is for you not to feel safe." Community councils are nonprofits, but their collaboration with police means that they facilitate traditional law enforcement solutions, like patrolling, which can be activated at any time. After the meeting, Eightieth Precinct officers spoke with Lyons and promised that they would visit her office on Friday.

I interviewed Lyons the following week. She told me that the officers never came, which was particularly frustrating because her office is otherwise closed on Fridays, so she'd been there, waiting unnecessarily (Dina Lyons, interview, May 29, 2019). It wasn't the first time she experienced police unresponsiveness. Five months earlier, she said, her home security camera captured footage of a shooting. After allowing detectives to borrow the footage, she went to the precinct station to retrieve it but endured a thirty- to forty-minute wait in the lobby. Lyons was not expecting preferential treatment as an elected official, though she mentioned she'd been the district's councilwoman just one year prior. She used to speak with the officers right before their roll call in that very precinct. Finally, she realized she "shouldn't have to be waiting this long"; she decided to phone Mr. Holloway. Soon after, "the captain came out, addressed me, went upstairs, took care of it, and it was done." Despite her political status, Lyons had to contact Mr. Holloway—the Eightieth Precinct Community Council president you met in the previous chapter—to facilitate police access. As she remembered, "The deputy inspector came right out his office, shook my hand, and then took me upstairs."

Interactions like these reveal a key dynamic in the Policing Machine: the most important constituents are *not* elected politicians but local brokers, such as Mr. Holloway, who have been empowered by police. By understanding this, it makes sense that District Leader Lyons received no deference from the police, whether as a former New York City Council member and now cooperative citizen waiting in the station or as an engaged resident bringing her local issues to a community council meeting. In contrast to elected politicians who constantly threaten top-down oversight and reform, nonstate actors like Mr. Holloway are more useful for police; they can be positioned as the most *authentic* neighborhood representatives and help police access and mobilize neighbors to participate in the police-community initiatives that sustain the Policing Machine. The Policing Machine seeks to untether police accountability from elected officials and the unpredictable whims of those whom politicians represent. Instead, by cultivating their own constituents and claiming accountability to them rather than elected officials, police accumulate political capital valuable toward optimizing public legitimacy with organizational independence.

—

The second stage of the Policing Machine is to *cultivate local constitu-ents*. Chapter 1 introduced stage one, in which the Policing Machine establishes department channels and directs heterogeneous commu-nity demands toward outlets that they control. These department-run community initiatives are open to the public, but the police are specifically seeking constituents who will serve their organization's strategic interests. In electoral politics, constituents are people who authorize representatives to act on their behalf. Similarly, police con-stituents provide legal authorization for enforcement to proceed, though they play an even more vital role in the Policing Machine by *conferring legitimacy*. They demand and consume police services in ways that police can represent as either explicitly or implicitly sup-porting greater investment in police power and resources. The legiti-macy conferred is from the bottom up, emerging from residents who can be represented as the most authentic neighborhood representa-tives. These processes advance the Policing Machine's goal of cen-tering police accountability on constituents—untethering it from the institutions designed to regulate them democratically.

This chapter identifies two ways that police cultivate constitu-ents, which form the basis of partner channels within the Policing Machine. First, police can establish alternative systems of neighbor-hood representatives over which they exercise outsized influence. For decades in New York City, the NYPD has pursued this strategy to form community councils in each of the city's seventy-seven police precincts. Other cities have similar systems, such as Community-Police Advisory Boards in Los Angeles (Gascón and Roussell 2019). Community councils hold monthly meetings and public events, elect their president and board members from the community, and are designed to represent and advance the community's interests to the local precinct. As described more below, a central strategy for how police cultivate constituents from community councils is by limiting the influence of newcomers.

A second way that police can cultivate constituents is by coor-dinating access to established audiences. The church is one of the most central neighborhood institutions, especially in African Ameri-can communities (Du Bois 1903; Lincoln and Mamiya 1990; Owens 2007; Pattillo-McCoy 1998; McRoberts 2003). In New York City, the NYPD has formalized relationships with local religious leaders across precincts by establishing clergy councils. These assemblies, which are like community councils but open only to religious leaders, are valuable because they provide police with access to clergy members' networks of faithful and engaged church attendees. Besides receptive audiences, churches provide a stage for information distribution, especially through an established, trustworthy leader like a pastor.

Both of these councils exemplify organizational brokers that police target as sources for constituents. In other words, these councils do not just provide spaces and contexts for community members to form social ties and obtain the resources available within them (Small 2009)—they do so for police as well. Police are not neutral participants in these spaces; they intimately shape their operations in ways that blur any clear lines between police as formal social controls and nonprofit councils as informal social controls. The Policing Machine is empowered the more that police permeate such organizations and direct the constituents cultivated in these partner channels into their own department channels.

Key to all this is the fact that as a selective process, cultivating constituents is necessarily *exclusionary.* Community members whose beliefs do not align with how police ascribe neighborhood problems—who cannot provide political capital to advance police's organizational goals—are more likely to be omitted, overlooked, and discouraged from coming to or returning to initiatives designed for cultivating constituents. The last section of this chapter thus describes how the Policing Machine establishes a social order wherein residents sort into the channels most likely to amplify their grievances. Such sorting diminishes interactions across channels and enables police to tailor their strategies for social control and political mobilization.

ESTABLISHING ALTERNATIVE NEIGHBORHOOD REPRESENTATIVES

In the mid-1900s, the NYPD helped institutionalize an alternative system of neighborhood representation over which it would exercise influence. Parallel to the traditional system of elected officials, which featured the city council and many community boards, police precincts across the New York City began to elect their own community council, featuring a president and a board. Unlike traditional elected officials, who often threatened the police department with greater oversight, police precincts could pursue organizational control over community councils by helping them build their capacity. As police empowered community councils as the alternative and authentic representatives of neighborhoods, they cultivated the constituents needed to contest the necessity of external oversight and institutional reform.

Historical Background on Community Councils

Between 1943 and 1944, the NYPD initiated a citywide plan to combat rising rates of juvenile delinquency. The department began "seeking and encouraging public participation,"[1] formalizing its outreach effort by establishing "citizens coordinating councils" in each of the city's eighty-one precincts. These councils comprised businessmen, clergymen, social workers, and representatives of city agencies (*New York Times* 1944a), all integral community stakeholders, given how the police department diagnosed the problem of juvenile delinquency. A department spokesperson explained that the plan was initiated "when it was discovered that the cause of juvenile delinquency centered around the home. The child's environment, including his family life, his school and his church, determines whether or not the child will be a delinquent" (*New York Times* 1944a). Police also believed that instituting a citizens coordinating council in each precinct would account for the local variation in juvenile delinquency, as each group would "come together, evaluate the condition in their community— determine how much delinquency there is—and coordinate the resources of the area to attack the problem" (*New York Times* 1944a).

Despite criticism from the very start, the mission of the citizens coordinating councils expanded over the years. New York Magistrate Judge Anna Kross critiqued at the outset how the "councils were created almost over night, without an organized plan and without a budget" (*New York Times* 1944b). Kross also argued that police departments were unqualified to handle juvenile delinquency, which fell more squarely within the scope of social work than police work. Nonetheless, the police department moved forward with the councils, as it described in the council guidelines: "What began as a crime prevention program for youth grew to a sound relationship involving all segments of the community."[2] In 1965, the NYPD renamed the citizens coordinating councils, expanding the mission of the newly designated community councils beyond delinquency to manage community problems more broadly.

Today, over seventy-five years after their creation, community councils operate with an organized plan but still without a budget. From conducting a meeting to removing a board member, the NYPD's twenty-three-page *Community Council Guidelines* is the publication that regulates the operation of each precinct's council. The guidelines define their own purpose as "serv[ing] as the standing rule governing the Community Council Executive Boards and its members," and they stipulate that "all other publications, constitutions and bylaws adopted independently shall be considered null and void."[3] Board members swear to uphold these police-supplied guidelines. When the NYPD's chief of community affairs swore in the fully reelected board of the Fifty-Fifth Precinct Community Council, she stated, "You guys promise to abide by our community council bylaws and continue to support the community, and continue to support the police department in all your endeavors" (Fifty-Fifth Precinct Community Council, September 2018). The fact that community councils today are still run by resident volunteers with financial support brought in primarily by fundraising renders the councils dependent on police department resources to accomplish even basic organizational tasks. As a matter of policy and practice, these realities dissolve any meaningful distinction between police and community councils, all the way from participant to president.

Meeting Newcomers and Elected Representatives

Community council boards feature a stable cast of members with long tenures. Table 2.1 shows the basic demographic information for the board of the Eightieth Precinct Community Council. The board's characteristics are broadly representative of its membership: participants in this council skew older, are largely African American and West Indian, and have long histories of engagement with the council. Board members are all volunteers, so they are largely either retired or hold day jobs in addition to their council service. For example, President Holloway of the Eightieth Precinct Community Council is retired and sits on the board of two nonprofits within the precinct.

TABLE 2.1. Eightieth Precinct Community Council board members: Demographic information

Position	Years in position	Age	Nationality	Education
President	22	67	African American	High school
Vice president	22	75	Trinidadian	College
Secretary	22	86	African American	Master's
Treasurer	4	59	African American	Master's
Corresponding secretary	1	47	Puerto Rican	Master's
Assistant secretary	18	77	Trinidadian	High school
Sergeant at arms	3	77	African American	High school
Chaplain	5	70	African American	College

His vice president, Laurette Simmonds (whom you also met in chapter 1), is a retired nurse, while the council's corresponding secretary still works at a social service agency.

Police invest substantive resources into cultivating constituents from community councils. The NYPD assigns a specific officer to manage the council of each precinct: the Community Affairs officer. Whereas the precinct's commanding officer is expected to attend every community council meeting to provide a report, Community Affairs officers serve as the go-to liaison between that officer and the council. In fact, in the NYPD's patrol guide, the very first duty listed for Community Affairs officers is to "attend community council meetings and assist in stimulating and coordinating council activities."[4] Their second duty is to forward monthly reports of council meetings and operations to NYPD executives, who use these to keep track of council activities.

The process of cultivating constituents is rooted in limiting the influence of newcomers. For instance, newcomers can shape community council operations by running for board positions; but unlike city government elections, police can directly shape the outcomes of community council elections. I met thirty-six-year-old African American James Jones at a Build the Block meeting—his first. While there, he called for greater youth involvement in such gatherings. I approached him afterward and learned that he'd recently moved into the Fifty-Fifth Precinct from a neighboring area. He was the founder of a nonprofit organization focusing on local youth empowerment and had been the sergeant at arms of his previous neighborhood's community council. But when he walked into his first executive board meeting, he "was just told or informed that I no longer sit on the council" (James Jones, interview, July 17, 2018). Jones learned that his position had been terminated because there was a "conflict of interest," given his affiliation with his nonprofit organization, which was interested in initiating a copwatching program. Even though he realized that "everyone on the council was a part of another nonprofit organization," the experience "turned me off to the whole thing." Rather than contest the decision, he decided to move on and focus on his own organization.

Jones's case was not unique. President Holloway recalled his first time running for a community council position in 1997: "First of all, the [Eightieth] precinct at the time, the commanding officer did not want me to become the president" (Holloway, interview, July 10, 2018). Mr. Holloway explained that it was a "battle trying to become the president of the precinct council because I wasn't in the so-called circle." Asked to clarify, he added, "Being 'friends,' so to speak . . . the cops basically ran everything, so the cops wanted to keep everything the way it was, so that way they don't have to answer questions. They run the show." The precinct even delayed elections for a month as it tried to work out a compromise with Mr. Holloway: "[They] tried to cut a deal with me to be the vice president, and be under the current president, which I said no. It's everything or nothing." Even though he ultimately was permitted to become the new president, the proposed deal underscores the importance police place on community councils and the influence they seek to exert on them.

Another way newcomers can shape community council operations is through their voice and vote. In the month before the 2018 elections in the Fifty-Fifth Precinct, when all but one board member were eventually reelected, an audience member contested the nomination process. The meeting minutes described how the resident "express[ed] concern that the process was limited, with positions geared to the same individuals every time" (Fifty-Fifth Precinct Community Council, May 2018). The nominating committee, a group appointed by the NYPD Community Affairs Bureau to oversee voter eligibility, replied that "the process was being followed per the bylaws," meaning the NYPD-produced *Council Guidelines*. In theory, the existence of these policies inscribed in police bylaws indicated that I could submit Freedom of Information Law requests to the NYPD to gain access to community council records. As it turned out, that was exactly what happened. The NYPD complied with my request, providing various historical records and thus confirming its organizational control over the community councils.

Historical meeting minutes complement my observations to confirm low voter participation in uncontested community council elections. Of the three I observed, only two out of twenty board positions were ever contested (neither were for the position of president). Lela Pessod, for instance, had been president of the Fifty-Fifth Precinct Community Council since 1998.[5] By the end of the study period, she had been elected for two-year terms *eleven* times, facing an opponent only twice. Her last contested election was in 2016, which she won, 21 votes to 5. In other words, only 26 people out of a population of approximately 150,000 residents in the Fifty-Fifth Precinct—*.02 percent*—decided who would serve as their precinct's community council president.

Eligibility policies point to procedural hurdles for those community members who want to participate in the elections. Newcomers must attend three out of ten council meetings within the fiscal year to be eligible to vote in that year's board elections, plus attend the particular meeting at which the elections are held. Looking again at the 2016 election in the Fifty-Fifth Precinct, the historical records indicated seventy residents in attendance at that meeting. The tally of twenty-six total votes in the presidential election thus indicates that only 37 percent of the people present were eligible to vote in the first place. These attendance records further show the stability of total attendees and newcomers over a four-year period, which improves the reliability of community council operations, decisions, and leadership (see fig. 2.1).

Data for total attendees and newcomers were available only for the Fifty-Fifth Precinct Community Council because of a unique meeting practice. At each meeting, President Pessod opened by asking, "For those of you who are here for the first time, would you stand, please? And I want you all to give your name and your affiliation to the community" (e.g., Fifty-Fifth Precinct Community Council, December 2018). As I will discuss later, some newcomers have identified this practice as creating an exclusionary environment, alongside this community council's norm of holding meetings in the precinct station.

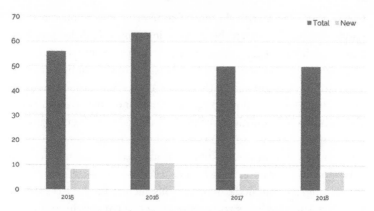

FIGURE 2.1 Average total and new attendees at Fifty-Fifth Precinct
Community Council meetings, 2015–18.
Source: Freedom of Information Law request; analysis conducted by author.

But I also observed other newcomers who were eager to introduce themselves. These residents usually came with an agenda in mind: to discuss a particular complaint, raise awareness of their next event, or announce themselves as the new school principal or community liaison for a nonprofit. Regardless, the board secretary recorded each introduction in the meeting minutes, which I combined with sign-in records to calculate total attendees.

These data highlight how community councils become consistent constituencies. The more the influence of newcomers is limited, the more reliable community councils become for police as sources of constituents. In support of the councils, later chapters describe how police distribute public resources to these "authentic" neighborhood representatives and rely on board members for public endorsements of police practices. Still, this is a relatively resource-intensive way for police to optimize legitimacy. Thus, another way the NYPD cultivates constituents is by pursuing formalized partnerships with those having access to already established audiences.

COORDINATING ACCESS TO
ESTABLISHED AUDIENCES

As with community councils, each precinct has a clergy council, although clergy councils vary in the degree to which they're active.

Clergy represent a critical point of contact between police and the wider community, given the durable legitimacy faith leaders have among their congregants. Police are certainly also pursuing relationships with a variety of neighborhood institutions, including business associations (Beckett and Herbert 2009) and school principals (Rios 2011). These "organizational brokers" (Small and Gose 2020) are valuable entryways for entities like police to access the residents who rely on them for services. Yet the unique significance of clergy in major cities is reflected in the existence of faith-based liaison officers in Chicago and elsewhere, clergy events such as police-clergy summits in Los Angeles, and dedicated divisions such as the NYPD's Clergy Outreach Unit, led by a sworn police officer who makes his rounds by observing clergy council meetings across precincts. These meetings are smaller than the community council meetings and open only to clergy and representatives of local political officials, service providers, and law enforcement organizations.

On a June morning in 2019, roughly ten faith leaders from across the precinct gathered in the police station for the monthly meeting of the Eightieth Precinct Clergy Council. (On the previous night, members of the community at large had convened for the precinct's community council meeting at a church six blocks away.) When it was time for the precinct's commanding officer to speak, he began with a parable: "There's a man walking down the street, and he sees three people laying bricks" (Eightieth Precinct Clergy Council, June 2019). It was striking to see him, a white police officer, open his remarks in this manner before an audience of Black clergy in the precinct station. "He goes up to the first and asks, 'What are you doing?' The first one says, 'I'm laying bricks.' He goes up to the second and asks, 'What are you doing?' He says, 'I'm building a wall.' Finally, he goes to the third and asks, 'What are you doing?' And he says, 'I'm building a house for God.'" The clergy members audibly murmured their affirmations: "Amen," "Wow," and "Mm." Then the commanding officer explained that the parable reflects the different "sense of purpose" people can have for their work. As a police officer, he believed that police have "a sense of purpose in building a relationship with the community." After finishing his report by sharing crime statistics and updates about the precinct's summer initiatives, he relinquished the lectern to the clergy council's vice president, Pastor Stuart, who said, "As pastors, we love parables—Jesus taught using parables." He turned to the commanding officer and commented, "We might have to give you a new name: Inspirational Inspector." He prompted his fellow clergy: "Amen?" They all attested: "Amen."

For the past quarter of a century, scholars and policy makers have described these types of interactions between local police departments and the Black church as efforts to improve police-community relations and advance violence prevention (Brunson et al. 2015; Meares 2002). African American clergy in particular have a long tradition of entrepreneurial collaboration with state institutions as a means of winning neighborhood resources like housing (Owens 2007). When it comes to public safety, the relevant state institution for collaboration is the police department. For example, activist Black clergy in Boston formed the Ten Point Coalition in the 1990s to help reduce youth violence by coordinating action among community institutions (Pegram, Brunson, and Braga 2016) and providing police with an "umbrella of legitimacy" (Berrien and Winship 2003). In New York City, the subset of activist Black clergy interested in violence prevention joins the clergy council.

For police, shared interests in violence prevention may be the impetus for collaboration, but access to the established infrastructure and audiences affiliated with religious institutions is crucial for police as political organizations. In New York City, about seven thousand churches are formally registered as nonprofit organizations; over half of them are located in Brooklyn. In African American communities, the religiously active are also historically more likely to be civically and politically engaged (Fitzgerald and Spohn 2005; Lincoln and Mamiya 1990; Little Edwards and Oyakawa 2022). Building relationships with the clergy who gatekeep access to these audiences represents a particularly promising source of constituents to further fuel the Policing Machine.

The former commanding officer (CO) of the Fifty-Fifth Precinct explained to me how today's version of the clergy council started in his precinct. After Bobby Banks was appointed CO, he received a list of pastors in the precinct. It was outdated: "Some of these people on the list was dead, some of the churches were closed, some of them didn't live in the community anymore" (Bobby Banks, interview, February 15, 2019). So CO Banks directed his Community Affairs officers to round up "all the prominent pastors in the precinct." I asked how Community Affairs officers would know all these faith leaders, and

Banks explained that they are the "heartbeat of the precinct—they're supposed to know every single person, or at least every single prominent person." In fact, one of the roles of Community Affairs officers is to bring rookie officers around to meet these prominent people. That's why it was "easy" for a Community Affairs officer to identify the prominent pastors.

With a revamped group of pastors, Banks began setting up meetings: "I had a room full of pastors every month, like twenty-five to thirty pastors in the room. Give them some coffee, give them some cheese—they were happy to sit and talk" (Bobby Banks, interview, February 15, 2019). This relationship with clergy was important, because "you can't forget that they have the biggest audience, they have the most influence, every Sunday. No matter where you go, church is on Sunday." Current members of the clergy council confirmed this story, with Pastor Greene even recalling how CO Banks "put up the first hundred dollars to help us" (Greene, interview, January 30, 2019). He recalled how the former counsel to the NYPD police commissioner had even prepared a proof of concept white paper to help the clergy council obtain additional grant money.

Unlike community councils, clergy councils do not have elections. In the Fifty-Fifth and Eightieth Precincts, the boards at the time of my research comprised the same people who had first formed the clergy councils. Interviewees told me the original board members were selected because they originally led the effort to establish their precinct's clergy council. For example, Pastor Young—president of the Fifty-Fifth Precinct Clergy Council—explained, "[CO Banks] appointed me to do the research about clergy councils. I did the research, and I gave them an idea as to what we can do. . . . So when I presented it, they said, 'Okay, now let's find a leader,' and they said, 'Since you did the research, we're gonna pick you.' And so they picked me" (Young, interview, September 19, 2018). To this day, clergy council boards are established through consensus, not election.

Police leverage the clergy councils' audience networks for law enforcement ends in at least two ways: to receive information and to distribute information for neighborhood mobilization. Representing about seventy churches within the precinct, interviewees estimated the Fifty-Fifth Precinct Clergy Council's audience network to be anywhere from "a couple thousand" (Young, interview, January 7, 2019) to "twenty thousand to thirty thousand" (Greene, interview, January 30, 2019) across all their congregations. Secretary Woodward of the council explained the informational value contained within this network: "We'll have people a part of our churches—whether it's a mother, a father, a grandfather, a sibling, an aunt, uncle, a neighbor—somebody typically knows the person that's been shot and that's been killed, and we'll get connected through the pastors of the church" (Woodward, interview, September 24, 2018). During a Fifty-Fifth Precinct Clergy Council meeting, Pastor Young explained how after a shooting, family members will find out "maybe within three hours, they would know who killed their son. Normally, the streets will tell them" (Fifty-Fifth Precinct Clergy Council, October 2018). As clergy, he noted, preventing the next shooting was part of every council member's job: "The best thing for us to do is to find a way to get in the middle, and tell the parents and the family members to go to the police with the information. We don't want to be carrying that information, we want to encourage them to go and give that information." In other words, clergy "get in the middle" in the sense of receiving information from the congregation's networks, potentially pass it to the family of shooting victims, and ask them to go to the police. Sharing information is one part of the clergy care they provide to victims and their families, which includes resources like free bereavement and burial services, referrals to legal services, and other forms of counseling.

Most helpful to police, the implicit part of providing clergy care is being conscious about gathering information and keeping an ear to the ground when it comes to talk about crimes. Over several meetings, pastors and precinct leadership debated whether police would (or could) guarantee no arrests if pastors forwarded surrendered guns from their congregants to the precinct. The pastors wanted assurances that the cops would not pursue enforcement action against the pastors or pressure them to share information about who had owned or possessed the firearm. Unsurprisingly, police refused. Their stated reason was that analyses of the firearms may link these weapons to crimes, and they feared this agreement would become a mechanism for offenders to "wash" weapons used in crimes and avoid repercussions. Some pastors suggested establishing a protocol to limit information sharing, but Bishop George, vice president of the clergy council, stood up to say that "there's something called common sense," and the council should not "overcomplicate the process" (Fifty-Fifth Precinct Clergy

Council, October 2018). The fifteen or so attendees listened as he continued: "If I hear any information, if my parishioners come across any information which I believe is valuable to the precinct, you bet I'm gonna get it to the precinct, because our safety is a shared responsibility. . . . This is why we come, we support, we're grateful for the leadership of [Clergy Council President] Pastor Young and of course the precinct commander. And this is a partnership worth building." In other words, Bishop George told his fellow faith leaders, it was imperative that, rather than limit their "partnership," they share any information related to crime and enforcement with the police.

The second way police leverage these networks is for audience access—the chance to distribute information and speak directly to church audiences. Throughout the year, churches within the Eightieth and Fifty-Fifth Precinct Clergy Councils routinely invite officers to speak with Vacation Bible School participants and church-organized senior citizen groups (Augustine, interview, February 20, 2019); religious education and youth groups (Joseph, interview, December 21, 2018); and congregants during pastoral anniversaries (Maurice, interview, January 7, 2019). Minister Augustine of the Fifty-Fifth Precinct Clergy Council saw these occasions as ways to rebuild trust, since "our kids don't run to the police anymore—they run away." In the Eightieth Precinct, Father Joseph explained how Community Affairs officers had spoken to his group of over one hundred Bible camp youth several times in recent years: "[Vacation Bible School is] an opportunity for us to teach the Bible, to teach them about life, to teach them about crafts, to build, to help them learn to build, how to develop relationships and work with others. And so we use that opportunity to bring in the Eightieth Precinct officers to speak to our children" (Joseph, interview, December 21, 2018). Father Joseph even welcomed the NYPD commissioner to speak at the first service he held after the NYPD killing of Eric Garner. He accepted, and as Father Joseph recounted, he "thanked everyone for their support during this difficult time." The invitation provided the commissioner with an opportunity in front of a church audience to reframe the tragedy as one for police instead of one for Garner and his family. Through clergy relations, police gain direct access to such audiences and can distribute information produced by the Policing Machine— the sort that affirms the quality of police services.

Take New Year's Eve as an example. Each year, the president of the

Fifty-Fifth Precinct Clergy Council accompanies the commanding officer and Community Affairs officers to three or four Black churches holding Watch Night Services. These are often the best-attended services of the year (Maurice, interview, January 7, 2019) and represent a tradition stretching back to the last night of 1862. It was the night before the Emancipation Proclamation was to be signed, and enslaved and free African Americans secretly gathered in churches, watching over the fragile moment. More than 250 years later, the Fifty-Fifth Precinct's Watch Night services feature police officers speaking about crime statistics and violence prevention as a shared responsibility, and offer prayers and blessings for law enforcement and community partners (Maurice, interview, January 7, 2019).

Pastor Greene, whose church was a stop for the clergy council and commanding officer's Watch Night visits, described how he texted with the Community Affairs officers to work out the timing of their arrival, because it's "not just a drive-by—hi and bye. They actually explain what we accomplished together." He detailed the typical schedule: "We start service. We have Praise and Worship, where we do songs and praise to God, and then we do Prayer, and then I have them come up" (Greene, interview, January 30, 2019). Immediately after the pastor conducts the prayer with the six hundred congregants, that is, the NYPD precinct commanding officer steps to the podium to list the precinct's recent accomplishments. Pastor Greene described the speech as mutually beneficial: by emphasizing the collaborative effort toward successfully reducing crime, each of the parties involved—police, Pastor Greene, and the clergy council—gains the congregation's confidence that police-community relations are improving their community.

These strategic interactions between police and clergy are precisely what CO Banks, who takes credit for connecting police representatives directly with the precinct's church congregations, envisioned. "I was really close to the religious sector because I knew if I could get the religious sect, then I could touch a lot of people" (Bobby Banks, interview, February 15, 2019). More specifically, "if you want to get a message out, you give it to the pastors." The commander recalled an incident when this had proved to be a powerful counter to media narratives: local media had reported a story about a nun raped by an African American bodega employee just as she was leaving her convent. Banks claimed that the shocking crime had the "police commissioner's office calling me . . . I mean, my phone, it was blazing." With news reports of a "nun being snatched off the street and brutally raped," he added, people were scared to go outside. But then he proudly noted that when investigations determined the sexual relationship had been consensual and ongoing, he could get the pastors to spread the word, quickly dispelling community fear.

Today, churches continue to represent central entry points into local neighborhoods for state actors and institutions (Owens 2007; Pattillo 2007; Rodríguez-Muñiz 2017). Pastor Maurice explained that "politicians, the government, as well as even the NYPD are starting to recognize the influence of churches" (Maurice, interview, January 7, 2019). Moreover, because Brooklyn is often referred to as the Borough of Churches and the Fifty-Fifth Precinct is home to many people of Caribbean descent, his church is a particularly influential neighborhood institution. "You normally see anybody running for office, anybody doing anything, they always come to the church," he marveled—recently, his church had visits from representatives from the US Census Bureau, voter registration volunteers, and a group providing mental health training, all there to get information out. The enduring centrality of neighborhood religious institutions positions them to attract various political mobilizers seeking access to their audience network.

Police cultivate constituents through community councils and clergy councils, where elected residents and local clergy leaders broker relationships with members of the broader community whose priorities align with theirs. Under the Policing Machine, police invest in these partner channels as a complementary strategy to establishing department channels like the Build the Block meetings offered through Neighborhood Policing. The relationships brokered through these councils across the years can now be leveraged to host and populate department channels, where police can cultivate direct ties with nonrandom constituents.

DRAWING CONSTITUENTS INTO
DEPARTMENT CHANNELS

Constituents cultivated through partner channels are directed into department channels like Build the Block meetings. Indeed, police relationships with community councils and clergy councils directly inform where Build the Blocks are held, to whom they are advertised, who is most likely to attend, and therefore what types of complaints are most likely to be raised. Drawing constituents from partner channels into department channels enables police to build direct relationships in spaces controlled by officers and credited to the department.

Analyzing where Neighborhood Coordination Officers (NCOs) choose to hold Build the Block meetings is helpful here. In the first quarter of 2019, NYPD headquarters issued a "location rotation guideline" that instructed NCOs to rotate Build the Block meetings among locations throughout their sector. This guideline indicates that NCOs never received instruction to rotate meeting locations—so in earlier years, the meetings were typically held in the exact same places. That routine had practical advantages: it offered consistency for residents who came to associate meetings with that particular location and to expect them, and it could take advantage of uniquely central and accessible locations. The disadvantages included biasing participation against residents living farther away, as well as those who could not travel to the site. The rootedness also represented a missed opportunity to form new relationships by, for instance, needing to find and secure new venues suitable for Build the Block gatherings. In issuing the location rotation guideline, the NYPD sided with the disadvantages.

To assess how the guideline affected meeting locations, I constructed a database of every Build the Block meeting site across New York City from the start of the program through the third quarter of 2019. Each NYPD precinct operates social media accounts, and for most Build the Blocks it posts the meeting information online as an invitation to residents. I scraped this information (date, time, and address) from each precinct's Twitter and Facebook pages. Then I used addresses to code for meeting venue—whether the Build the Block was held in a church, library, or other location type. When precincts did not post meeting information for a quarter, I coded these observations as missing. I erred on the side of caution in calculating the percentage of Build the Block meetings my dataset covers. Although the NYPD publicizes the date Neighborhood Policing was rolled out in each precinct, it is unknown when a specific precinct or sector held its first quarterly Build the Block meeting. For instance, if Neighborhood Policing was launched in a precinct in March and the precinct did not post Build the Block meeting information on its social media page, it is unknown whether the precinct held meetings in some, all, or none of its sectors during the first quarter. I coded these observations as missing—that the precinct should have held meetings across all its sectors, but my dataset does not account for them. Based on the department's approximation of holding "over 1,500 meetings" through 2018 (NYPD 2018), the most liberal estimate of total meetings held during the study period is 2,406. My dataset contains 92 percent of this estimate of total meetings.

My analysis indicates that NCOs were consistent in choosing meeting locations. On the surface, these officers did abide by the location rotation guideline: before the guideline was issued, 1,319 meetings were held at just 651 unique addresses. After it was issued, 888 meetings were held in 732 different locations. Thus, the guideline effectively altered location decisions. At the same time, however, NCOs remained consistent in that they held meetings in the same *types* of venues (table 2.2). Before and after the location rotation guideline, most NCOs hosted most Build the Block meetings in religious spaces. Only about half as often were the meetings sited in housing complexes,

TABLE 2.2. Frequency of Build the Block meetings by venue type before vs. after location rotation guideline

Venue type	Pre-guideline		Post-guideline		Total	
	N	%	N	%	N	%
Religious institution	400	30.3	273	30.7	673	30.5
Housing complex	206	15.6	127	14.3	333	15.1
Educational institution	174	13.2	138	15.5	312	14.1
Community center	165	12.5	85	9.6	250	11.3
Commercial business	119	9.0	116	13.1	235	10.6
Charity/Social service provider	65	4.9	30	3.4	95	4.3
Hospital/Health center	36	2.7	22	2.5	58	2.6
Civic/Fraternal association	24	1.8	17	1.9	41	1.9
Government agency office	30	2.3	11	1.2	41	1.9
Cultural association	7	0.5	6	0.7	13	0.6
Museum	3	0.2	6	0.7	9	0.4
Precinct stationhouse	4	0.3	0	0.0	4	0.2
Total	1,319		888		2,207	

educational institutions, or community centers. In addition, while the NYPD as an organization may prioritize the number of attendees at each meeting (the mandatory form that NCOs fill out has a spot for them to report that number), NCOs running the meetings likely care as much about the "who" as the "how many." Citywide, their insistence on holding meetings in religious institutions when other venues were available as well indicates a belief that clergy relationships will provide them with the quantity and quality attendees they seek.

Religious Institutions

Religious institutions represent an ideal site for Build the Block meetings, in part for practical reasons. Beyond their use of social media, NCOs rely on venue hosts to put up flyers and otherwise draw a crowd to the meetings. (During the course of fieldwork, I saw an individual physical flyer only four times—on three of these occasions, they had been posted inside the actual venue.) Moreover, churches, synagogues, and mosques can be reserved weeks in advance, giving the precincts time to get the word out; they can accommodate large audiences; and they can be high-traffic spaces where many will see flyers or hear announcements about the meetings.

But a closer look at the unique dynamics of meetings held in religious institutions reveals the more substantive advantages of choosing venues with hierarchical structures and motivated audiences—the very same factors that initially drew police to establish clergy councils and begin speaking at church services. Besides the capacity of houses of worship, NCOs prefer to hold meetings in them to take advantage of their engaged audiences, especially within African American communities (Pattillo-McCoy 1998; Meares 2002), and their faith-based leadership, which facilitates relationship-building through trusted leaders.

Build the Block meetings held inside churches often open and close with prayers led by the resident pastor, who channels blessings and protection over officers through a familiar cultural practice (Pattillo-McCoy 1998). Pastors do not have to provide instructions to the audience on how to proceed; most automatically stand, bow their heads, and hold hands with their neighbor. A typical prayer to begin a Build the Block meeting: "We recognize that every day, our officers place their lives in the line of danger for our community, and so we pray for your continued grace and protection" (Sector 55C, May 2018). Infusing prayers for police into community meetings blurs the distinction between meeting experiences and church-sponsored events. Being in a church and observing a pastor lead a prayer—especially if it's *your* church and *your* pastor—helps orient attendees to the spirit of collaboration and police appreciation that both NCOs and pastors aim to cultivate. As faith leaders, these pastors endorse police's actions and encourage their congregants to do the same.

Just as NCOs cultivate relationships with faith leaders, so pastors endorse NCOs to congregants as solutions to neighborhood problems. Anywhere from one to three times a week, NCOs visit places like clergy council member Pastor Henry's church to personally check in and make their services directly available (Henry, interview, December 12, 2018). During Build the Block meetings, pastors then recount their positive interactions with police and encourage their congregants to assist police efforts. At a meeting held in Pastor Henry's church, attendees remained quiet when the NCOs asked whether anyone had issues to raise. Pastor Henry then stood up, walked into the church's center aisle, and stood in between the officers and the audience. He explained that there was drug dealing on the block, and "the way to stomp it [out] is to foster that relationship between the police. We're not just to see the police as the enemy but we see the police as our ally, that we work together" (Sector 55C, November 2018). Next, he recounted how he gave the NCOs access to the church's surveillance system and reported that he'd already seen a decline in drug activity on the block. The temperament of the meeting then changed as the audience gradually opened up and began voicing complaints.

Police value and want to protect these clergy relationships. Even when residents seek enforcement action *against* religious institutions for rule violations, police choose *non*enforcement in these instances. At a Sector 80B meeting, an elderly resident named Eva introduced herself as president of her building's tenant association. She explained how "dealing with the church is a delicate issue," but "for fifteen years, they have abused a privilege of double-parking" (Sector 80B, May 2019). Specifically, Eva complained, congregants double-parked outside her building during every church service, thereby impeding disabled tenants from entering and exiting, preventing deliveries, and forcing a caterer who lives there to carry her food across the street to load her vehicle.

After asking questions to clarify the issue, the NCOs proposed to arrange a meeting between the building and the pastor. Eva balked; this was the same solution they proposed six months earlier, when she emailed them and the NCOs met with her in her apartment. The NCOs reiterated: "I want to set up a meeting between you and the head of the church, and that's the answer that I can give you at this moment." They cemented this solution in their formal write-up of the meeting. In an interview afterward, however, Eva's attitude was defeatist: the issue would likely go unresolved, because the precinct's Community Affairs officers attended the specific church she had complained about (Eva, interview, May 14, 2019). In fact, the church had ties to the Fifty-Fifth Precinct Clergy Council and was part of the NCOs' rotating list of locations to hold Build the Block meetings. While this was the final meeting that I observed Eva attend, this was not the last Build the Block meeting held in that particular church.

Housing Complexes

Besides religious institutions, NCOs often hold meetings in housing complexes ($N = 333, 15.1\%$). In the Fifty-Fifth Precinct, the major complex is Brooklyn Gardens, introduced in this book's opening vignette. Its 2,500 apartments on four square blocks house twelve thousand to fifteen thousand tenants (Jeffrey Rosen, interview, October 31, 2018). Historically known for murders that would make both the front and back pages of city newspapers, Brooklyn Gardens had more recently been sold to private investors. From the time I began this project up until the location rotation guideline in 2019, every Sector 55B Build the Block meeting was held on the property. Just as Build the Blocks in churches seek to draw already active congregants, so Build the Blocks in Brooklyn Gardens tend to draw the already active members of the complex's tenant association. Alisha Grey, the seventy-three-year-old association president and newest member of the Fifty-Fifth Precinct Community Council, explained how the NCOs referred to the tenant association as their "support group" and frequently checked in with Alisha's office as they drove around the sector (Alisha Grey, interview, March 9, 2019). The NCOs also attended the various events held within the Brooklyn Gardens community center, including three out of ten tenant meetings that Alisha runs per year. The officers even frequently stopped by just to use the bathroom—easier than driving back to the precinct station.

Also present at each Build the Block meeting was Brooklyn Gardens' director of security, Jeffrey Rosen—the Fifty-Fifth Precinct Community Council's Community Service Award recipient. When one of the NCOs introduced me to the building management, that officer described their relationship as "cereal and milk." Jeffrey, along with Brooklyn Gardens property manager Sean Spiegel, spearheaded the installation of fifteen hundred cameras costing $2.5 million; a central command center monitored twenty-four hours a day; two Smart cars to patrol the courtyards; and five hundred LED lights to illuminate the property as if "you're walking into a baseball field" (Jeffrey Rosen, interview, October 31, 2018). What Jeffrey described as his "close relationship" with the Fifty-Fifth Precinct translated in practice to prioritized access to police services. Just the other day, he called a sergeant because "we had a whole group of guys hanging out and blocking the entrance, playing dice, smoking marijuana, littering." Whereas calling 911 "takes a while" because "they put you in a queue," he proudly shared his ability to make a direct phone call to ask the sergeant for immediate help. Jeffrey estimated that he has worked with the Fifty-Fifth Precinct to execute over 150 arrests on the property in just two years. "We've done a lot of evictions and identified problematic apartments, and done no-knock warrants with the NYPD, we've recovered handguns and identified very dangerous people, and they've been removed from this property." Not only does the precinct keep a patrol car stationed outside Brooklyn Gardens, but NCOs have key fobs and "unlimited access to where they want" within the property.

The Socialization of Constituents

As I attended meetings, over time I observed one particularly salient indicator of police effectiveness in forming a constituency: returning residents gradually adopting police vernacular. For instance, when identifying locations, core attendees would often state each individual digit within numbers the same way that officers did—instead of referring to their address as "One Hundred Twenty-Fifth Street" or to the "Eighty-First Precinct," they would say "one-two-five" or the "eight-one precinct." These attendees not only familiarized themselves with the hierarchy in the police department's command structure, but they referred to precinct leadership by the abbreviated titles used by NCOs to denote their supervisors: CO for commanding officer and XO for executive officer. Such social mirroring reflects how meetings socialize certain residents, transforming those receptive to police services into reliable returnees, even allies.

NCOs began noticing the familiar faces. At the start of a 55D meeting, the NCO explained, "The Build the Block is if anybody has any questions, most of you guys are familiar faces, but anything, any questions or concerns" (Sector 55D, June 2018). In Sector 55B, the NCOs similarly cut their introduction short after pointing out that "most of you guys are our usual guests, so you understand what's going on" (Sector 55B, December 2018). NCO introductions across sectors grew briefer, no longer welcomes but welcome backs.

The return attendees began to take on a key role within meetings. After a while, it was constituents—not NCOs—who contested newcomers offering alternative ways of assessing and resolving neighborhood problems. At an 80D meeting, a middle-aged African American building superintendent complained about groups of teenagers going onto the roof of his building to smoke, drink, and do drugs. NCO Perez requested footage from the building's security cameras as well as a key fob to gain continued access. An older African American resident named Israel, attending his first meeting, then asked, "I'm just curious, the people going on the roof, under the age of fifteen, is it possible, before we put their names into the system for the first time, is it possible to notify these kids that it's illegal to be on the rooftop?" (Sector 80D, June 2018). The superintendent responded, "They never listen," but Israel pushed back against the generalization: "No, no, I don't want to assume that they're not gonna listen. You give them the benefit of the doubt. Tell them up front."

That's when other residents—not the NCOs—joined the conversation to contest Israel. One pointed out, "But it's not their building, why would they be going on the roof?" Another referenced the "no trespassing signage" in buildings and put herself in the superintendent's shoes: "If you come into our building, you know you don't live here, [then] you know damn well you're not supposed to be on the roof." A third stated the implication: "So you're trespassing." This was the last meeting I saw Israel attend. As voices like his drop out of department channels, the Policing Machine further succeeds in consolidating constituents.

SORTING INTO CHANNELS

"So, when we call 911, are you guys coming with guns, or not?"

An audience member shouted this question during the monthly meeting of the Seventy-First Precinct Community Council. This meeting was different from those held in previous months. Just two weeks earlier, on April 4, 2018, four officers had fired ten shots, killing thirty-four-year-old Saheed Vassell. Police were responding to a pair of 911 calls reporting an individual pointing something at pedestrians, but rather than a gun, Vassell was found to have been holding a "small metal object" (New York State Office of the Attorney General 2019, 1). A larger than usual crowd gathered at this month's community council meeting to participate in what the NYPD has referred to as the "oldest and most successful expression of 'community policing.'"[6]

On the stage, the commanding officer of the Seventy-First Precinct, Deputy Inspector Frank Giordano, apparently did not understand the question: "Can you just repeat that question, sir? So, you're just asking if we respond with guns?"

Another audience member yelled, "Are you coming with weapons to somebody in crisis?"

"Sure, our weapon on our belt is our weapon on our belt."

Sensing the flippant undertone in Inspector Giordano's reply, the audience member countered: "What? It's not funny, it's not a joke, somebody is dead."

The inspector's confusion returned: "I don't understand the question you're asking, sir."

Then the president of the Seventy-First Precinct Community Council intervened. He was an older, dark-skinned man wearing an NYPD-blue-colored crossing guard vest labeled Volunteer NYPD Community Council President on the back. At one point during the meeting, he claimed, "I'm the representative of the people to the police department." He suggested rephrasing the question.

"The question I'm asking is, when you respond to people in mental crisis . . . are you gonna respond to them without weapons?"

Inspector Giordano answered, "Sir, we respond to all situations with respect and dignity." The audience laughed, and various people interjected with versions of "That's not true." Nonetheless, Giordano was finished with the line of questioning: "We respond to every situation with respect and dignity, sir. There are certain elements of a situation that cause us to take certain actions. Every situation is different."

The next month, at the May meeting, the activists in the audience returned—this time with Vassell's father, who asked, "I hear you say that the names of these officers cannot be released because it's under investigation. But hours after Saheed Vassell was murdered, videos of him was on the media, pictures of him was on the media. Why is there a double standard, that even though there's an investigation, there were pictures of him in the media? Is it right for the police department to put out pictures and videos of someone while it is under investigation?" This time, Inspector Giordano responded dryly: "The police department regrets the loss of life under any circumstances. The incident that occurred that day was very difficult for us to handle as a police department."

By the June meeting, the Seventy-First Precinct Community Council had begun resuming its routine procedures. The Community Affairs officer began the meeting by summarizing: "Obviously, we've had a couple of rough meetings, things got a little contentious" (Seventy-First Precinct Community Council, June 2018). But that day, the atmosphere was calm in the sense that most of the activists who had attended the previous two meetings were otherwise occupied—they were in Manhattan showing solidarity with colleagues and staging a protest at the Immigration and Customs Enforcement headquarters. June's meeting audience was a third of the size of the previous two.

And by the end of June, the council was no longer having discussions about Saheed Vassell. It held its annual Harmony Day picnic, a quarter-century-old event "to strengthen the bonds within the community, among the community, and between the police officers and the community" (field note, June 2018). After marching from the police precinct station to a nearby basketball court, officers grilled and gave out free food. The NYPD Community Affairs Bureau brought a rock-climbing wall, McGruff the Crime Dog, and a bouncy house embellished with a cartoon police car. Just three months after Vassell had been killed, Inspector Giordano announced, "We stand here as a community, tall and proud." He'd be made deputy by June 2019.

The Policing Machine imposes a particular social order on neighborhood life that is organized around the promise of police services in exchange for public support. Everyone at these events is a community member. However, some share the stage with the deputy inspector, while others must shout from the audience. Within the audience, some are invited to attend each and every police-community meeting; in contrast, the absence of others enables the meeting to resume course. These distinctions align with divergent community demands, hence the presence or absence of healing after the police killing of Vassell. While some could put the Vassell case behind them with the upcoming Harmony Day picnic, others continued mobilizing beyond these events to end the practice of armed police responding to mental health crises. The Policing Machine emerges from this variation.

Interviews with the alternative voices from the audience provide context as to why their presence at police-community meetings is strategic rather than routine. I asked Nasir, the aforementioned founding director of a member organization of RALLY (Reforms Advancing Long Lives for our Youth), whether he had attended a community council meeting previously: "We've gone—as a way to counter them" (Nasir, interview, July 6, 2018). He gave the Vassell meeting in May as an example. It began just like any other one, with representatives from various offices and organizations providing updates and announcements. One elected official explained how he just passed a new ordinance that restricted people with domestic violence offenses from owning firearms. Then Nasir shouted from the audience: "What about the cops? They have the highest rate of sexual and domestic violence of any workforce. Why do they have guns?" He imitated how the representative stumbled over his words at the unexpected pushback. But the contestation was just the precursor to demanding justice for Vassell and questioning the logic and ethics of police policies that had led to his violent death. By contesting or contextualizing the information provided in meetings, RALLY members seek to intervene in the routine socialization of council meeting attendees.

If RALLY members were to actually attend each meeting, however, it would involve a trade-off. Engaging in the organized disruption of meeting information does not directly translate into either justice or accountability. Corey, the white elementary schoolteacher and organizational campaign coordinator from chapter 1, had attended community council meetings "where people have criticized the police, and have basically been told by the elected council members that this is not the appropriate venue for that," that community councils are "not here to criticize the police. We're not here to ask them about complaints against officers. . . . That's not what this is about. This is about celebrating the police" (Corey, interview, August 2, 2018). Similarly, Michelle, the director of RALLY, described Build the Block and community council meetings as "not a site where we're gonna change [police], it's not a site that's gonna decrease police violence" (Michelle, interview, November 20, 2019). Neither department channels (e.g., Build the Blocks) nor partner channels (e.g., community and clergy councils) are outlets where Corey, Michelle, and others believe they can substantively transform police.

An older activist named Tanya remembered that in 2014, after Eric Garner's murder, RALLY members attended the Seventy-First Precinct Community Council meeting to demand a separate meeting with the police. They complained, "You got these cops, they constantly coming into the community, they constantly harassing us. Their presence is intimidating to the residents—people don't want to show up because you got, like, twenty cops standing outside. Clearly, there's something wrong happening" (Tanya, interview, June 27, 2018). The council president promised to set up the meeting Tanya wanted, but after a year had passed, she got the message: "We're not gonna set up the meeting, because we don't like the way you behave." Eventually, her demands for a private meeting ended, because she stopped attending community council meetings.

Nor could RALLY members reliably turn to clergy councils for help in amplifying their complaints against police. At the national level, the Black church has been largely absent from the front lines of the Black Lives Matter movement, especially when compared with their prominence during the Civil Rights movement (Little Edwards and Oyakawa 2022). In Brooklyn, only a select few clergy members substantively supported RALLY's cause. For instance, Nasir described Pastor Larry as a "radical" who actually opened his church building to meetings and copwatch trainings, even when others advised against it (Nasir, interview, July 6, 2018). He also organized panels where people like Nasir were invited to sit alongside elected officials;

as Nasir attested, he "never tried to police our politics." Beyond Pastor Larry, however, most neighborhood clergy who were active in policing issues were members of the clergy council, about which Nasir declared, "They don't speak for everybody."

As residents sorted themselves into channels based on where they believed their complaints were most likely to be amplified, interactions across channels diminished. Mobilizing for justice for Saheed Vassell was the central campaign for RALLY groups for months, and it remains a priority as I write. However, despite the Eightieth Precinct's proximity to the precinct in which Vassell was murdered, neither the president nor the vice president of the Eightieth Precinct Community Council recognized the name or the incident when I brought them up. RALLY had held protests and vigils for Vassell within the Eightieth Precinct itself, and still they were unfamiliar. This reflects just how little exposure those participating in community councils had to the central policing concerns of other groups within the same neighborhood.

At the same time, RALLY members often formed strong perceptions against community councils without ever having attended a single meeting. After I asked Bill whether he had specific changes he wanted to see, he cited the Garner case and began listing what the NYPD commissioner should have done differently: "naming the police officers, suspending them (he has the power to suspend without pay any police officer), and having an investigation conducted (not by the NYPD, but by an outside agency)" (Bill, interview, July 30, 2018). Echoing his view toward Build the Block meetings, Bill suggested that raising these issues at community council meetings would be useless. In his mind, the meetings were mere "distractions," enabling, "at best, little tweaks around the edges of the problem and at worst, actually provid[ing] a cover for what the NYPD is doing on a regular basis." By cover, Bill meant that the meetings allowed police to "defuse some of the pressure on them," since they distracted the public from the underlying issue of abusive policing. But when I asked him whether he had ever attended a community council meeting, he said, "No, I have not." He was simply *sure* that the meetings were ineffective channels to get his concerns heard.

The sorting of constituents and their complaints into different channels, as will be explained in the next chapter, positions police to adopt targeted strategies for social control over each of them.

—

This chapter focused on the second stage of the Policing Machine: cultivating local constituents. It identified two ways that police do so: establishing alternative neighborhood representatives and coordinating access to established audiences. These strategies helped solidify community councils and clergy councils as sources of constituents that police can draw from in furthering their own department channels. The scene of engaged residents is small, and these strategies helped cultivate a set of familiar faces across community councils, clergy councils, and Build the Block meetings. In fact, many residents and NCOs even remarked how they were seeing *me* "everywhere."

Cultivating constituents is an exclusionary process. Ideal constituents enable police to claim community legitimacy without challenging police authority. Police seek to provide services to those who demand them. These are the voices invited to community initiatives, elevated to leadership positions on councils, and mobilized to invite peers to get their networks involved too. These relationships are thus unrepresentative of the range of community preferences regarding police. The voices, perspectives, and preferences that go unheard must organize and sort themselves into independent channels to amplify their demands.

As police cultivate constituents, however, a new set of challenges arises. Specifically, police must simultaneously empower their partnering organizations—like community councils and clergy councils—while containing the influence of independent channels like RALLY. The following chapter discusses how, in the third stage of the Policing Machine, police selectively distribute public resources, regulatory leniency, and coercive force to empower partners and contain independent organizers.

3

Distributing Power and Privilege

James Jones, the thirty-six-year-old African American activist I met at a Build the Block meeting, invited me to his youth empowerment organization's Summer Kick-Off event: an outdoor barbeque in a neighborhood park that featured a talent show, a dance competition, and other activities for young people in the community (field note, April 2018). As introduced in chapter 2, James had been previously elected but then dismissed as sergeant at arms of his community council, given that the nonprofit he founded was interested in starting a copwatch patrol. Still, he believed that officers could and should have positive relationships with neighborhood youth, so each year he has continued to invite the police precinct to attend the Summer Kick-Off. As we stood talking in the park, he noted that the officers had yet to arrive. I suggested that perhaps they never actually received the invitation, but he explained that since he was required to apply for an amplified sound permit and the precinct had to sign off on that, "they had to know it was going on" (James Jones, interview, July 17, 2018). Frustrated, he returned to his preparations.

I spent the morning helping James set up: unfolding tables and chairs, arranging balloons, and using a laundry basket to move frozen food from his aunt's apartment to the park. The most memorable task we had was securing electricity, a key resource for the outdoor event's DJ equipment, microphone, and sound system. A seemingly trivial undertaking, the logistics involved had actually taken days to coordinate (field note, July 17, 2018). First, James had to persuade a family friend to power the Summer Kick-Off with electricity from their third-floor apartment. Then, he needed a series of extension cords and some dedicated helpers. From the apartment window, a "tosser" had to throw the extension cords down to "catchers" waiting inside the park. But it wasn't that easy. The window was barred, forcing the tosser to stick his hand through a narrow opening; the park was perpendicular to the building, so the tosser had to throw the cord about twenty feet to his left; and the cord had to clear the fence surrounding the park, which prevented the catchers from coming any closer.

The first try at electrification failed. The cord slapped the ground and did not clear the fence. Painstakingly, the tosser reeled the cord hand over hand, pulling it back up to the third floor.

The second toss also failed. The tosser retracted the cord once more as catchers began congregating around the fence and yelling out chaotic directions. "You gotta lasso it. Make it into a ring," they shouted while using gestures to accentuate their ideas. It was unclear whether the tosser saw or heard them, given the distance and the background din of the city.

The third try failed too, but finally, after several more attempts, the lasso technique worked. After days of coordination, we had power. We rushed to finish the remaining tasks.

In contrast to these challenges, I asked Mr. Holloway, the Eightieth Precinct Community Council president, how the council gets electricity for its events. He replied, "We can go to one of the officers, and they'll come out and help us get electricity from the light pole" (Holloway, interview, July 10, 2018). Because police departments are a city agency that can provide access to public utilities like streetlights, obtaining electricity for community council events is as easy as asking an officer to plug the extension cord into the nearest light pole. In the aggregate, such assistance eases the execution of public events for certain organizations. Based on how police exercise their discretion, their help can enable community organizations to avoid logistical hurdles and resource burdens to focus more on the substantive goals of their events. This chapter explains how police departments selectively distribute public resources, regulatory leniency, and coercive force—and how their doing so is fundamental to the strategic relationship-building that undergirds the Policing Machine.

—

Far from neutral actors, police are powerful decision-makers in the distribution of key public resources. In the classic principal-agent sense, there is a misalignment between the *public* as owners of these resources and the *police* as the distributors of them. On the one hand, police control material resources, as with officers who might serve as event volunteers and offer precinct stations as meeting spaces for select community groups. These assets are uniquely available to police departments as opposed to other local institutions, because for decades cities have concentrated public resources in policing organizations (Auxier 2020). Police are now positioned to strategically distribute these resources to empower partner channels and the constituents within them, amplifying their demands for police services. The Policing Machine highlights how public resources continuously distributed through officers' hands become police resources instead and part of the project of naturalizing police power.

At the same time, the police as a coercive force is also a public resource. Routine decisions regarding where to focus its attention shape the regulatory landscape for neighborhood groups (Fassin 2013). The mere presence of uniformed police, flashing light bars on patrol vehicles, and specialized transport vans can even create second-order costs for certain neighborhood organizations holding public events, as it can deter residents from participating in independent channels by increasing the anticipated costs of both police contact and being associated with an event surrounded by police. For these reasons, how police distribute regulatory leniency matters as much as how they distribute coercive force. *Regulatory leniency* refers to situations where police have the authority, capacity, and opportunity to enforce the law but tolerate its violation instead. Such tolerance is a political choice and a subset of nonenforcement, wherein police have the opportunity to enforce a violation but decide not to (Holland 2016). Regulatory leniency is also conditional, as its withdrawal can allow enforcement to proceed. The conditionality of enforcement means that the threat of enforcement permanently lingers for constituents and nonconstituents alike.

Each of these decisions is essential to the Policing Machine, because the strategic distribution of public resources, regulatory leniency, and coercive force helps police retain the constituents they cultivate. But the targeted distribution of power and privilege advances more substantive goals than "mere" retention of constituents—it empowers certain groups in ways that underwrite their organizational survival, provides a stage that amplifies their voices, and in the aggregate, maintains an organizational landscape supportive of police practices. It ensures that neighborhood organizations that do not receive this largesse encounter greater struggles in terms of organizational survival, amplifying their concerns, and mobilizing momentum to fundamentally challenge policing institutions. And it means that police accumulate political capital along the way, since the strategic distribution of resources engenders goodwill, influence, and favors that can be mobilized for future gain.

The first portion of this chapter focuses on how police approach resource distribution across neighborhood organizations. How the Policing Machine deploys resources to gain influence over potential partners varies depending on the community entity's existing organizational capacity. I argue that the NYPD takes two different approaches: *capacity-building*, direct, hands-on assistance and resource transfers to facilitate an organization's operations; and *cooptation*, avoidance of substantive organizational change by incorporating stakeholders who are credible to key constituents. The former is aimed at those organizations, like community councils run by volunteers, with otherwise low capacity independent of the police department. The latter is aimed at groups already endowed with organizational capacity independent of the police department—in this case, for example, each clergy council member already leads a church with staff, meeting spaces, and other resources. Whereas police provide basic organizational resources to build the capacity of community councils, cultivating and co-opting the legitimacy of clergy councils require even more valuable resources like priority police access and attention.

In the second portion of the chapter, I turn to the ways police strategically distribute regulatory leniency and coercive force. Partner channels like community and clergy councils directly benefit from having the state's regulatory enforcers as an ally. From electric access to event permits, police provide regulatory leniency that eases the execution of council events—occasions that provide a stage for police and other partners to endorse the quality of current policing. In contrast, independent channels, like those organized by RALLY

(Reforms Advancing Long Lives for Our Youth), not only must abide by strictly enforced regulations for each public event they hold but face an ideological dilemma: rule-break and lack recourse, or affirm the power of the very institution they seek to transform. These decisions around public resources and regulatory leniency demonstrate just how intimately police shape the landscape of voices, events, and organizations mobilizing around policing in local neighborhoods.

DISTRIBUTING PUBLIC RESOURCES

Under the Policing Machine, police adopt different approaches to gain influence over community groups organizing partner channels: capacity-building and cooptation.

Capacity-Building

Capacity-building involves direct, hands-on assistance and resource transfers to facilitate an organization's operations. For instance, to advance the missions, events, and tasks of community organizations having low organizational capacity, police provide a variety of resources: material (meeting space, basic supplies), human (workers), and informational (bureaucratic insights into how to hold public events) (see Cress and Snow 1996). Lacking independent capacity, these groups can become reliant on police assistance over time; this helps police gain influence and control over the groups' everyday operations.

The benefits of capacity-building are clearest when contrasted with the obstacles that independent channels endure. RALLY director Michelle explained the importance of securing a fiscal sponsor—a practice where a more established nonprofit offers its tax-exempt and legal status to other groups, becoming able to accept, administer, and manage funds on the subsidiary's behalf (Michelle, interview, November 20, 2019). Now renting office space from its fiscal sponsor, RALLY finally has reliable access to a copy machine and meeting space. Previously, it had moved offices four times in seven years and often relied on its member organizations to book meeting rooms for event planning: "If we had a meeting or a big event, we'd call one of the organizations who might have a little more money or access to copiers. It's not gonna hurt them to make five hundred copies of something, and then we'd say you need to bring five hundred copies of this—or split it up among a bunch of organizations."

RALLY's fiscal sponsor could not solve every administrative need, however. For instance, it could not assist with managing transportation. Covering the costs of public transportation is important so that members can attend meetings, demonstrations, and other events that advance RALLY's organizational goals of police transformation. As a coalition of small, grassroots organizations representing communities of color, Michelle emphasized how "informally, we do a lot of resource sharing to try to make sure that different things can be accessible to folks"; when one group or another can fit it into its budget, for instance, it orders extra metro cards for distribution. Similarly, when some organizations cannot afford paid staff, RALLY fundraises for collaborative projects and shares its staff with member organizations. As groups worked, planned, and used informal resource sharing to solve problems, with or without fiscal sponsors, the problem-solving itself was a "logistical hassle" that added an additional layer of administrative strain.

In contrast, for community councils local police precincts fulfilled many of the services provided by fiscal sponsors. For instance, the primary event defining community councils is its monthly police-community meeting; meeting information is posted on each police precinct's web page alongside the precinct's contact information, the community council president's name, and general meeting information such as "Community Council meetings typically take place on the second Monday of each month at 7:30 p.m. in the precinct." On that point, I was particularly interested: across precincts, almost every community council meeting was listed as taking place inside the precinct station. Yet out of six random precincts I selected at the beginning of this study, only one actually held its community council inside the station. Most were, in fact, held either in a consistent location outside the precinct station or in rotating locations around the precinct. This further solidified the police department's monopoly on community council access: newcomers seeking to determine meeting locations needed to contact the precinct's Community Affairs officers, as the volunteer board members of community councils lacked the capacity to field phone calls and inquiries. More recently, some precincts have begun posting upcoming community council meeting locations on Twitter, but even then the information remains in the hands of the police department itself—not the community council.

Police provide other mundane resources that are nonetheless integral to facilitating organizational operations. Whereas RALLY must ask favors to access printers and copy machines, community councils simply use the ones in the precinct station. And before each community council meeting in the Eightieth Precinct, the Community Affairs officer calls the council secretary to obtain the agenda by dictation (Holloway, interview, March 8, 2019). Over the phone, the secretary reads the agenda to the officer, who types it up, prints it, and distributes a copy to each meeting attendee. Community Affairs officers even arrive at the meetings bearing requested sound equipment, projectors, and tables.

Neither RALLY nor community councils had their own permanent meeting spaces, yet community councils could always hold them inside the police precinct station itself. The *Community Council Guidelines* state that "at least two (2) Council meetings should be held at an alternate location other than the designated meeting location; this ensures that consideration may be given to other members as well as attaining maximum participation at Community Council meetings."[1] However, the Fifty-Fifth Precinct holds every single monthly meeting inside the precinct station—a choice that shapes the meeting experiences of attendees. In a field note, I described my first time arriving at that precinct's community council meeting:

> I arrived at 7 p.m. for the 7:30 p.m. meeting, since it was my first one. I entered with a woman in front of me, and the officer at the desk asked if he could help her. When she replied that she was there to attend the community meeting, he said okay and asked for her ID. She said she was a new resident and was invited to the meeting, and wasn't told she needed ID. The officer apologized and said he just can't let anyone in. After a few more back-and-forths, the officer said he would need to ask a sergeant. He got the sergeant, they explained the lack of ID, and he said okay, but she cannot come in until 7:30 p.m.—"that's when we start letting people in and go upstairs." (Fifty-Fifth Precinct Community Council, April 2018)

Given that the meeting space is in a nonpublic area of the Fifty-Fifth's station, officers ask newcomers to present identification and prohibit them from entering until the precise meeting time. A former gang member who attended the meeting to inquire about activities for local youth commented on this practice directly during a council meeting I observed: "One more thing, my kids are scared to come in here, because every time we were in here prior to today, it's like panic attacks—we were arrested. Every time we came in here, we were in handcuffs. So it feels very uncomfortable to come to a community meeting" (Fifty-Fifth Precinct Community Council, April 2019). Opting to meet in station houses alienates those individuals most skeptical of police intentions, again limiting the possibility of complaints calling for reform.

The Eightieth Precinct Community Council rotates its meetings among various locations outside the precinct station. Out of a dozen council meetings I attended, eight were held in churches, one in a medical facility, two in a residential substance abuse rehabilitation center, and one in the precinct station. The council president, Mr. Holloway, explained the board members' awareness that the meeting location is a barrier to some in the community: "A lot of our people thought that by inviting them to come to the precinct, they thought it was like an operation, like you'd go to the precinct, you'd get arrested 'cause you coming for a meeting; a lot of people didn't want to come to the precinct to talk about their business" (Holloway, interview, March 8, 2019). Precinct leadership, he recalled, had welcomed the council's decision to hold meetings outside the precinct station, because it would increase meeting attendance—itself an important signal of police-community relations for supervisors. Mr. Holloway recounted, "When I took over, there was something like maybe fifteen people would show up at the meetings—maybe. So they [police department] was looking to get more people involved, because at that time, they wanted the higher-ups to say, 'Well, they're working with the community.'"

Transportation proved to be a challenge for the councils, just as it did for groups like RALLY. Holding meetings outside the precinct station, for instance, potentially cut down the attendance of senior citizens, one of police's most reliable constituents (Goldstein 2021). Rather than stockpiling metro cards, however, community councils

offered transportation from the precinct station to the meeting location. Before every meeting, a police van in each precinct picks up
and drops off groups of seniors and residents with disabilities at designated locations within the precinct. In practice, the van service is
open to anyone who has developed a relationship with the driver from
the Community Affairs Bureau.

Individual officers also coordinate rides for community council
members. For example, the president of the Fifty-Fifth Precinct Community Council received a ride from a Community Affairs officer to
get to the precinct station for my interview and an executive community council board meeting afterward. Another time, after a meeting I
was talking with the vice president of the Eightieth Precinct Community Council, and she complained that taxis would not stop for her. A
Neighborhood Coordination Officer overheard and interjected, "Oh,
my god!" Then the officer presented her business card and promised,
"Here's my cell phone number; if you need a ride next time, give me
a call, and if I'm working, I can come get you" (Eightieth Precinct
Community Council, November 2018). The precinct even arranges
for the police van to drive community council members to organizational events, such as a trip to observe night court (Fifty-Fifth Precinct Community Council, April 2019). By providing transportation,
police assure steady attendance by reliable constituents at community
council events.

Another reason precinct leadership welcomes community council
meetings outside the precinct station is because the location change
allows police to broker relationships with new potential partners. In
February 2019, the Eightieth Precinct Community Council held a
meeting for the first time in the New Grace Tabernacle Christian Center. To open the meeting, the senior pastor welcomed the fifty-two
attendees to his church and explained its history and mission. When
Mr. Holloway spoke next, he told Reverend Wright in front the audience, "The Precinct Community Council comes with the commanding officer of the Eightieth Precinct. We like to think that we bring
resources, so I'm gonna get ready to introduce you to a big resource,
alright?" (Eightieth Precinct Community Council, February 2019).
Before the meeting ended, he had personally introduced the reverend
to the commanding officer and a representative from the Brooklyn
District Attorney's Office, making sure that they exchanged contact
information. In an interview, Mr. Holloway explained:

We make sure to tell the police right in your presence—the pastor's presence—that "Hey, you now going to have a relationship with the commanding officer here." Prior to that, they don't even know who their commanding officer is—they don't have a clue. And by us, the mere fact of our presence at your place, your stock goes up, because now you got the CO's telephone number, you know who the Community Affairs officers are, and you have an open door now. . . . And plus, you can always call me. And if you're having a problem, we'll go in and try to be the buffer to make that situation disappear. And plus, we're letting the CO know that hey, that's my friend. Look out for them. (Holloway, interview, March 8, 2019)

These new contacts increase the political capital of each of the parties involved. The community council presents itself as a resource broker that bridges the precinct to the neighborhood groups; the church gains access to the community council and police precinct to help resolve any issues that arise; and most important, the Policing Machine is advanced the more police cultivate constituents among those who view them as a valuable public resource.

Cooptation

For neighborhood organizations that already have high organizational capacity, police primarily pursue a strategy of cooptation. Unable to offer capacity to gain influence, police departments instead offer prioritized access to police services to build strategic relationships and accumulate political capital that can be mobilized for future public endorsements. High-capacity community organizations thus represent cooptation targets, or actors who can act as "credible to key constituents, yet who are unlikely to demand dramatic changes in organizational activities" (Suchman 1995, 589).

Cooptation succeeds when strategic targets are symbolically incorporated into the organization yet lack substantive influence. From federal agencies like the Tennessee Valley Authority (Selznick 1949) to local governments deciding about land-use projects (Levine 2017), state institutions routinely co-opt community representatives to legitimize decision-making. In this case, cooptation enables police to reappropriate the sources of the neighborhood group's high capacity and local legitimacy for the purposes of the Policing Machine.

As noted earlier, clergy councils have, independent of the police, a wide and reliable congregational volunteer base, ample meeting spaces, dedicated administrative staff, and sanctified routines for running events. Unlike community councils, clergy councils do not need police's help with capacity-building. Instead, police gain influence over clergy councils by offering them heightened police access and complaint priority. In other words, police co-opt by providing prioritized access to police services.

Clergy councils have more police access than community councils in basic ways. For example, while community council meetings are open to all members of the public, clergy council meetings are more intimate, designed for open conversation between the commanding officer and a recurrent group of ten to twenty pastors. Without the general public present, the pastors and the police are free to discuss specific case details without fear of consequences for their candor. Often, clergy council meetings focus on police reports about gun violence and how clergy can help police reduce it. The Fifty-Fifth Precinct Clergy Council distributes a list of all the fatal and nonfatal shootings across Brooklyn, including a brief synopsis of relevant details, such as the victim's demographics, the shooting location, and the suspect's assumed motive. Though Pastor Young invited me to attend these clergy-only meetings, I was not permitted to attend the even more sensitive meetings that the clergy council sometimes held with the commanding officer in the hour beforehand. In those hypersensitive meetings, police and pastors discuss upcoming actions, such as taking a joint approach toward a "problematic" building where pastors would "occupy" public spaces inside and around it in anticipation of enforcement action.

Another example of the clergy council's heightened police access involves identification cards, which the NYPD issues only to the presidents of community councils but to every member of the clergy council. What does the ID do? Reverend Powell explained: "It gives you access to talk to the police. And when you have an ID issued by the police department . . . the police honor it and they know that you're, you know, not their enemy" (Powell, interview, August 29, 2018). By presenting their cards to officers on the street, they can gain access to crime scenes or material and informational resources that people unaffiliated with the police department cannot. Identification cards materialize the clergy council's police affiliation, facilitating introductions whenever and wherever clergy encounter police.

More informally, police also grant clergy council members walk-in access to the precinct station to discuss issues with officers. At a Fifty-Fifth Precinct Clergy Council meeting, the council president and a Community Affairs officer jointly explained to pastors that if they ever want to come to the precinct "for any matter whatsoever," they should "never walk into this precinct cold" (Fifty-Fifth Precinct Clergy Council, September 2018). Instead, they were instructed to call the Community Affairs officers directly. The officers will come out, secure otherwise impossible to obtain street parking, and accompany them into the building. President Pastor Young emphasized the importance of calling ahead several times in the meeting, saying that he had the two Community Affairs officers' phone numbers on speed dial. He prompted the assembly: "If you come into the precinct, always what?" In unison, the clergy council responded, "Call ahead."

Pastor Young described one valuable occasion to phone their police contacts: "If you have an issue at your church, and you can't get anyone, and it's something that's really serious, you can always get in touch with the captain: Captain Milton." Captain Milton was the precinct's executive officer, or the second-highest-ranking officer within the precinct. He would know how to respond to the clergy's situation, since he oversaw the precinct's personnel decisions. This relationship was particularly important on weekends, when church services are held, Pastor Young emphasized, before giving the assembly Captain Milton's cell phone number.

All this amplified police access means that clergy council complaints receive prioritized attention. It's actually formalized by the NYPD's Clergy Liaison program, which typically features the most active members of clergy councils. These liaisons, the NYPD claims, are an "invaluable ally," because their "close connections to the community place them in a unique position to identify and intervene in community issues early on, acting as a link between the department and the people they serve."[2] Like auxiliary officers (see chapter 1), the Clergy Liaison program represents another mechanism for recruiting community stakeholders into the project of policing as essentially volunteer officers. To become a liaison, local clergy must be nominated by precinct leadership, approved by NYPD headquarters, attend a ten-week Citizen's Police Academy, and then participate in various activities to "improve public safety and police community relations throughout New York City."[3] Police thus recognize clergy as an important partner channel through which community complaints will be voiced.

In addition to calling if "you have an issue at your church," Pastor Young provided another example of when members should call their Community Affairs contacts within the department: "A member [of your church] arrested? Don't know what to do in the Fifty-Fifth? Call me. Call them. Alright? When we call them, they will tell us exactly what's the deal, what's the case, what's the charges, and what do we do next. Alright?" (Fifty-Fifth Precinct Clergy Council, September 2018). When church affiliates encounter police trouble, that is, Pastor Young advised the clergy to rely on Community Affairs to provide information, which is at a premium when someone is, for instance, taken into police custody; these same officers will be their advocates in these circumstances. In an interview, Pastor Maurice explained that he receives about two requests for help per month from his congregants—three to four requests during busier months: "Pastor, there's this man outside my house, I've called the precinct so many times, nobody's responding, they're being rude to me"; "Pastor, my son was taken here [by police]"; "My son felt like he was attacked, he unfortunately had to call the police, but they told me he was taken to one place, I don't know where he is" (Maurice, interview, March 7, 2019). In these situations, Pastor Maurice would call his contacts in the precinct, locate his congregant's loved ones, and figure out how best to navigate the situation.

Underscoring the value of this access, Pastor Maurice spoke of a Friday evening the summer prior. That night, a young man leaving Pastor Maurice's church youth group noticed two men running up behind him. Neither man announced "Police!" or ordered "Freeze!" (Maurice, interview, March 7, 2019). The youth, who had been robbed of his belt the previous month, ran out of fear. The two men tackled him, demanded "Where's the gun?" and searched him. He responded that he did not know what they were referring to, and after the search came up empty, the two men simply walked away. The youth told his mother, who called the precinct; she got the runaround. So the next day, she called Pastor Maurice. By Sunday, these concerns were being aired by the pastor in a face-to-face meeting with the chief of the NYPD Community Affairs Bureau:

> I have this concern that was lifted up last night, concerning this young man who was coming from youth group, Bible study, who was assaulted, who was taken advantage of, who feels afraid, scared, nervous, distrustful of this department that's trying to build these bridges. And now you not only have this young man, but an entire youth group that has brought forth trauma—that the police is not there to protect, but rather to bully and to intimidate. . . . This is not an isolated incident, but it's incidents like these that cause policing to become even more problematic, because you're not able to have access when you want witnesses, when you want information. It's not gonna be freely given if the community feels as though the police are not there with them and for them, but rather against them. (Maurice, interview, March 7, 2019)

After the meeting, officers from the chief's office took down Pastor Maurice's information and promised they would apologize in person. Indeed, the chief of Community Affairs personally came to the Fifty-Fifth Precinct, met with the youth's family and the church youth group, and apologized. Though Pastor Maurice helped the family file a complaint with the police department, the precinct took no disciplinary actions—without badge numbers, it claimed, it couldn't determine which plainclothes officers had searched the youth. In addition, it made no changes to policy or practice. But a direct apology from a high-ranking NYPD officer smoothed things over and kept the relationships between the cops and the clergy council intact.

I asked Pastor Maurice how his congregants know about his police access. First, he said, he infuses references into the church services: "I include narratives, stories, or things that have happened in my sermons." He cites specific situations based on what he's learned from clergy council meetings, and he asks the congregation to pray: "So I say listen, this is what happened in the community this week, this is what's going on. Let us pray as a congregation. We're working with so-and-so." Second, Pastor Maurice figured that congregants could connect the dots based on the guests he invites to his church: "They know just from who they see come here and who they've seen me with and things that have taken place previously. And you must have access to be able to do that." He views his police access as just another way he can assist his congregants in need.

Father Joseph, of the Eightieth Precinct Clergy Council, detailed the benefits of having police present at all his church services. As people enter the church, they are often greeted by officers. The presence of police deters disruptions that might warrant a police response— these happen "very rarely" now, "because as [people] come in, they see police" (Joseph, interview, December 21, 2018). Once, when Father Joseph wanted police help with a disturbance and the officers happened not to be there, they personally called him to apologize: "Sorry, Father Joseph, we got called away to another job." Unsure how this arrangement with police began, the priest remembered only that "they asked one time what was the schedule and I told them, and they've been there since." Father Joseph was even confident that no matter how many houses of worship dotted the precinct, "if you go to any of them during their worship times, there's somebody from the Eightieth Precinct there. They really are there. They really are very, very good." At the end of each year, the precinct makes sure to ask Father Joseph for any updates to service times. "It's really, really great. It's like automatic now." He felt honored to invite officers and firefighters to attend service every September 11 so that parishioners could pray for these first responders.

Emphasizing that police responses are rarely needed during church service, Father Joseph had nonetheless used his police contacts to resolve several issues for himself and his congregants. For instance, a car had been left parked outside his church—"one of those cars where they have a phone number plastered on the side of the car as an advertisement for a cell phone service." After several days, Father Joseph called his contacts in the precinct, and the very next day "it was gone. I don't know what they did, but it was gone." Similarly, there was a Sunday when police closed off traffic in one direction on the street where his church is located, but Father Joseph had obtained permission to travel the opposite way for just the brief distance to get to his church. Nonetheless, he was pulled over and lectured: "You know, you could've hit somebody." The pastor countered that he'd received permission, to which the officer responded, "Just so you know, I think that's wrong." At that, Father Joseph said boldly, "Do me a favor. Call

[Commanding Officer] Christian Morris, tell him you spoke to the pastor of St. Augustine's like that." By the time the pastor parked his car, went upstairs, and looked out the window, the police officer had left—no longer stationed near the church.

Father Joseph's police access also aided in getting his congregants' complaints prioritized. One church member who "wanted to check on someone living in their building who they hadn't heard from in a while" came to him, because the police had told her that other cases were higher priority, so they needed additional cause to conduct a wellness check. At first, Father Joseph got the same response, but after reiterating his request, the Eightieth Precinct agreed: "Okay, let me see what we can do." Officers checked on the apartment, and the tenant was inside—previously, they had simply declined to open the door. And so, whether it was outright help or an "okay-let-me-see-what-we-can-do," Father Joseph regarded the precinct as accommodating and responsive to him and to his congregants.

Yet there are limits to the prioritized access that police can provide clergy. Pastor Maurice explained that if an individual has received a DWI or is "already in the system," then his help becomes primarily informational (Maurice, interview, March 7, 2019). He can help locate the family member—the clergy council has contacts in the district attorney's office as well—and provide his congregant with "information, guidance, as well as peace that they're okay, they're being taken care of." He can also provide direction on next steps, and sometimes he can even "go in [to the jail] and speak with them in areas because of clergy access." Though he emphasized that he cannot "obstruct justice" or otherwise circumvent the criminal justice system, these affordances are no small thing: aside from bail bondsmen (Page, Piehowski, and Soss 2019), few others hold the sorts of information that families so desperately need when a loved one is locked up.

In return, clergy councils help the police officers who take their calls and otherwise advance their interests. The Fifty-Fifth Precinct Clergy Council regularly campaigns for the promotion of specific officers, like Dayana White. Officer White had been a Community Affairs officer in the Fifty-Fifth Precinct since CO Bobby Banks convened the council (see chapter 2). Pastor Maurice characterized her as someone from the neighborhood who worked "well with us, very accessible, gave us insight and direction as to what's going on—like, 'it looks this way, but this is what's really happening'" (Maurice, interview, March 7, 2019). He described the council's campaign efforts on her behalf, hoping she would be promoted to detective:

> We campaigned to every commanding officer, to every deputy chief, to the chief and the commissioner. Whenever we had meetings, whenever we had opportunities, that would be part of our agenda. . . . Now, we didn't have to tell them what they had to do, but they understood and recognized that this was somebody who has been with us and for us, and we continued to just lift that name up. . . . We also gave her an award from the clergy council just to honor her as well, and she was elevated [to detective] and we continue to celebrate her elevation. (Maurice, interview, March 7, 2019)

The campaign paid off: White was not only promoted to detective, she was assigned to be one of NYPD Commissioner James O'Neill's liaisons. Now when Detective White regularly attends Fifty-Fifth Precinct Clergy Council meetings, it is as a formal representative of the commissioner's office—and it is frequent. I observed Detective White attend three times as many Fifty-Fifth Precinct Clergy Council meetings as any other clergy council or community council meeting. With its direct contact in the commissioner's office, Pastor Maurice said that the council's demands were given even higher priority: "She's the one who got us a meeting with the commissioner when he first came in, as well as access so we can say: 'This is on our agenda. These are the things we want to champion.'"

The campaign to promote Detective White was not an isolated success. Each year, the Fifty-Fifth Precinct Clergy Council sponsors a Violence Reduction Summit. It invites police officers, elected officials, and survivors to gather and discuss how they can collaborate to reduce gun violence. After the 2018 summit, the clergy council announced two demands: one for a survivor advocate at the Brooklyn District Attorney's Office and the other for the NYPD to appoint a detective first grade to act as a contact in the Detectives Squad for the victim's family members. These demands were rooted in the clergy council's gun violence activism as well as its goal to improve the experiences of, and services to, homicide victims' families as police investigate cases. The council submitted these demands to the NYPD commissioner in August. By December, Pastor Young announced that Commissioner O'Neill had complied and assigned a "top-level inspector to [unsolved homicide] cases" (Fifty-Fifth Precinct Clergy Council, December 2018).

From another perspective, the success of these clergy campaigns represents successful cooptation by police. By prioritizing issues of crime and violence rather than police accountability, clergy council demands focus on improving police administration and expanding law enforcement, not reforming the institution or its practices. Besides the examples of hiring and promotion described above, clergy councils lead in the political organization of crime victims—a time-tested strategy for advancing the power of criminal justice institutions to punish (Page 2011). Religious leaders interact with these victims, especially the surviving family members of homicide victims, during one of the most sensitive and private times in their lives. By offering pastoral care and free burial services for victims of gun violence, members of the Fifty-Fifth Precinct Clergy Council form close relationships with mothers, fathers, and other family and friends. Even after the funerals, clergy councils in both the Fifty-Fifth and Eightieth Precincts support families with a group called Mothers for Hope and Healing, which enables mothers to meet together monthly, managing their grief and their paths forward through social and police services.

Grieving mothers searching for justice for their murdered child epitomize the symbolic significance of victims in the criminal justice system. Historically, policy makers have recurrently referred to crime victims to justify increased enforcement action (Simon 2007). In fact, at the Fifty-Fifth Precinct Clergy Council meetings, debates arose about whether the precinct would require clergy to submit information about the gun owners who asked them to turn over their weapons on their behalf to the police (see chapter 2). In response, officers repeatedly emphasized, "What about the mothers who lost their sons, and this person just killed her son? Because you want to gain the trust of one person, so now she can't find out who killed her son." Indeed, the mothers associated with Mothers for Hope and Healing have become prominent advocates of the controversial NYPD practice called stop-and-frisk, because they view it as a violence reduction strategy that can prevent other mothers from losing their children. As Secretary Woodward of the Fifty-Fifth Precinct Clergy Council explained, police departments fully support clergy councils organizing crime victims and initiating violence reduction strategies, because "we're helping them. So anyone who has good sense, you're not gonna work against anybody that's going to help you and help make your job easier" (Woodward, interview, September 24, 2018). Clergy councils make police's jobs easier by amplifying complementary sets of demands aimed at activating the criminal justice machinery to reduce violence and secure justice for victims.

That said, not *all* grieving mothers and crime victims make for suitable constituents who can serve law enforcement ends. Several years before my research, plainclothes officers from the Fifty-Fifth Precinct had fatally shot an African American teenager named Christopher Grant. It was nighttime, and the officers reported that the teen had moved in a suspicious manner. Of the seven shots that killed the boy, three entered his back. Police recovered a firearm from the scene, though forensics revealed it had never been fired. In the "first couple days, I was working with the family, very specifically," said Clergy Council President Pastor Young (Young, interview, January 7, 2019). It would seem that Grant's mother would be an excellent fit for the Mothers for Hope and Healing group and its services. Yet, when I asked Council Secretary Woodward about the grieving woman, she said, "I am not sure. I'm not sure. She's still around. Whether she attends Mothers for Hope and Healing, I'm not sure" (Woodward, interview, September 24, 2018). In fact, Grant's mother did *not* participate. She became instead an active participant in events organized by Reforms Advancing Long Lives for our Youth (RALLY). As a victim of police violence rather than community gun violence, she advocated for transformations that would have impeded cooptation by demanding police accountability and reform. Her voice was not one that would fit neatly into the narratives that best served the police. Toward the dissenting voices exemplified by Grant's mother, police deploy more coercive strategies to contain them as much as possible.

DISTRIBUTING REGULATORY LENIENCY AND COERCIVE FORCE

Police complement the strategic distribution of public resources by selectively deploying regulatory leniency and coercive force. Recall that regulatory leniency refers to situations in which police have the authority, capacity, and opportunity to enforce the law but tolerate its violation instead. Rules, laws, and policies can go unenforced to simultaneously empower neighborhood groups organizing partner channels, such as community and clergy councils, and strain the capacity of those entities convening independent channels, such as RALLY organizations. By exclusively pursuing regulatory enforcement against independent channels, police further increase the actual and perceived costs of participating and voicing complaints against them. Here, police's pursuit of political mobilization may include enforcement tools like citations and arrests, but the ends are not, strictly speaking, about law enforcement. Instead, police are drawing from their powers as agents of the administrative state to shape the politics of who can hold public events within neighborhoods and at what level of regulatory resistance.

Public events are important ways that neighborhood groups attract participants, increase audiences, and mobilize for organizational goals. For partner channels, police may facilitate public events by offering volunteer officers dressed in casual wear, approving requests to close streets, and granting leniency over event regulations. In contrast, police often deploy a heavier enforcement presence at the public events organized by independent channels: parked squad cars, flashing police lights, and uniformed officers stationed as both negative signals and tangible threats to participants and onlookers alike. Officers make sure participants are complying with every administrative code regulating *these* public events. Differential enforcement practices thus shape the capacity of community organizations to mobilize supporters for the channels of public input they represent— with implications for the organizational success of those groups and the complaints they channel. Local groups must differentially manage funding needs, legitimacy concerns, and core operations in response to strategic variation in police presence and prohibitions.

Event Permits and the Dilemma of Police Permission

With their formal authority over event permits, police differentially facilitate public events through both regulatory enforcement and administrative leniency. Two events held on the same date and time, just three blocks apart and in the same precinct, demonstrate police's

differential approach to local organizations. The first, an annual basketball tournament called Basketball for Accountability, honors two
young victims fatally shot by police in the Fifty-Fifth Precinct within
nine months of each other in the early 2010s. Families gather to mourn
and remember each year, renewing their commitment to demands for
police accountability. The second event, called the Peace Tour, is a
two-and-a-half-mile walk along two main avenues in Central Brooklyn. It starts on a main commercial thoroughfare a quarter mile from
the concurrent Basketball for Accountability event, and it ends in
the Fifty-Fifth Precinct with a street fair demarcated by police vans
and featuring a rock-climbing wall in the NYPD Community Affairs
booth. Whereas the Basketball for Accountability banner displayed
"#stoppolicebrutality," the Peace Tour aimed at uniting police and
community. Reverend Powell, an NYPD Clergy Liaison and member of the Fifty-Fifth Precinct Clergy Council, told me he had been
organizing the Peace Tour since 1997. He was familiar with Basketball for Accountability, but he never thought of combining the events,
because "I don't know if the messages and those who coming out to
support that, that's a decision that would have to be made by the family since their son was killed by a cop, I don't know if they want to
come out and play with a cop" (Powell, interview, August 29, 2018). In
another moment, I asked whether the reverend had obtained amplified sound permits for the Peace Tour: "Normally you should, yeah."
In fact, my Freedom of Information Law request for all sound permit
applications for August 4, 2018, in the Fifty-Fifth Precinct returned
the Basketball for Accountability application, but there was *no* application for the Peace Tour.

RALLY organizations face an ideological and a practical dilemma:
apply for sound permits, pay forty-five dollars to the police precinct,
and reinforce the power of the very organization they seek to transform, or forgo sound permits, risk enforcement action that would shut
down their event, and lack recourse for holding an event without a
permit. Some RALLY organizers decide to obtain the sound and other
permits required to hold sizable public events. For some demonstrations and marches I attended honoring victims of police violence—for
instance, Sandra Bland (field note, July 13, 2018) and Kyam Livingston
(field note, July 21, 2018)—the organizers had obtained sound permits,
parade permits, and other types of authorization from the precinct.

Most of the time, however, RALLY organizers skip the permits and accept the risk of having their events shut down by the police, with no recourse. Erickah Lewis, the organizer for Basketball for Accountability, was arranging an anniversary vigil for her sister who was fatally shot by Fifty-Fifth Precinct officers. In 2019, as they had done for several years, Erickah and her supporters gathered at the location where her sister was killed, entered the intersection in a circle formation, and released balloons. Unlike Basketball for Accountability, an event geared toward community youth, Erickah did not get permits for her sister's vigil. As she put it, "My sister was killed by police, I'm not gonna now go ask them for *permission* to have a vigil for her" (Erickah Lewis, interview, August 7, 2019). However, after Erickah and her supporters stayed in the intersection for over five minutes, Community Affairs Officer Hines began ordering, even pushing participants to clear the street. Hines and several other officers had been at the memorial for the past hour simply observing the event, which until then had taken place on the sidewalk. As tensions escalated, Hines called for backup and unmarked squad cars arrived—disrupting the spirit of the vigil and ending the memorial. While Officer Hines had initially granted Erickah regulatory leniency, it was immediately revoked at the first sign of dissatisfaction from the motorists in traffic.

For the first time ever, Erickah decided to voice her frustrations at the Fifty-Fifth Precinct Community Council meeting—the group that always meets inside the precinct station. It was only the second time she had entered that building since her sister was killed, and she described going into it as "nerve-wrecking," because "it felt like, I could see the Detective [who killed my sister] at any moment—even though he don't work there anymore—it's like, I feel like I'm gonna run into him." Nonetheless, she and her friend Steven were two of the first community members to arrive at the meeting. They immediately introduced themselves to President Lela Pessod and explained why they were there. Erickah recalled how the president informed them that they did not follow the "proper chain"—that they should have "spoke to the captain, or speak to their [Officer Hines's] supervisor, then you come to the council meeting." Erickah suspected that Pessod invoked this supposed norm of a proper chain because she preferred to handle the matter away from the eyes and ears of the public meeting. Nonetheless, she thanked Pessod for the information and explained that they wished to raise the issue at the public community meeting.

According to the meeting agenda, the appropriate time for Erickah to speak was during agenda item "Number 10. Issues from the floor and open discussion" (Fifty-Fifth Precinct Community Council, June 2019). This agenda item was third to last, immediately before "Number 11. Spring fling raffle drawing." The meeting began at 7:30 p.m., and by 8:30 Erickah and Steven were growing impatient. As President Pessod moved through the agenda, Steven made audible remarks about how their voice was being "suppressed." At 9:30 p.m., the meeting was finishing the ninth agenda item when Pessod pointed to the raffle materials and announced, "We're gonna do this." Steven shot up from his seat and contested: "Point of order, point of order. Point of order is will you be addressing number ten on your agenda? Which is 'issues from the floor and open discussion'?" Pessod responded that they would do the raffle first, but Steven pressed: "It's just that raffle appears as number 11, and the open discussion is number 10." Pessod responded, "I know, I can read. Remember what I told you before?" She was referring to their conversation at the beginning of the meeting, which Erickah did not recall specifically, only that "the tone was not welcoming at all" (Erickah Lewis, interview, August 7, 2019). The raffle proceeded for the next thirty minutes. As Pessod went around the room inviting attendees to pick the winning ball from the raffle spinner, she asked Erickah to participate. Erickah responded, "I don't want to pick. I want to speak." Pessod replied, "Okay, fine, no problem. No problem. Stay there." Steven chimed in: "Why aren't you letting her speak?" Pessod answered, "I didn't say that. I wanted her to pick." Steven tried one more time: "You're skipping your own agenda item." Pessod ended the conversation abruptly: "That's okay. That's okay."

At 10:00 p.m., three hours after Erickah and Steven arrived, President Pessod finally began taking questions from the floor. By this point, however, attendees—including the highest-ranking officers from the precinct—were already leaving. Trying to rush through the remainder of the agenda as another wave of people noisily left, Pessod announced, "Listen, everybody, we need to go home. We need to get out of here. On the agenda, it says issues from the floor, and he's [Steven] insisting, so I'll allow him to talk" (Fifty-Fifth Precinct Community Council, June 2019). Despite her awareness of Erickah's complaint, Pessod permitted her to raise the issue only at the very end of a meeting that had already run too long. As Erickah expressed in an interview later on, "Everything almost seem[ed] like a conspiracy" (Erickah Lewis, interview, August 7, 2019).

At Pessod's begrudging cue, Erickah went to the front of the room. Only a thinly scattered audience remained.

> When my sister was murdered, traffic was diverted down Broadway, traffic was completely stopped. I wanted five minutes. . . . So five minutes for one day of the year, you couldn't respect my family? . . . So if you're pushing supporters out of the street, what do you expect them to do now? Now they're turning around and they're videotaping you, and they're yelling, and you're going back and forth, and it's a whole situation that has nothing to do with my sister. (Fifty-Fifth Precinct Community Council, June 2019).

Now we see the ideological and practical dilemmas around permits come to the fore. The few audience members remaining replied by focusing on permits: "I understand you had a vigil, but if the streets were cut off, did you get permission from the precinct to cut off those streets?" (Fifty-Fifth Precinct Community Council, June 2019). Erickah responded that she had not, reiterating that it was an annual, five-minute vigil that hadn't had any disruptions from the police department in the past. Now audience members asked whether Erickah had "notif[ied] the precinct" and had obtained "a permit for that particular area, because I just want to know who was wrong in this instance?" Erickah reiterated: "My sister was killed by police; I will not notify the precinct of a memorial. They know. They know. She was murdered by this precinct." Audience members expressed their condolences, yet countered that without notification, "how are they [the precinct] to assume, or I to assume as a person, that it's not a riot or anything happening?" Officer Hines, who was standing quietly in the back, walked to the front and explained: "I gave you guys five minutes, they wanted to carry it even further. That's why we got involved, that was the reason. . . . But they failed to tell you that they blocked traffic and people were blowing their horns." At this, President Pessod intervened, concluding the meeting. "Now we know both sides from hearing it." She invited Erickah to "keep in touch, and we can see what we can do to work with you and help you. Thank you." The meeting was over.

As a partner channel, the Fifty-Fifth Precinct Community Council had the power to, but did not, amplify Erickah's demand for police accountability for shutting down her sister's memorial. Pessod's decision to end the meeting simply by encouraging Erickah to stay in touch—rather than ordering remedial steps from Officer Hines or his supervisors—should not be surprising, given the close collaborative relationship between the Fifty-Fifth Precinct and its community council. Officer Hines is the council's point person for requests to the precinct and its commanding officer, including getting police help for fundraisers or police enforcement to resolve particular neighborhood issues. Hines also provides transportation for Pessod to and from the precinct station for council meetings. And just a few months earlier, he and his fellow officers had presented her with a cake and balloons at a meeting held near her birthday. The strong relationships with and influence over community council members that Officer Hines has developed shields him from opposition in Fifty-Fifth Precinct Community Council meetings. And it was true that rather than accommodate the vigil, police had forced Erickah and her supporters out of the intersection after five minutes, because the gathering lacked authorization—authorization which the precinct itself provides. These interactions contravene the idea that police-community relations need to be cultivated; instead, preexisting relationships protect police against neighborhood grievances.

In contrast to their approach to vigils for victims of police violence, Officer Hines and his partner routinely facilitated the Fifty-Fifth Precinct Clergy Council's no-permit events. A core activity of the clergy council is a "shooting response": its public presence at the scene of every violent crime occurring within the precinct. Just like the prayers that begin police-community meetings, shooting responses repurpose classic evangelizing for violence reduction. The clergy council canvasses the scene of the shooting or stabbing, denounces the violence over an amplified megaphone, and distributes information to passersby. Despite such events ordinarily needing an amplified sound permit, the clergy council simply "coordinate[s]" with the precinct by contacting its Community Affairs officers directly and informing them of the council's plans. The council secretary explained: "We'll call the police department—hey, we're gonna do a shooting response over here in response to the shooting that just happened yesterday or the day before or whatever. But there's no paperwork that we need to fill out, no documentation, nothing. Having a working relationship with the police department, we'll tell them we're doing it here" (Woodward, interview, September 24, 2018). The clergy council president described the process as a "courtesy call" (Young, interview, September 19, 2018).

In one shooting response I attended at a historically violent housing project within the Fifty-Fifth Precinct, a Community Affairs officer even accompanied the clergy to their destination: a playground where a stabbing had occurred. Whereas officers at events rallying for police reform or memorializing victims of police violence focus attention on the demonstrators themselves, the officer here faced outward, observing pedestrians rather than the clergy gathered. The Fifty-Fifth Precinct Clergy Council thus not only coordinates with the precinct to organize a recurring event knowingly without a permit, but the officers in charge of permits—Community Affairs officers—attend these events to oversee their smooth execution.

Event Execution and the Burden of Aggressive Regulation

The major annual event for most community councils in New York City is National Night Out. Since the mid-1980s, police departments across the United States have celebrated National Night Out on the first Tuesday of August by holding parades, barbeques, and other festivities aimed at enhancing police-community relations (see Carr 2005). In New York City, each precinct's community council takes responsibility for fundraising, selecting the location, coordinating activities, hiring the DJ, determining the program, and publicizing the event.

With police's help, the entire precinct accommodates community council events like National Night Out. In 2018, the Eightieth Precinct Community Council decided to hold its National Night Out in a park centrally located within the precinct. Leading up to that evening, the police department put up No Parking signs on the park's adjacent streets. On the day of the event, a pair of police tow trucks removed the cars that were still present. Police assistance in enforcing street closings was critical, because this particular park did not permit barbequing on its premises, so all cooking had to take place on the surrounding streets—and those streets needed to be cleared. At the two other National Night Outs I attended in the Seventy-

First and Fifty-Fifth precincts, police officers also acted as the event workforce—setting up tables, cooking and distributing food, and managing information booths for distributing crime prevention tips (field note, August 7, 2018). These interactions provided ample photo opportunities: snaps of smiling officers grilling and passing out food and water to community members. Though the officers executing the event were still armed, they wore jeans and National Night Out T-shirts, making them somewhat less intimidating than if they had been fully uniformed. On the 2019 National Night Out I attended in the Fifty-Fifth Precinct, buses were rerouted because the event occurred on a central street within the neighborhood (field note, August 6, 2019). These extensive accommodations are simply unavailable to those community organizations demanding police transformation, consequently restricting the comparative scale of the public events they can hold.

Police accommodations also extend to events held by clergy council members. In the Eightieth Precinct, Father Joseph explained how church attendance is typically higher on Father's Day (Joseph, interview, December 21, 2018). At the same time of the year, however, other clergy council members of a different faith usually request that the roads be closed in observance of a religious holiday. With Father Joseph wanting roads open and other members wanting roads closed, the precinct works closely with the clergy council to coordinate which streets will be accessible to accommodate all the parties involved. In fact, the precinct even introduces its rookie officers to these "religious quirks" from their very first day on the force, as the Community Affairs Bureau brings newly assigned officers around to meet Father Joseph and the rest of the clergy council.

The accommodative approach police take to community and clergy council events contrasts with their aggressive approach to RALLY events. At the latter, marked and unmarked squad cars and officers form perimeters around participants to contain them and enforce their compliance. At an anniversary memorial for Sandra Bland and several other Black women killed by law enforcement, police erected metal barricades that enclosed roughly seventy participants within a corner section of sidewalk (field note, July 13, 2018). Across the street, I counted fifteen uniformed officers lined up to monitor the event, and an additional twenty-five acted as extra hands on the scene, directing traffic and reinforcing the metal barricade positions. Multiple com-

munity leaders and residents spoke on a megaphone, including one
mother demanding justice for her daughter, who had died in a police
holding cell after officers declined to provide her with medical attention. As an independent channel for public input, events like this are
met with police enforcement—not resources, leniency, and accommodations. In fact, as participants began marching down the street,
officers marched alongside them carrying zip ties—needed for mass
arrests—while police vans stood at the ready. Figures 3.1 and 3.2 illus-

FIGURE 3.1 Policing of community council event.
Source: NYPD Twitter account.

FIGURE 3.2 Policing of RALLY event.
Source: Author's photo.

trate the differential policing: whereas officers distribute free food to residents at community council events, at events sponsored by independent channels they carry the notorious plastic handcuffs to communicate to onlookers the risk of participating in such activity.

The police approach to RALLY organizers adds work beyond the normal logistics of holding a public event. These organizers must prepare security plans, map out contingencies, and think through how they will respond when police present hurdles. RALLY director Michelle explained how several affiliated organizations wanted to arrange for a march to mark the anniversary of Eric Garner's death (Michelle, interview, November 20, 2019). The march was supposed to be to city hall, less than a mile's walk, and the primary organizers—various youth organizations in collaboration with Garner's mother—wanted to march on the street itself. Police wanted them to stay on the sidewalk. As the short march proceeded, police and organizers paused roughly every twenty-five feet, disputing how to proceed. Then, when marchers arrived at NYPD headquarters at 1 Police Plaza, they wanted to enter. But police had erected barricades—even though the area was public property, and marchers only wanted to proceed another twenty-five feet into the plaza's park area. Michelle interpreted these small forms of resistance as police seeking to exert control: "So that kind of ridiculousness is just a sign of—it's not like they wouldn't shut us down, I don't think—but I think the threat for them in each moment was that they wanted to control how people protested and how people expressed their anger." She contrasted the police's approach to RALLY events with how police manage other marches—like the first Women's March in New York City—which the mayor supported, and "so they made all the accommodations to make sure it was able to proceed in whatever way it was able to proceed." Instead, police resistance to RALLY events strains the group's capacity, pulling it away from more organizationally productive efforts.

RALLY events draw not only more police officers but different types of officers. Unlike at community and clergy council events, RALLY events are frequented by members of the NYPD's Strategic Response Group (SRG) and Technical Assistance Response Unit (TARU). The SRG is the department's rapid response unit, designed for deployment during terrorist incidents, city emergencies, and, increasingly, civil unrest. TARU provides NYPD units with investigative equipment and tactical support. At RALLY events, the SRG is ready to shut down the event with mass arrests, while TARU provides technical assistance, gathers intelligence, and films interactions to collect and preserve evidence. Michelle believes that the decisive factor in whether police interactions during rallies escalate into violent arrests is not the level of disruption stemming from the rally itself, which is relatively constant each time. Instead, she points to "who the commanding officer is on the scene and how hotheaded they are" (Michelle, interview, November 20, 2019). The very way their events are policed forces RALLY to account for an additional layer of contingencies and concerns at every step.

To further exert social control over RALLY and other independent channels, police actually deputize and deploy clergy. Secretary Woodward of the Fifty-Fifth Precinct Clergy Council explained that after the street protests that erupted after police killed Christopher Grant, the police and clergy relationship "formalized more," because police "saw their need" (Woodward, interview, September 24, 2018). For seven days after Grant's death, residents protested in the streets. The Fifty-Fifth Precinct Clergy Council had just formed, and Pastor Young, who remains its only president to date, referred to the protests as the "first Ferguson" (Young, interview, January 7, 2019). He recalled the chaos of the initial nights, including stores being "ransacked" and fruit stands being "turned upside down."

The clergy council tried to alleviate tensions. Young explained how it worked with Grant's family and "had meetings at churches with the organizer of the protest, saying listen, 'You can protest, but you're not gonna trash our community. You can protest, but you're not gonna do something stupid'" (Young, interview, January 7, 2019). The council told police that they had to let people march, and it told protesters to respect the police and the community. Secretary Woodward described how the council was "able to talk to people who [it] knew were part of [its] churches" (Woodward, interview, September 24, 2018). Pastor Maurice confirmed that it was able to "step into that to defuse the situation"—creating "healthy outlets for the community to express their concern and outrage" and convincing the police to "take it down one notch in regards to not overreacting" (Maurice, interview, March 7, 2019).

Since the Grant protests, the clergy council and Community Affairs officers have organized a WhatsApp group to notify clergy of shootings within the precinct. Pastor Young then issues a response level depending on the urgency at the scene: level 1 (emergency), 2 (urgent), or 3 (nonemergency). Police have also requested clergy responses to issues beyond gun violence: "There are times when the Community Affairs officers will say, hey, you know this is going down, can you guys come out and help with this and this" (Woodward, interview, September 24, 2018). For instance, after an incident in which store owners attacked two Black customers, community members deemed the incident a hate crime and protested outside the store for days. Secretary Woodward explained how "we were called [by police], we have to assist in the tension, in deescalating the tension in the community around that case."

Finally, police even deploy the Fifty-Fifth Precinct Clergy Council to identify and patrol hot spots during major festivities like J'Ouvert—an annual daybreak celebration around Labor Day weekend that is rooted in the nineteenth-century emancipation of slaves in Trinidad. I followed the clergy council to some of the hot spots, where their status granted them regulatory leniency to enter through the strict security measures. At one point, when officers began towing cars to clear the parade route, the council president ran across the street, yelling, "Hello, police officer—that's my car! That's my car. That's my car. Don't touch it. That's my car" (field note, September 2, 2018). When the officer asked how many cars belonged to the group—just two—he moved on down and began to tow the *third* car. As we settled into the location, the president began proselytizing over a megaphone: "Our main responsibility is for the safety of our city. . . . As you can see, there's three thousand police officers who have come into our community this evening to make sure that not one person gets shot. And we appreciate that. We appreciate their service." Membership in the clergy council earned access behind parade barricades and permitted the use of amplified sound over a megaphone without a permit. Together with the NYPD, the Fifty-Fifth Precinct Clergy Council policed the parade.

Whereas the clergy council aided police in watching for wrongdoing among the parade onlookers, RALLY members attended J'Ouvert with their gazes fixed on the police themselves. With the influx of police into the area, RALLY's priority was to maintain community safety. To its members, that meant overseeing police officers. So first, they held a special copwatch training for J'Ouvert. Copwatching is the organized practice of observing, monitoring, and video recording police interactions, with the goal of holding police accountable for their actions (Stuart 2011; Simonson 2016). In the training, RALLY leaders discussed specific team formations, real-life scenarios, the lawyers on standby to contact, and scripts to use in police interactions. They also circulated a Google form among the J'Ouvert attendees, encouraging them to document all police interactions over the weekend. The goal was to learn about police harassment, both on and off the parade route. No mere exercise, these preparations came into play during J'Ouvert. At 5:30 a.m., a copwatcher was recording a video of a police checkpoint when twenty-five officers surrounded him and ejected him from the parade. After the parade, RALLY worked with others who experienced various levels of police harassment and brutality—including one who posted a video of officers restraining and punching her brother on a sidewalk. Whereas the NYPD granted the clergy council president access and leniency, copwatchers faced enforcement that oftentimes blurred the line between aggressive and abusive.

—

Each of the chapters thus far has documented a stage within the Policing Machine. Chapter 1 described how police begin the process of building consensus and coalescing power by channeling heterogeneous demands from community members toward the department channels they control. Chapter 2 explained how police cultivate and then draw constituents into their own department channels by establishing neighborhood representatives and coordinating access to established audiences. And the current chapter has chronicled how police simultaneously empower constituents and control alternative voices by selectively distributing public resources, regulatory leniency, and coercive force. As both the state's coercive arm and the recipient of concentrated resources across recent decades, police departments are uniquely positioned to allocate *public* resources—as if those resources were theirs to distribute—to amplify the constituents they have cultivated. Whether through resources or coercion, police fundamentally shape the channels through which community grievances and demands are articulated.

These chapters reflect a level of police commitment to and investment in community relations that would contravene arguments that either such relationships still need to be built or they are inconsequential to community affairs. In the next chapter, I turn to the payoff of the Policing Machine: how police convert the political capital they have accumulated into public endorsements of the quality of current policing—successfully exchanging the promise of problem-solving for public support.

4

Inducing Public Endorsements

On June 17, 2012, thousands marched down Manhattan's Fifth Avenue to protest NYPD Commissioner Ray Kelly and Mayor Michael Bloomberg's use of stop-and-frisk. In New York City, what was officially known as the Stop, Question, and Frisk program was a gun violence reduction strategy. It produced masses of Terry stops (named for *Terry v. Ohio*, a 1968 landmark decision by the US Supreme Court), incidents in which police with reasonable suspicion that someone was involved in criminal activity could briefly detain that individual to conduct a pat-down search of outer clothing. While the mayor and the commissioner persistently defended stop-and-frisks as a productive strategy for reducing crime and protecting lives in minority neighborhoods, activists called it an institutionalized program of racial injustice. Indeed, in practice the NYPD was clearing six hundred thousand stops at its height in 2011, with these stops concentrated among Black (53 percent) and Latinx (34 percent) residents and 88 percent of them involving innocent pedestrians.[1] The marchers on Fifth Avenue that hot summer day carried signs but otherwise marched in silence as planned. Newspaper reports would describe how at moments, the only audible sounds were "feet slapping pavement, birds chirping, and the occasional crackle of a police radio" (Devereaux 2012).

Three days after the march, the NYPD posted a video to Facebook and YouTube—social media channels that police can use as highly visible and highly controlled spaces for distributing information directly to the public. This video clip was a local news station's interview of the Eightieth Precinct Community Council president. The accompanying post credentialed Mr. Holloway, whom you've met in previous chapters, as a community resident since age thirteen, and suggested he was "invited by" the news station to "discuss his support for police presence and NYPD programs." In the interview, the president acknowledges the stop-and-frisk "numbers" and the possibility of "bad police officers out there," but argues that people in his neighborhood are no longer walking around in fear. Mr. Holloway also expresses the community's support for the NYPD's impact zones—a policing program that flooded high-crime areas with officers, but produced harmful effects on the educational performance of school-aged children (Legewie and Fagan 2019). In the years since this interview, he has gone on to be featured in NYPD annual reports, where he is similarly presented as a community representative supportive of current police practices.

When I asked Mr. Holloway how the 2012 televised interview had been arranged, he revealed, "[NYPD] Commissioner Kelly had his people get in touch with me to go on to defend stop-and-frisk" (Holloway, interview, July 10, 2018). In other words, the NYPD activated and mobilized its political capital. Even though Mr. Holloway had not publicly supported stop-and-frisk previously, Commissioner Kelly tapped him for the interview on the advice of a liaison in his office. Holloway understood as well that it was significant that he, an African American community leader, was being asked to publicly endorse stop-and-frisk, Operation Impact, and policing in general. It was, he figured, a favor to Commissioner Kelly, who had called when he was in the hospital and, in another moment, gifted him a pair of cuff links. Moreover, Mr. Holloway was not being disingenuous. He truly believes that community members must tell police's side of the story: "Our job is to tell their story—it's the community job." In other words, police cannot credibly defend controversial decisions directly to the public. Instead, they rely on community members like Mr. Holloway to articulate the positive aspects of policing, a favor he can leverage as his own form of political capital to advance community council goals in the future.

With systems like community councils and clergy councils in every precinct across New York City, police have options when they're in need of endorsements. That's helpful, because even someone like the Eightieth Precinct Community Council president was not always considered a cooperative voice. For example, while Holloway had a mutually beneficial relationship with Commissioner Kelly, that with the next commissioner—Bill Bratton—turned sour after Holloway made a negative statement about the police department that got published in the local newspaper. It was 2014, when youth crimes were rising in the community, and Holloway told a reporter that it was the fault of the mayor and the police commissioner's insufficient investments there. After the story reached the mayor's office and Commissioner Bratton through an associate of the civil rights activist Rev. Al Sharpton, the newspaper conducted a follow-up interview in which Holloway charged that the bigwigs "don't like dealing with the little people, they like dealing with the big Black folks" like Sharpton (Holloway, interview, March 8, 2019).

A couple of years after Holloway's pointed critique, Commissioner Bratton organized a raffle for community council presidents in Brooklyn. The prize was a police boat ride with Bratton, his wife, and three others from the community. Holloway got the winning ticket. He never received details about the trip, however, so he decided to call the police commissioner's office. A sergeant "told me straight up, straight up . . . told me—he [Bratton] wasn't going." Holloway noticed that the NYPD leadership who previously attended the Eightieth Precinct Community Council's annual fundraiser had stopped coming, and it was becoming harder to coordinate guest speakers from police headquarters for his community council meetings. Over in the Fifty-Fifth Precinct, these things hadn't changed. Its community council president, Lela Pessod, told me, "Everybody keeps telling me, 'Lela, the commissioner loves you, you know?' And I say, 'Well, I can't help that'" (Lela Pessod, interview, March 7, 2019).

Inevitably, the leadership and relationships in community councils, clergy councils, and the police department change over time. Yet like a formal bureaucracy, the structure and positions outlast the people. Maintaining these formalized systems of cultivating constituents across precincts requires work, and the vignette above reveals why police are willing to invest the resources to do so. As a department and as individuals, police officers at every level from commissioner down to patrol seek validation and vindication. As it was built to do,

the Policing Machine provides police with options for inducing public endorsements.

—

Public endorsements are the payoff of the Policing Machine. I define
endorsements as indications of support or approval expressed toward
another actor. The strategic actions detailed in the previous chapters—
channeling heterogeneous demands, cultivating local constituents, and
distributing power and privilege—are the stages by which the Policing Machine positions police to induce public endorsements that help
stave off institutional reform under intensifying public scrutiny. As Mr.
Holloway recognized, police rely on external entities like him for such
endorsements, because they represent credible voices with community legitimacy. They represent the sorts of constituents to whom police
want to be held accountable—those who agree that initiatives focusing on oversight and reform only divert resources from the expanded
capacity police need to satisfy *community* demands for more enforcement. Were police to achieve widespread acceptance of these endorsements as representative and accurate indicators of policing quality, it
would affirm a fundamental realignment of police accountability—one
that tethers police to the constituents they have cultivated from the
bottom up rather than the institutions designed to regulate them.

Public endorsements of organizations can take many forms, which
I categorize into explicit and implicit endorsements. Explicit endorsements refer to direct indications of external approval and come in two
forms: *awards*, or material recognition, and *testimonials*, or verbalized
or transcribed statements of support. Each provides direct evidence
that the endorser is, in fact, an endorser: the certificate, quotation,
or other award or testimonial verifies the endorsement's source and
intentions. These are the classic forms of commendation that organizations use to communicate approval to and from salient stakeholders.

In contrast, implicit endorsements feature indications of external
approval that are claimed rather than verified. Two forms are relevant
for organizations: *collaborations*, which feature joint endeavors that
imply approval from affiliates, and *demand*, which provides evidence
of service provision and meeting needs. Compared to explicit endorsements, the burden of proof is lower when claiming implicit endorsements. Organizations suggest that the endorsement be inferred based
on evidence that they—rather than endorsers—have provided.

In the contemporary era, organizations use social media to expand their capacities for claims-making (Bail 2016; Leonardi and Vaast 2017). I introduce the concept of "digital omissions" to describe processes of strategic exclusion in the representation of real-world phenomena in digitally distributed content. Researchers typically analyze social media according to the "affordances" for their users (Treem and Leonardi 2013), but their "avoidances" are equally important for how state institutions use social media. In other words, social media provide users with a variety of benefits while also permitting users to strategically evade and circumvent things that are unwanted. The concept of digital omissions emphasizes how digital technologies are being used within a social context, not in lieu of it, and provides a comparative framework for analyzing the sociological action unfolding in between the online and the offline. Ethnography is particularly suitable for uncovering these meanings (e.g., Lane 2018; Schradie 2019; Stuart 2020).

In this case, by engaging in digital omissions, the Policing Machine strategically generates circumstantial evidence of collaborations and demand that guarantees an implicit endorsement can be claimed from any community event or exchange. While police departments continue to provide evidence of public endorsements in budget hearings, annual reports, and other established outlets, this chapter emphasizes the rising significance of social media as forms of state media, allowing officials to strategically construct the public record based on public unknowing.

The key takeaway I show is that the public endorsements generated under the Policing Machine are problematic: explicit endorsements are earned from cultivated constituents and are thus unrepresentative, and implicit endorsements are claimed and thus possibly misrepresentative. Disseminating these public endorsements establishes an unreliable public record of community interactions with the coercive arm of the state. Social media empower police to pursue these goals at scale.

EXPLICIT ENDORSEMENTS

Explicit endorsements feature direct indications of external approval. The sections below describe two forms of these: awards and testimonials. Explicit endorsements leave less room for ambiguity than implicit endorsements, as the support has been materialized through objects like plaques and television news interviews. Effectively, they are valuable pieces of concrete evidence that police departments can mobilize to defend the quality of and community demand for status quo policing.

Awards

In the minutes before a community council meeting, officers and residents arrive and sign in at a table littered with Wanted posters, crime safety tips, and other materials from the NYPD, as well as flyers for local elected officials' upcoming events and literature from community groups in attendance. The cops either make small talk with meeting regulars and fellow officers or immerse themselves in their department-issued cell phones.

When the meeting begins, it flows through a succession of speakers: president's welcome, commanding officer's report, updates from board members, and news from the representatives of elected officials. Rather than community complaints, community council meetings are geared toward community updates, with complaints typically handled by the precinct commanding officer asking the resident to "stay around afterwards" so he can speak with them directly. As I learned, a focus of community council presidents is on arranging for special guest speakers—maybe a representative from a local bank to discuss reverse mortgages, housing judges to discuss landlord-tenant issues, or, if they are fortunate, NYPD leadership. When the Fifty-Fifth Precinct Community Council landed NYPD Commissioner James O'Neill as a meeting speaker, three of my past interviewees contacted me to tell me the news—and that was before it was announced.

The main event of the council meeting is the commanding officer's report. To accommodate a CO's schedule, meeting agendas are commonly reorganized at the last minute. The commanding officer's report involves monthly updates about crime statistics and noteworthy incidents within the precinct. The Fifty-Fifth Precinct's commanding officer has a sort-of trademark move: printing out and presenting a photo of every gun recovered by the officers in the precinct since the last meeting. This show-and-tell is expected by council members and regular meeting attendees alike; at one meeting, as the president finished her remarks, she assured the audience: "One more thing before we go into the commander's report so you guys can see the guns" (Fifty-Fifth Precinct Community Council, September 2018). As he displays each photo, the CO proudly announces the type of firearm (e.g., a .45 caliber), the date of its recovery and the street it was recovered from, how it was recovered (e.g., vehicle stop, search warrant), and whether lab tests have tied it to any shootings. He adds context in only one instance—if the gun was recovered from a gang member: "July fourth, East Eightieth and Broadway, we had a 9 millimeter, gang member arrested in this one. Crip gang member." The Community Affairs officer solemnly holds up the photo, turning so the entire audience gets a look. Attendees crane their necks to catch a glimpse, with each photo eliciting whispers: "Damn!"; ".45 caliber, that's a big gun"; "Thank god"; and "Whoa." The audience always applauds the show-and-tell. About a third stand, their ovation communicating extra appreciation to the law enforcement members in the room.

Both the police department and the community councils often reiterate that community councils are "independent" (Holloway, interview, July 10, 2018) and "advocates" for the community's best interest (Eightieth Precinct Community Council, February 2019). At the October 2018 meeting of the Eightieth Precinct Community Council, the president stressed the importance of caring for one another and reaching out to others in times of need. When it was time for the commanding officer to provide his report, he began by stating,

> Mr. Holloway, you asked a question. You said, "Who's looking out for you?" Well, I think we have the answer loud and clear: it's you. You're a very powerful voice. . . . He's great to have as a partner, and I can't say—what he does for the community, it's amazing. Mr. Holloway, you absolutely transcend what leadership means. And you're an extremely important person in this community, and we're so, so lucky to have him. So, thank you to Mr. Holloway. (Eightieth Precinct Community Council, October 2018)

Before the meeting ended, the CO reiterated, "[Mr. Holloway]'s really your voice out here." Holloway, however, was always careful not to wear anything reflecting his NYPD affiliation—besides an NYPD pin that all community council presidents receive—because people would "feel that you're one-sided, you're not really blending in with the community" (Holloway, interview, March 8, 2019). Although community councils and local precincts often promoted their collaborative partnership, these two entities also stress that community councils are independent local advocates who objectively fight for the community's best interest.

Emphasizing the independence of community councils is important, because it makes them more meaningful as platforms for endorsements of police. Across all community council meetings, the Cop-of-the-Month award is an important staple. The following is a full speech given by the Fifty-Fifth Precinct's commanding officer for Cop-of-the-Month in October 2018.

So, this month's Cop-of-the-Month goes out to Officer Jon Jones. Officer Jones's been with me since my last command. The fact that I brought him over with me shows that he's a very dedicated officer. I'm going to tell you why. This is one incident, of the many incidents he's done throughout the year for the Fifty-Fifth, so, a few days ago, Officer Jones was working—a lot people were off, it was over the weekend—and the Warrant Squad comes in with an arrest. For those of you who don't know the Warrant Squad, they basically pick up people with active warrants. They don't really do much more than knock on the door; if the individual is there, they pick him up and they arrest him. Not to take away from anything that they do, but that's pretty much what they do.

So, Officer Jones was working that day, he overhears how the event went down, and his knowledge of the command, he knows there's a lot more to this than just the warrant. So, he does a very extensive investigation, and as a result he was able to seize a .40-caliber firearm, a .38-caliber firearm, a PS-90 assault rifle, and four hundred glasses of heroin. This is just a prime example of what he does every day, what his team does every day. At the last community council meeting, a member from his team, I was able to tell you about the assault rifle that they recovered, it was a submachine gun that was picked up in a car stop. This is just a few incidents of the many, many things that they do here. And for that, due to his commitment and his proactive work, these deadly weapons are no longer in our community and that poison is no longer here, and it's not gonna make the streets. So, the individual is currently in on a $50,000 bail, and for that, thanks, Jones. (Fifty-Fifth Precinct Community Council, October 2018)

As the audience began to stand and applaud, the commanding officer read the inscription on the plaque: "'For your tireless and loyal efforts in performing your duties over and beyond to protect the residents of the community you serve,' from myself and Community Council President Lela Pessod, thank you."

With descriptive phrases like "extensive investigation" and "proactive work," the CO presented a narrative of heroics that simultaneously recognized the exceptional act while normalizing it as "what he does every day, what his team does every day" (Fifty-Fifth Precinct Community Council, October 2018). At other meetings, I've documented COs who claimed, "New York City cops, we run toward the danger to protect our communities that we serve" (Fifty-Fifth Precinct Community Council, February 2019); commended an officer's "eagle eyes" when he spotted a car that fit the description of one being sought by police (Eightieth Precinct Community Council, May 2019); and described an officer's "very, very dangerous assignment" as he pursued and arrested individuals wanted for a commercial robbery (Eighty-Ninth Precinct Community Council, June 2018). Moments like these allow the NYPD to communicate its narratives directly to officers and the community members motivated enough to attend (and return to) community council meetings—communicating precisely *what* constitutes quality policing and *what actions* deserve commendation.

While Cop-of-the-Month is an internal award decided by the CO (Rim, Ba, and Rivera 2020), its presentation occurs publicly at community council meetings. Like clockwork, each month brings a new laudable officer to the lectern. There's always a winner. And the fact that the plaque states that it is co-awarded by the commanding officer and the community council president imbues the honor with the community's explicit endorsement, which is replicated for the public through photos posted on social media. These online posts are oftentimes the *only* public record of what happened during community council meetings.

Photo opportunities are a critical part of these meetings. Whenever awards are distributed or guest speakers finish their speech, audi-

FIGURE 4.1 Photo-taking at community council meetings in the
Fifty-Fifth (*left*) and Eightieth (*right*) Precincts.
Source: Author's photos.

ence members scramble, like amateur paparazzi, to take pictures of
the community council president, the commanding officer, and the
honoree or guest (see fig. 4.1). They jostle for the best angles, competing for attention and eye contact with the local luminaries. Even
though the photos are meant to recognize the honoree, the photo tak-
ers gain from them too: community organizations, elected officials,
and the police department itself can post them online or in news-
letters as evidence of their community participation. Community
council presidents recognize the importance of photos to the precinct and help stage them: "Now what we're gonna do, here's how
we gonna take the picture, because the CO loves to tweet, he tweets
a lot" (Eightieth Precinct Community Council, December 2018). The
president then directed the guest speaker and the CO to stand in the
middle of the audience, so "when he tweet, he's gonna be tweeting
everybody out."

The high value that precincts place on awards, especially those
that can be framed as *community* awards, is indicated by their efforts
to shape the winners. During National Night Out, for instance, the
Eightieth Precinct Community Council distributes awards to recognize those who have made significant contributions to the community in the previous year. In 2018, as the council considered its
nominees, the president received a call from the commanding officer.
Vice President Laurette Simmonds recounted: "When Mr. Holloway
got the call, he was sitting here [in Simmonds's living room]. And
he said, 'Okay, alright, yes sir.' I said, 'Oh, boy, something's up.' So,
when he was finished, [Holloway] said, 'I have two awards to give

out, and they want it to be given to the Community Affairs [officers]'" (Laurette Simmonds, interview, September 5, 2018). The CO's direct call reflects his enormous stake in publicly presenting the community council's endorsement of the precinct's performance.

During the event, the Eightieth Precinct tweeted a montage of four photos: (1) the community council president and vice president sharing the stage with the CO; (2) the award being presented by the community council vice president to the first Community Affairs officer; (3) the second award being presented to the other Community Affairs officer; and (4) a local elected official speaking. Not only did the Eightieth Precinct provide the resources to execute National Night Out, it arranged to have the community council award the precinct's Community Affairs officers during the event.

Testimonials

During the very first Build the Block meeting I ever attended, the Neighborhood Coordinating Officers (NCOs) stalled with small talk as they waited for their guest speaker to arrive. They reminded people to sign in, handed out small plastic bottles of water, and jokingly invited the audience to eat the grocery store doughnuts and cookies so they "wouldn't have to." An attendee's phone rang; after a minute-long conversation, she reported to the NCOs: "Mr. H is on his way up." I was surprised, since I assumed that most of the attendees had no prior relationship with the NCOs and were attending as relative newcomers like me. When the speaker finally arrived—Mr. Holloway, president of the Eightieth Precinct Community Council—he was unfamiliar to me at the time; I assumed that his presence was merely coincidental or convenient.

But at this point the NCOs started the meeting and immediately invited Mr. Holloway to take the floor. "My mother has been living here for over seventy years. I've been here for approximately forty-five years," he began (Sector 80A, April 11, 2018). After establishing these community credentials, he positioned himself as a legitimate authority on the evolution of local policing: "Webster Avenue, back in the day, you couldn't even walk up Webster. Now they call it 'baby-stroller-ready.'" Next, just as in the chapter's introductory vignette, he explicitly endorsed the police department: "This is a really good time for the community, and mainly because we have the world-famous NYPD police department, which is the best in the—not only the nation, but the world. We have a lot to be thankful for."

Besides awards, explicit endorsements can take the form of testimonials like Mr. Holloway's. Testimonials can come from proclamations, announcements, recommendations, or other explicit articulations of approval, and they hinge on the legitimacy of the endorser. Put differently, those who provide testimonials put their own legitimacy on the line to vouch, on the record, for positive experiences with police. Their testimonials imply that audiences should also join, participate, or take similar action. But the testimonials are not random. Collecting them is a highly curated process that starts with one key decision: *who* should provide the needed endorsement?

Clergy are a particularly coveted source. On the NYPD website and in the 2018 *Police Commissioner's Report* online, the department posted a video explaining Neighborhood Policing. In it, just one community member is named: Senior Pastor Gwen Dingle of the Pentecostal House of Prayer. Pastor Dingle testifies to the impact of NCOs: "The NCOs are definitely changing the neighborhood. There's more interaction with the community. . . . Walking around, talking to people, and that's what we need. That's what we need."[2] As Pastor Dingle provides her testimony from within her church, the video pans to the church's outdoor sign and then back inside to the front of the pulpit, where the pastor is having a conversation with two officers. Pastor Dingle's endorsement frames the problem of policing as insufficient community interaction, a problem the police department is now addressing through Neighborhood Policing.

In the 2016 *Police Commissioner's Report*, Rev. Dr. J. Loren Russell provides a comparable endorsement: "The partnership program allows ordinary, community-based people like me to take an active part in how our community is policed" (NYPD 2016b, 21). His testimonial appears next to a photograph of a police officer and a community member engaging in conversation. By suggesting that he is an "ordinary" and "community-based" person, Reverend Russell asserts his legitimacy and, by encouraging readers like him to get involved in Neighborhood Policing, validates the program. Endorsements from faith leaders are so valuable because their status lends moral objectivity to their testimonials.

Clergy also provide police testimonials during church services.

Reverend Harris explained how his sermons often drew "from my own personal experiences on how [to form] a good relationship with the cop" (Harris, interview, February 28, 2019). If police can rely on clergy to provide testimonials, they do not need to speak at church services themselves. Pastor Greene noted that while officers speak at his church service about three times a year, there is not much of a "need" beyond that, because he can distribute information on their behalf about "crime trends, what to watch out for, [and] what to be cautious of" (Greene, interview, January 30, 2019). And in the Eightieth Precinct, Pastor Campbell referred to himself as a "spokesperson" for the precinct (Campbell, interview, September 17, 2018).

Moreover, clergy provide positive police recommendations whenever they encourage their congregants to become auxiliary officers or sign up their children for the NYPD's youth programs. Pastor Greene estimated that over a decade into his current position, he has helped twenty members of his church sign up as auxiliary officers (Greene, interview, January 30, 2019). As explained in previous chapters, these testimonials for police take on heightened significance when communicated by one's religious leader in a house of worship.

IMPLICIT ENDORSEMENTS

Unlike explicit endorsements, implicit endorsements are claimed rather than verified. They rely on the audience to infer the endorsement based on the information provided (and, as I show, the information *not provided*). The sections below identify two forms of implicit endorsements that are particularly relevant for service providers: collaborations and demand. When organizations publicize information about joint endeavors and partnered projects, they seek to convey an implicit endorsement—that the affiliate's approval underlies the agreement to collaborate. Similarly, when organizations promote the consumption of their services, they seek to imply demand for those services—in this instance, that police are meeting community needs. Either way, note how the source of these endorsements has switched: the endorsee is claiming them implicitly rather than endorsers providing them explicitly.

The Policing Machine incorporates social media as particularly valuable vehicles for publicizing implicit endorsements. The concept of digital omissions clarifies why these media suit implicit endorsements so well: digital omissions enable police to communicate collaborations and demand without relying on affiliates and consumers to provide an explicit endorsement (which, of course, they might or might not be inclined to give). Digital omissions transform every public exchange into a guaranteed source of implicit endorsements.

Collaborations

Coffee with a Cop is a national event. Every year on the first Wednesday of October, over 125 policing agencies partner with a local coffee shop to provide a space for officers and community members to share informal conversations over a cup of coffee. Started by the Hawthorne, California, Police Department in 2011, Coffee with a Cop is now a 501(c)(3) nonprofit organization that offers resources, training, and promotional items for any police department to hold its own Coffee with a Cop. The goal, as Officer Marshall, one of the East Coast instructors, explained to me, is to "combat that negative image of the police with a positive, local—not advertisement—but a display of what we're doing out there. So, what better way to do that—to humanize police officers—than to just sit down and have a cup of coffee with them?" (Marshall, interview, October 26, 2018). In a separate interview, another East Coast instructor, Officer Jake, expressed a similar aim to "humanize the officers and humanize people for officers." He told me that most of his days were about people saying, "'Fuck you, I'm not talking to you.'" With Coffee with a Cop, however, "it's nice to go to these and hear people say, 'No, we're the majority. Thank you. Thank you for your service and for keeping us safe'" (Jake, interview, November 12, 2018). For officers like Marshall and Jake, Coffee with a Cop is valuable in overcoming what they perceive as miscommunication between police and community (Rivera-Cuadrado 2021)—an event where they assume the participants are de facto endorsers.

In the Eightieth Precinct, Coffee with a Cop was held at a coffee truck called La Patisserie Mobile. I arrived at 9:30 a.m., just as six officers were parking their cars and placing their pastry orders. After they ate, they waited for customers to approach the coffee truck and place their own orders. A designated officer would approach to ask some variation of "Miss, do you want to take a picture with us? Today is Coffee with Cops day." All eight of the customers I observed the officers approaching agreed to a photo, as they were all either tourists or regulars toting strollers or dogs to La Patisserie Mobile—unsurprising, given the weekday morning timing. Though the event is supposed to last an hour, the officers quickly secured their photos and the NCOs were gone within twenty minutes. By 10:03 a.m., the remaining Community Affairs officers were gone. And minutes later, the precinct had posted the photos on Twitter with the hashtag #NYPDConnecting.

The decision to hold Coffee with a Cop at La Patisserie Mobile was not random. As a Sector A NCO explained to me before a Build the Block meeting, the venue is a "community asset." Months earlier, the Beanery, a nearby coffee shop, had called the NCOs and asked them to write summonses against La Patisserie Mobile for parking in front of a hydrant. Seeing through the pretext of the request (the truck was siphoning business from the brick-and-mortar shop), the officers refused: "Yeah, right, I told him we'd have to take care of Starbucks [next to it] first." The NCOs also reasoned that Pierre, the owner of La Patisserie Mobile, is "in the car all the time, so if there's an emergency, he can move his car." So when they called Pierre to hold Coffee with a Cop the weekend before the event, he agreed—he'd been granted regulatory leniency by the officers now asking to use his business for the event.

Coffee with a Cop generates content for social media, which in turn communicates an implicit endorsement as the collaboration is publicized. The shop itself, appearing on the precinct's social media channels, indicated a collaboration, and the people in the photos indicated their corroboration—though my observations evidenced a great deal of convenience. Occasionally, the officers exchanged conversation with passersby, but it mostly involved explaining why they were present and the nature of the event. The citizens in the photos may have expressed approval toward the police or not, but the point is that it didn't matter for the officers—they did not need the confirmation to generate the social media content to imply the endorsements.

In one interaction, a man illegally parked behind the coffee truck and quickly dashed out to place his order. When officers asked whether he wanted his picture taken, he answered, "As long as I don't get a ticket here." Laughing, an NCO responded, "Nah, you're fine." Pierre, too, joked with the man, saying that his wife had come by earlier and already purchased two coffees: "She's probably waiting for you!" The customer thanked Pierre and was running back to his car when the NCO intervened to ask about the photo—an endorsement in exchange for the leniency granted. With Pierre's encouragement, the man agreed, then waited while the NCOs then guided the Community Affairs officer on how the photo should be taken—making sure to capture the coffee truck's logo and taking one with everyone as a group. Later, the NCOs asked Pierre whether they could enter his coffee truck, just to get some photos of police officers serving his customers. Soon thereafter, the NCOs were done at La Patisserie Mobile and on to their next stop: a local cathedral, where they joined in praying the Rosary. In fact, I only learned about the NCOs' next stop through Twitter, because they posted photos with the bishop and about fifty parochial schoolchildren in front of the church. Like La Patisserie Mobile, the church's endorsement was implied through the collaboration publicized online.

Another method for producing collaborations as implicit endorsements is by coordinating roll-call prayers with local clergy. The NYPD conducts roll call three times a day, each instance officially beginning a new shift of patrol officers. Supervisors take attendance, inform the officers of outstanding incidents from the previous shift, and update them on any assignments and priorities. Clergy council members are encouraged to visit during roll call to pray for the officers' safe return as well as on special religious occasions: Father Joseph is called into the Eightieth Precinct every Ash Wednesday to "say a prayer, read a section from scripture, and then ask who wants ashes" (Joseph, interview, December 21, 2018). Outside their home precincts, clergy council members are further encouraged to present their identification cards and offer prayer at the nearest precinct. Reverend Powell described how he once entered a precinct in the Bronx and more than fifty officers applauded as he started his prayer: "Hello, officers. Praise the Lord. I'm Reverend Powell. I'd like to say a prayer for all of our officers. Let's hold hands" (Powell, interview, August 29, 2018). Reverend Powell told me that he remained in that precinct after the prayer, talking to the officers about the community and explaining that "people like us are out there—making sure that all police officers are safe. All lives matter. Black lives matter. White lives matter. Yellow lives matter. Blue lives matter."

Roll-call practices strengthen the partnership between police and clergy. The clergy provide one of their core services during a pivotal period of the day for officers; the invitation to do so encourages them to develop a stake in police's success, as the dangers of policing are emphasized to them and the officers alike during roll call (see Sierra-Arévalo 2021). In return, clergy know that roll-call prayers are important to maintaining the council's relationship with the precinct. The practice familiarizes officers with council members, which can prevent misunderstandings on the street: "When we come to the roll call . . . you and the police officer will then recognize, 'Oh, I remember those guys that came to pray—they're part of the clergy council'" (Young, interview, September 19, 2018). Indeed, while the clergy council primarily holds meetings inside its members' churches, they purposefully hold two to three meetings per year inside the precinct station so "people can come into the precinct, the precinct can see us, they can house us, so you can have that interaction, they can tell the layout of the precinct." The more face time clergy can get with the precinct, the more they can remind police that the clergy council exists, that it cares for police, and that this partnership is worth further developing (and further supporting through resource allocations).

These mutual advantages are cultivated from an officer's first day on the job. When a precinct receives its allotment of new recruits from the police academy, the Community Affairs officers take the recruits to meet the precinct's community partners around the neighborhood, especially the clergy council churches. Pastor Greene explained how he would "talk to them about his church, get to know them and have them get to know me, thank them, and give them a blessing—that's relationship-building" (Greene, interview, January 30, 2019). As new recruits make their rounds and receive blessing after blessing, they foreseeably internalize the dangers of their work and begin to appreciate the spiritual protection and community connection that clergy provide.

These otherwise private prayers become implicit endorsements when they are publicized. In an Urban Institute report titled *Social Media Guidebook for Law Enforcement Agencies*, one of the effective strategies it identifies is to "develop relationships with community members and organizations that have large audiences" (Tiry, Oglesby-Neal, and KiDeuk 2019, 17). Precincts do just that with local clergy. Police routinely tweet photographs showing new recruits meeting local pastors, uniformed officers attending church events, and precinct officers huddled during roll-call prayer. For example, the Fifty-Fifth Precinct tweeted a video of a roll-call prayer and thanked the clergy council for its "prayers and inspiration." Heads bowed and hands clasped, the cops listen as the pastor leads them in prayer: "We pray God that you bring comfort to their homes, pray for every officer in the Five-Five Precinct and beyond, that they will be safe. God, we want to thank you for the effort that they put in every single day and night. God, let us remember that as they keep us safe, you keep them safe. This is our prayer. In Jesus' name we pray and we say thank you. Amen."

Tweets such as these demonstrate to community members that police are woven into the same moral fabric as they are, that clergy are active and engaged in protecting and caring for the community, and that police do dangerous, appreciated work. Precinct tweets on other dates similarly thanked the clergy council for conducting roll-call prayers, including one post about how Fifty-Fifth Precinct officers can now "go out and enjoy knowing that we will be here protecting you." Although the Fifty-Fifth Precinct posts these tweets first, the clergy council and its members always retweet them, sometimes transforming the precinct's tweets into explicit endorsements in the form of testimonials. Clergy retweets describe their commitment to clergy care, the importance of their partnership, and how the clergy council is active on the ground. Roll-call prayers are thus mutually beneficial—providing, enacting, and reinforcing legitimacy for both parties.

But police can also use social media to promote narratives that strategically omit the full context of a "collaboration." In 2018, the mayor, the NYPD, and elected officials announced a plan to invest over $1 million in renovating four precinct stations in Brooklyn. Mayor de Blasio made the announcement in front of about fifteen community members and a banner that read, "Bringing Police and Community Together." After acknowledging the people behind him for "doing important work . . . to bring police and community together," he explained that the renovations were needed to "create the kinds of facilities that really foster dialogue and respect—that's what this city needs" (de Blasio 2018). While none of the community or clergy council members onstage spoke at the press conference, their mere presence signaled an implicit endorsement of the collaboration. Police tweets afterward emphasized how community leaders announced the plan with city and police officials together.

Following the press conference, I asked one of the clergy I had spotted onstage how he had received his invitation. Pastor Campbell replied that he received a general email from the Eightieth Precinct inviting local clergy, political figures, and others who liaise with it to join the mayor on the podium: "They just invited me. I was just invited. They invite a lot of people, so they invite me" (Campbell, interview, September 17, 2018). I followed up by asking whether the Eightieth Precinct invited all clergy members, and he clarified that they invited "some of the clergy council members and those involved in the [Clergy] Liaison [program] with the precinct." Then I asked about his role in selecting, planning, or executing the initiative. As he put it, he was invited to join in the announcement but "not so much on the development [of the] project."

Social media provide police with the technological capacity to imply endorsements. In other words, they enable police to purposefully avoid disclosing the full context of the initiative's genesis by letting the post and photos imply coordination between police, politicians, and the community. Even if community members like Pastor Campbell would have been willing to provide an explicit endorsement, social media eliminates the need for it.[3] Instead, police can simply post photos featuring coffee shop logos, church exteriors, or community stakeholders as an indication of approval that typically comes with collaborations. Yet situating these online posts within their offline social context can complicate the strength of these endorsements in ways police prefer to avoid through their digital omissions. These dynamics are even more salient with implicit endorsements that seek to demonstrate demand.

Demand

Besides collaborations, implicit endorsements can also be communicated by publicizing demand for organizational services. Demonstrating demand implies endorsements, because it shows that the organization is meeting public needs. If core services are being consumed, then organizations can advance claims that those services require investment if not expansion. But because these are implicit endorsements, evidence of actual consumption is unnecessary. Practicing digital omissions on social media represents an ideal strategy for publicizing demand.

From the moment a resident comes through the door of a police-community meeting, the NYPD begins to accrue evidence of demand, regardless of *why* the resident has come. They may be there to complain about police, but at the departmental level, merely holding meetings and attracting attendees are represented as demand for police services. In a statement before the New York City Council Committee on Public Safety to discuss the department's 2020 preliminary budget of $5.6 billion, Commissioner O'Neill described how the NYPD's NCOs had held "more than 1,500 Build-the-Block meetings to address problems, help fight crime, and build stronger relationships between officers and community members" (O'Neill 2019). This same message was broadcasted to the public through tweets like the one depicted in figure 4.2. With photos of residents sitting quietly and listening intently to officers' presentations, the NYPD chief of patrol tweeted that "more than 30,000 New Yorkers have attended a #BuildtheBlock meeting."[4]

Implicit in these numbers—the 1,500 meetings and 30,000 attendees—is high community demand for police services. Whether posting visuals online or defending the police budget to the city council, the NYPD claims implicit endorsements by invoking mere attendance

FIGURE 4.2 NYPD tweet by Chief of Patrol Rodney Harrison.

FIGURE 4.3 Two @nypdnews tweets about community council meetings.

at police-run meetings as evidence of community demand for its services.

However, situating NYPD tweets in their offline context highlights how police can engage in digital omissions through strategic concealment in routine posts. Figure 4.3 illustrates two NYPD tweets that simultaneously communicate the current demand for police services and the value of attending community council meetings. The two posts also provide visual evidence of "#NYPDconnecting." On the left, the tweeted photo is zoomed out, showing a room full of seated community members listening to the officer and community council board members at the front of the room. On the right, the tweeted photo is zoomed in, focused only on the front of the room, omitting the audience altogether. This distinction aligns with the dominant ways officers strategically photographed and posted about meetings throughout my fieldwork. Given the NYPD directives for its precincts to post more social media content,[5] almost every community meeting I attended was photographed and tweeted. In the middle of a meeting, an officer from the Community Affairs Bureau would begin the search for the best camera angle: photos of meetings that happened to be well attended depicted the entire room, while photos of those with too few attendees showed officers pointing, lecturing, and even just smiling before an audience outside the frame. Other photos that communicated engagement while concealing low attendance included tables with informational pamphlets, snacks provided at the meeting, and the sightline of officers in front of residents who happened to be sitting clustered together—especially after officers instructed attendees to move forward and squeeze together. Regardless of meeting turnout and whether the subset of attendees actually demanded police services, digital omissions enable police to generate implicit endorsements all the same.

Comparing online posts with the meeting dynamics they claim to capture undermines the implicit endorsements of police services. In contrast to the chief of patrol's tweet above, a Sector 55B meeting I attended in Brooklyn Gardens began with only three residents in attendance, including me (Sector 55B, April 2018). Seeing the low turnout, the NCOs encouraged the residents to text and phone their neighbors. One of the NCOs then went outside to see whether he could "grab people off the street." He was successful: with the promise of free doughnuts, he persuaded five additional locals to attend. "Please grab some coffee and some doughnuts, and sit down for five minutes and hear what this program is about. If you don't have nothing to say, leave and take a doughnut for your girl or your mom. All right? We're good? You guys wanna call up some friends, tell them get a cup and doughnut too, because I see a lot of doughnuts still here." But these inadvertent attendees *did* have questions: Do police officers shoot to kill or shoot to maim? Can officers even name the differences between buildings within public housing developments? Why don't officers ever come to events held by young people, at locations where youth feel more comfortable? The ensuing discussion extended through the majority of the one-hour meeting.

At one point, Travis, one of the inadvertent attendees, stood up and explained, "If you're speaking to me, and every time you go to speak, your hand is on your holster. That says a lot." For youth who are already fearful when approached by police, Travis described the added threat of officers placing their hands on their belts near their service weapons. Even as he spoke, the NCOs kept their hands on their belts when speaking at the front of the room, a fact to which Travis implicitly pointed: "Even in this meeting, I'm pretty sure you guys don't think anybody here is a threat—I would hope not, at least."

Multiple officers responded. The first NCO to comment acknowledged that he understood Travis's point—and it was a good one—but minimized it by explaining that "the truth of the matter is, it's a hand rest." A second NCO rationalized how their gun holsters are simply "right by our pocket." A third officer in the room, from the

Community Affairs Bureau, added, "It's comfortable." The first NCO then resumed: "I'm not trying to threaten anybody, but you know, you can't put your hand in your pocket." The officers' explanations, in other words, focused on explaining the misunderstanding—not changing the underlying behavior.

Travis pointed out a contradiction: "Likewise, a lot of young people keep their hands in their pocket. You understand? So when they put their hands in their pocket, you may look at it like that's a threat, or they may have a gun, but it can be misinterpreted is what I'm saying. So I think we should work on things of that nature." As he emphasized the contradiction in the policing of hand motions and their own gestures, the NCOs focused on the importance of mutual respect. They spoke at cross-purposes until finally, Alisha Grey, president of the Brooklyn Gardens Tenant Association, concluded the back-and-forth: "This is why meetings like this are so important . . . and we wanted to thank the Fifty-Fifth Precinct again. They're working extremely hard with Brooklyn Garden to solve the issues. . . . Yes, we want their courtesy, professionalism, and respect, but we also have to teach our people how to give that."

After the meeting concluded, the Fifty-Fifth Precinct posted a tweet summarizing the discussions that had taken place. Despite the meeting's having been dominated by complaints against police (constantly feeling threatened by police, concerns about police use of force and body language), the tweet summing up the night focused on quality-of-life issues aligning with police as service providers—community complaints about automobile safety, illegal parking, and crime prevention strategies. The tweet ended with the hashtag #NYP-Dislistening. Like the photos in figure 4.2, the visuals within this tweet showed NCOs in discussion with a semicircle of residents surrounding them. Photos of crowded rooms like this visually communicate the demand for police services—even though these attendees, pulled in at the last minute, were actually critiquing police services. For the duration of my fieldwork, I never saw anyone from this group of inadvertent attendees return to another Build the Block meeting.

In the organizational records of this Sector 55B meeting, the NCOs summarized the issues raised by the inadvertent attendees as follows: "Attendees discussed general policing matters. What it is to be an officer and asked questions about tactics and community. Questions included why do officers not shoot to injure but shoot to kill. How long does it take an officer to truly know a sector and all its residents. Body language why do officers put their hands on the gun belt." For each issue recorded, NCOs must articulate a plan of action. In this case, the NCOs wrote, "Answered the questions to the best of my ability." In other words, the NCOs interpreted these issues as questions asked and answered rather than as underlying critiques requiring an action plan. Supervisors receiving these write-ups will understand these issues the same way—as misunderstandings that the NCOs have already clarified.

I should note that by including these "questions" in the formal write-ups, the NCOs in Sector 55B demonstrated greater inclusivity than was typical. For example, in a completely separate meeting in Sector D of the Eightieth Precinct, I saw Jessica, an older Black woman who was in charge of a youth organization, raise the same issue as Travis in the Fifty-Fifth Precinct: "You can't expect the community to be friendly to you when you walking down the street with your hand on your gun—that's not necessary, and it psychologically shows a bad attitude, because now you're telling me, you're not coming here to be friends, when I got my hand on my gun" (Sector 80D, September 2018). The NCOs in Sector 80D offered more of the same: Officer Perez explained that "this is our uniform," and "the best way for me to rest my hands and my arms, the best way, is to just lay them there. This is not an attitude or a threat, it's just to rest, it's a habit that we have, and I do it myself." When Jessica described how youth associated with her program often ask why officers walk the streets with their hands on their weapons, NCO Perez reiterated: "So my explanation as to how you see many officers resting their hand is because sometimes they get tired, and they have to rest their hands somewhere—that's the only explanation I can give you." Persistent, Jessica repeated that she did not want to see a "gung ho" attitude among police in her community, especially because it influences the children. Officer Perez ended the conversation: "I'm gonna spread the word of your concern."

However, unlike the NCOs' write-up of the Sector 55B meeting, Perez completely omitted this issue from the formal records. The only complaints he included were homelessness issues, controlled substance use/sale, noise, lighting/scaffolding conditions, and parking issues. Similarly, the precinct's tweet of the meeting—which referred to "productive conversations" about police-community relations—similarly omitted Jessica's complaint about police's threatening self-presentations in favor of a photo of residents clustered around NCO Perez. With it, the precinct communicated police's responsiveness to community requests and implied that community relations were improving as a result. Despite the social context of the interaction, police publicized the implicit endorsement and communicated community demand for their services.

—

Successful operation of the Policing Machine culminates in public endorsements. Whether explicit or implicit, such affirmations equip police to contest the necessity of institutional changes. Endorsements posted on social media, cited in annual reports, and testified about in city council budget hearings provide evidence of the quality of current policing, and platforms like Twitter empower police with the technology to strategically publicize these endorsements widely—guaranteeing that any community exchange can be represented as an implicit endorsement through digital omissions.

Endorsements generated through the Policing Machine are problematic, however. Explicit endorsements are only representative of the constituents police have cultivated, such as those from community councils and clergy councils. At the same time, implicit endorsements undermine collective understandings about the coercive arm of the state by suggesting a degree of public approval that may not exist. When police have the power to both cultivate explicit endorsements and claim implicit endorsements, the public record of police and community interactions becomes both unrepresentative and misrepresentative. The public cannot be well informed if the Policing Machine undermines the good-faith distribution of information.

The chapters thus far have focused on identifying the mechanics of the Policing Machine, especially as a set of strategies imposed on community members, and laying out the rewards of the Machine's successful operation. But how do neighborhood groups operate within and against the Policing Machine? How do they motivate the particular police actions they want, especially when these conflict with the Policing Machine? While some residents seek the expansion of service provision and others seek the redistribution of state power, their shared goal is to hold police accountable whenever police's inactions or actions diverge from their demands. The next chapter details how residents pursue strategies of resistance, guided by what they believe is the optimal type of police relationship, given their circumstances. As long as the Policing Machine has existed, community members have responded to it with agency and contestation.

5

Resisting the Policing Machine

Seeking justice is expensive. When someone is a victim of violence, the surviving family members must take off from work to manage everything from court appearances to new caretaking responsibilities. Yet for victims of police violence specifically, law enforcement agencies are no longer allies in advocating for the laws to be enforced. For those surviving police violence, the pursuit of justice takes on new dimensions: rallies, marches, interviews, and other obligations attract a spotlight that many would decline but for the possibility of securing justice for themselves or their loved one.

Andre, whom you met in chapter 1, began organizing in the Tri-State area after police killed his brother. He provided a snippet of the intrafamily dynamics that arise. As parents continue to grieve and rally over the years, the victim's younger siblings begin to complain that the parents "don't care about us"—seeing that their parents' attention remained focused on their deceased siblings (Andre, interview, July 19, 2018). Ultimately, Andre summarized, police "steal our loved one and then we have to deal with it."

I asked Andre whether he ever expressed these experiences at a community council meeting. "In my experience, they all got the same bullshit. It's all the same shit." He described the typical sequence of events: "[The police] come in, they talk about how many robberies happened in an area, how many break-ins in an area, they say they've gotten X amount of people off the streets, they bring these fucking Wanted posters of young men they're looking for—same song and dance every fucking time. Literally."

Andre is not unique in his perception that police-community meetings are worthless at best. June, whom you also met in chapter 1, described how "people who are afraid of the police are not gonna go to precinct meetings" (June, interview, August 4, 2018). Stakeholders who go unrepresented at these meetings include victims of police violence, their family members, and "anyone who is disenchanted with the system or doesn't feel like that's gonna be a productive space." In contrast, the most well-represented constituencies are those who "don't actually have a systemic understanding of where issues like poverty and homeless[ness] and violence and quote-unquote 'crime' actually come from." For these reasons, June felt justified: "I actually personally haven't [been] for a while."

But while Andre's perception is not uncommon among proponents of police transformation, what he said next is: "Truthfully, it's really nothing worth going for, to be honest. *But I still do*" (Andre, interview, July 19, 2018; emphasis added). Despite the NYPD's broad sorting of complaints from the public into different channels, Andre recognized the risk of siloing his voice in independent channels. An occasional precinct meeting attendee, he said he went in order to "combat what they're saying." He distinguished this from *derailing* the meeting, as he attended "not to really disrupt it, I'm really not trying to disrupt it." Instead, he believes that his specific attendance is important in that he asks questions to contextualize police claims. Despite police never "really answer[ing] community members' questions—they kinda give some vague fucking answers," Andre tries to challenge information that would otherwise be accepted without question.

Implicit in Andre's dilemma over disengagement is an important reality about the Policing Machine. He knows that the police will pursue the Policing Machine regardless of his attendance, and he understands that the Policing Machine will continue diffusing a set of public safety frameworks that other residents will internalize. In other words, his absence at police-community meetings would better enable the machine to proceed uncontested. Any resistance to it must thus assume its inevitability and operate alongside the social order that it imposes—a social order organized around the attractive promise of police services in exchange for public support.

In fact, no matter how racialized the consequences of policing, the Policing Machine seeds its vision across communities such that residents of color can often become some of its staunchest defenders.

At a Build the Block meeting held in a gentrifying area within Sector 80A, a younger white woman named Lindsey asked the Neighborhood Coordination Officers (NCOs) about the police killing of Saheed Vassell. "So in [a similar] situation, I would never call the police, because I worry. I can't live with [death] being the ultimate outcome. I just won't do it" (Sector 80A, April 2019). To Lindsey, the 911 calls that summoned the police who shot Vassell upon their arrival had amounted to a directed killing of a fellow community member. "I think of these scenarios a lot, and I feel very privileged as a white person [that] I don't worry about being shot by police." An NCO responded that "that's your personal choice."

Then Monica, a Black woman in her forties, interjected, directing her words to Lindsey:

> While I understand your principle, I think it needs to perhaps be a little more nuanced, because there are certain African American community members who are not that psyched about this violence either in their community. And so, I think that's really the focus. The focus is keeping our children safe. And yes, there may be kids in hoodies, and we'll push back on that, but I don't think we can make a blatant statement of "I'm white, I'm not gonna pick up the phone to call." That's sort of horrifying to me. And I apologize if it sounds like I'm speaking for the whole race, but I think to a certain extent, the one thing that we all have in common in this room is that we have children and we have families on these blocks, and we want them to be in safe environments. And I don't think that has any racial connotations. (Sector 80A, April 2019)

Monica's reaction to Lindsey's blanket refusal to call 911 reflects the complexity of community preferences regarding police (Doering 2020). To her, eliminating racial profiling of Black kids in hoodies and calling police in emergencies are entirely compatible. Indeed, police-community meetings can represent valuable opportunities for residents like Monica to demand the public safety resources that they deserve, as Skogan (2006) noted, without losing ground on enduring struggles for reducing racial inequalities.

Scholars and activists alike often dichotomize strategies of resistance as being centered either within or outside the system. Whereas strategies inside the system seek change by working within institutionalized channels, those outside the system employ protests, rallies, and other tactics viewed as external to established channels (Burstein 1991; Ewick and Silbey 1998). This dichotomy understands participation as reinforcing existing power and hegemonic structures, and protest as the primary legitimate means of challenging them.

But Andre and Monica complicate this dichotomous framework in different ways. On the one hand, Andre demonstrates the drawbacks of operating from outside official channels. He recognizes that disengagement with police-community efforts is risky, because police will pursue the Policing Machine anyway. His absence advances its success. On the other hand, Monica demonstrates the benefits of operating from within. She views the Policing Machine as a welcomed mechanism for obtaining the protective services in her neighborhood that complement broader movements for racial equality. The goal of this chapter is not to adjudicate whose position is more defensible but to identify convergent strategies for motivating action, irrespective of one's vision for the future of policing. This chapter asks: How can communities resist the Policing Machine when its services offer benefits and their disengagement risks enablement?

—

The classic American political machines of the twentieth century targeted poor new immigrants, whose short time horizons made the material rewards of machine politics attractive (Scott 1969). In fact, one reason political machines faded late in the century was that the majority of the electorate had moved above the poverty line. Before that point, droves of poor newcomers responded to tangible incentives, seeing no alternative but to participate in these relationships of patronage exchange.

These insights still apply when it comes to resisting the Policing Machine. As previously described, the Policing Machine imposes a social order organized around exchanging the promise of police services for public support. On the one hand, police cultivate reliance on the Policing Machine as they amplify the threat of crime and other neighborhood problems. Maximizing the attractiveness of police services motivates public participation in the Policing Machine and aims to generate public displays of support. On the other hand, as residents internalize alternative ways to diagnose and resolve neighborhood problems, the Policing Machine loses steam. While residents are not monolithic in their preferences regarding police, their preferences converge in ways that present possibilities for strategic resistance across the spectrum. The Policing Machine's constituents thus converge with its challengers when the promises of police services are unmet. In these situations, both constituents and challengers want to hold police responsible for actions or inactions that diverged from their demands. Resistance strategies emerged at these intersections and took shape essentially by introducing competition to the Policing Machine in order to reduce reliance on it.

Across organizations, I saw residents employ four resistance strategies on the ground: infusing scarce resources with community significance, pursuing services from nonpolice providers, reestablishing democratic oversight, and forming nonstate protective services. Strategies of resistance thus feature both cognitive and material dimensions. Residents must make the cognitive connection and commitment to alternative resolutions that may be unfamiliar and take longer to effectuate, while being presented with resources for actually resolving those problems. Though in the following pages I discuss the particular goals of the residents in my study, I caution that it is more important to focus on the "how" than the "what," since these strategies can be productively deployed by stakeholders having dissimilar visions of policing.

Throughout, this chapter makes explicit something only implied in the previous chapters. Each of the residents encountered through this study was broadly aware of the dynamics I have termed the Policing Machine. Their actions and decisions discussed in earlier pages, as much as those discussed below, were strategic in the sense that each believed their approach was the appropriate one to achieve their goals. Whether individuals and organizations resisted or shielded the Policing Machine, these agentic decisions were always informed by their experience and judgment regarding how to improve their—and their community's—livelihoods.

INFUSING SCARCE RESOURCES WITH
COMMUNITY SIGNIFICANCE

One method of reducing reliance on the Policing Machine is to develop independent resources. In chapter 3, we saw how the Policing Machine pursues capacity-building to establish control over community councils. As volunteer groups whose organizational funds depend on fundraising, community councils rely on police precincts to provide the basic resources for them to operate. In turn, such capacity-building facilitates police influence over community council operations. However, community councils can begin to resist by differentially infusing their scarce resources with community significance.

For instance, event volunteers are a scarce resource. During major events like National Night Out, the precinct offers its officers as volunteers to set up tables, grill food, distribute water, and assist with all other aspects of event execution. This arrangement means that National Night Out is an annual source for implicit endorsements of police. In the Fifty-Fifth Precinct, officers wear uniforms or National Night Out T-shirts as they provide the labor to execute the entire event. The social media photos, newspaper articles, and blog posts covering the collaborative event implicitly affirm the affinity between officers and residents and signal the success of police-sponsored efforts to connect with community. Previous chapters highlighted this predicament.

Police are less dominant, however, in the Eightieth Precinct's National Night Out. To reduce reliance on police, the Eightieth Precinct Community Council recruits independent volunteers who can benefit by accruing community service hours. The Hope House, a residential substance abuse rehabilitation program, is one consistent source of volunteers. To take on the tasks officers fulfill in the Fifty-Fifth Precinct, such as managing the sound system, National Night Out in the Eightieth required roughly twelve volunteers. In exchange, as I witnessed during the September 2018 meeting, the Eightieth Precinct Community Council awarded community service letters recognizing the hours each person volunteered and how their "efforts were crucial in helping to improve cohesiveness, and to fortify the bond between the police and community" (Eightieth Precinct Community Council, September 2018). Produced on council letterhead, these verification letters infused community significance into volunteering at community council events and initiated a direct relationship between the council and the Hope House independent of the police department. These letters were also valuable to the volunteers as indicators of rehabilitation, whether for programmatic, legal, or personal reasons.

Both the Hope House and the Eightieth Precinct Community Council continued to benefit from this relationship throughout the year. The Hope House not only hosts community council meetings (providing chairs, setting up meeting equipment, and cleaning up), it also prepares full dinners to feed the usual fifty to sixty attendees who come to community council meetings. The council finds ways to return these favors. For instance, at one meeting, Mr. Holloway— both the council's president and a board member for another neighborhood nonprofit—announced he was purchasing seven tickets (at seventy-five dollars each) to the Hope House's graduation ceremony, then encouraged the rest of the council meeting's audience to follow suit (Eightieth Precinct Community Council, September 2018).

Mr. Holloway understands and leverages the community stock that a precinct community council offers to other nonprofits: "Keep in mind, they're a 501(c)(3), and that's something that they can put in their portfolio too—about how we work with the community. One of the biggest agencies in the city is the police department—and that's something. That's good to have the NYPD down on your proposals, this, that, what have you" (Holloway, interview, March 8, 2019). Mr. Holloway recognizes, in other words, that his connection to the NYPD can be attractive to certain community partners and provide credence to their projects. By figuring out ways to innovatively develop nonpolice resources, he reduces reliance on the Eightieth Precinct while retaining the benefits that accrue from collaboration with it.

Another way to create value from scarce resources is to publicly recognize them with awards in the name of the community. The Policing Machine understands the value of such awards, which is why police have privately and routinely influenced community councils to give recognition in this manner to precinct officers (see chapter 4). Luckily, community councils have two options for granting an unlimited number of awards: apply for them or invent them.

In the first instance, community councils can nominate awardees and present them on behalf of the borough president's office, the public advocate, and other elected officials in the city. Applying for these awards is a burdensome process, and many community councils lack the interest, resources, or capacity to pursue these projects. At least two weeks before a meeting, the community council must submit an application for the award to the elected official's office: "You gotta write a story up, you gotta tell it, because elected officials don't know hardly anything about the individual, so we have to put all of that together and pass it on to them and do it according to the way they want it done" (Holloway, interview, March 8, 2019). Providing awards not only promotes goodwill from the recipient, but also, "if you're trying to build relationships with people in the community, you have to do positive things, because nowadays, we have social media, people talking on phones, 'hey, let me tell you what happened the other night'—people talk." Giving these awards generates both political capital and valuable publicity. The trade-off between the time-intensive process of applying for them versus the community council publicity created by presenting meaningful awards from elected officials works out in the favor of those willing to navigate the bureaucracy.

A second option is to invent awards to hand out. This similarly allows the council to formally recognize the resources they receive from nonpolice sources. For instance, local restaurants frequently receive council awards. One reason why the average audience size is larger in the Eightieth Precinct Community Council than in the Fifty-Fifth Precinct's is because it has provided full meals to its audiences for every meeting, every month for the past two decades. This is no small thing, given the meetings' start time—7:30 p.m. "When people come to meetings, especially when you're meeting at the time we do, they wanna eat. They want something cold to drink" (Holloway, interview, July 10, 2018). The Eightieth Precinct Community Council not only obtains enough food for the fifty to sixty meeting attendees to eat, it provides Styrofoam takeout containers for people to take extra food home.

Even if they wanted to, community councils could not cook and serve enough meals for meeting attendees; instead, they persuade local restaurants to donate the food and service to "the community." During a council meeting, as we indulged in stewed chicken and rice, Mr. Holloway invited the owner of Sanaa's Caribbean Food to announce the restaurant's name, location, and commitment to the community (Eightieth Precinct Community Council, February 2019). In an interview afterward, I asked Holloway how his relationship with Sanaa's began. He remembered that he'd simply walked in and asked the owner whether they were willing to donate food to National Night Out.

Introductions to other restaurants were even more serendipitous and transactional. Holloway's relationship with Guyana Gardens began when it got shut down by the city Board of Health due to an inspection disagreement that resulted in a failing grade. The owner happened to explain the situation to the same bank teller who handles the Eightieth Precinct Community Council's funds, and the teller recommended he call Mr. Holloway. Holloway met with the owner, explained how to navigate the health board, and introduced them to local elected officials who called the board on their behalf. The fine was reduced, and Guyana Gardens reopened. The owner did not hesitate to donate lo mein and chicken to the next community council meeting. In total, the Eightieth Precinct Community Council has several restaurants to which it submits donation requests on a rotating basis every three to four months, because "you don't want to beat nobody down" (Holloway, interview, March 8, 2019).

When the community council cannot arrange for a local restaurant to donate food for a particular meeting, it turns to a major supermarket to provide food, utensils, and other supplies on credit. "Sometimes it took us a couple years to pay them back. We got them paid back, though," Holloway remarked. In exchange, the council recognized the supermarket's management with community appreciation awards. The store held a block party as part of its anniversary celebration, and Mr. Holloway devised three awards for the occasion. Each was named for the council's vice president, secretary, and sergeant at arms, respectively. The supermarket publicized the council board as the featured guests at the celebration and went on to display these three plaques prominently by its checkout registers, where all the customers could see them. Although initiating these relationships with restaurants and supermarkets, coordinating food orders, and making plaques to publicly recognize them all require uncompensated labor, the Eightieth Precinct Community Council leverages those hours to feed the community and expand the council's resources and relationships.

But who receives these awards matters. Whereas awards to neighborhood entities independent of the Policing Machine can facilitate relationships for resistance, those to the Policing Machine's partners further sustain the enterprise. During the Fifty-Fifth Precinct Community Council's annual fundraiser described in the book's introduction, the council recognized all eleven of the precinct's NCOs, the NCO supervisor, and Jeffrey Rosen, the director of security of one of the largest apartment complexes within the precinct. Another award, the Ecumenical Award, was given to Pastor Young, president of the Fifty-Fifth Precinct Clergy Council. In an interview, Fifty-Fifth Precinct Community Council President Lela Pessod explained that the awards often varied, depending on the recipient. In past years, the council has given the Entrepreneurial Award to honor local businesspeople. Since it selected Pastor Young as this year's honoree, the award was called the Ecumenical Award.

I asked President Pessod why Pastor Young was top of mind for recognition. First, she noted, he "does a lot with the community as far as when somebody dies" by going with the Fifty-Fifth Precinct Clergy Council to console and pray with the victim's family (Lela Pessod, interview, March 7, 2019). Then she described the clergy council's crowd control function: "If they [community members] are upset, especially if it's a police shooting, he tries to calm it down and keep everybody in control so it doesn't blow out of proportion." While these awards are imbued with just as much community significance as those in the Eightieth Precinct, the Fifty-Fifth's recognition of officers and their partners sustains rather than resists the Policing Machine.

By developing resources independent of the police department and infusing them with community significance, the Eightieth Precinct Community Council is better able than the Fifty-Fifth to mobilize its network of supporters as "the community's voice." Both the Eightieth Precinct Community Council president and a former Fifty-Fifth Precinct commanding officer independently described these two historically high-crime precincts as high-status assignments within the NYPD. According to the president, the Eightieth is a "fast track: you want to get promoted, you come to the Eightieth. Because you know there's an opportunity for you to become deputy inspector or full inspector" (Holloway, interview, September 21, 2018). Along similar lines, the former Fifty-Fifth Precinct commanding officer explained: "There's certain precincts that's a very prestigious assignment—the Fifty-Fifth Precinct is one of them. Everybody that's been there has been a chief of police" (Bobby Banks, interview, February 15, 2019). Like other professionals, officers are career oriented. Therefore, furnishing evidence of community support is viewed as an asset, especially in an era when police prioritize political mobilization.

Yet although both precincts are prestigious assignments, the Eightieth Precinct Community Council is better able to leverage its wide network of community supporters to promote the specific police officers who advance the council's interests. For example, when the Fifty-Fifth Precinct Community Council president wanted a particular community member appointed as an NYPD auxiliary officer, she nominated him to the commanding officer at the time:

> She came to my office and was, like, "I want to put Joe Smith as an auxiliary police officer"—and I thought she was joking, 'cause I know there's only one commander in this, there's only one person who can make decisions. And I was, like, "You serious?" She was, like, "Yeah, I've been talking a lot to people, and we think we should have him." And I'm like, "It's not gonna happen, ma'am." [NYPD Commissioner] Ray Kelly put me here to make those personnel decisions, I make personnel decisions. (Bobby Banks, interview, February 15, 2019)

Even as a former auxiliary officer nominating someone for the volunteer position, the community council president could not exert her influence to contest the commanding officer's decision.

In contrast, the Eightieth Precinct Community Council estimates having helped promote between eight and fifteen officers (Holloway, interview, September 21, 2018; Laurette Simmonds, interview, September 21, 2018). When officers in that precinct seek promotions, those with community council relations ask for its support: "Officers, they know, their own way, they know how to come to you and put that request in—'Hey, can you help me?' And generally I answer—you're not gonna say no. We always, 'Okay, we'll see what we can do'" (Holloway, interview, September 21, 2018). Whether it is supporting an officer's promotion to detective or demanding an officer not be terminated or reassigned to another precinct, the Eightieth Precinct Community Council begins with a letter to the NYPD commissioner formally endorsing the officer and providing examples of their community-oriented acts. Writing the letter is important, because "we want it on record." Concurrently, the council begins collecting signatures to demonstrate community support for the request. In most cases,

Mr. Holloway aims to collect five hundred to six hundred signatures. The president has also announced the NYPD commissioner's office phone number during meetings and asked attendees to "jam the phone line, because the commissioner's not used to having people calling and saying, 'We want this'" (Eightieth Precinct Community Council, June 2019). In these and other ways, the Eightieth Precinct Community Council has created value in its community voice and has mobilized it to shape personnel decisions within the police department.

Infusing scarce resources with community significance is not automatically a mechanism for resistance. Nonetheless, the Eightieth Precinct Community Council did so to create low-cost currencies that it exchanged to mobilize support independent of the police department. While labor intensive, initiatives like recruiting nonpolice volunteers and creating awards for restaurants and supermarkets help reduce reliance on police and begin building the council's own base of audience members and resource providers. This network of supports can then be mobilized as "the community's voice" to shape the promotion and placement of officers within the precinct.

PURSUING SERVICES FROM NONPOLICE PROVIDERS

Resisting the Policing Machine both requires and is advanced by pursuing services offered by nonpolice providers. Police's ability to shuffle citizen complaints to other city agencies implies that there is overlap in the tasks that agencies can cover (Herring 2019). When the Policing Machine is unwilling to provide services, community councils can initiate relationships with other state institutions to get the job done. As I will explain, building relationships with alternative service providers can help de-monopolize the Policing Machine.

A series of events in the Eightieth Precinct shows how the community council pursued relationships with competing service providers to motivate police action on animal-related issues. It began when a family sought help getting their cat back after it accidentally fell out their apartment window. A neighbor had retrieved the cat and forwarded it to an animal abuse organization. Ezra, the son, tracked the cat over the course of six months as it was moved throughout the city. He explained at a Build the Block meeting how he "called the precinct like a hundred times," with no response. Then he decided to walk to the precinct station to fetch a stolen property form, but he was given a lost property form instead—a mistake he discovered only later, when he sought help from the American Society for the Prevention of Cruelty to Animals (ASPCA), which handles lost animal cases in the city. After returning to the precinct twice more, trying to obtain the stolen property form, Ezra finally decided to contact his councilperson, who forwarded him to Mr. Holloway and the Eightieth Precinct Community Council (Sector 80D, September 2018).

Mr. Holloway realized that the precinct was "fumbling with it" because it did not appreciate the significance of a cat to its owner—"they referred to that cat like it was a couch, as property" (Holloway, interview, September 21, 2018). He decided to approach the Brooklyn District Attorney's Office's Animal Cruelty Unit, with which he had connections. Soon, investigators from the DA's office located the cat and arranged for an NCO to pick it up, but even that began to turn into an administrative hassle. The Brooklyn-based NCOs explained that they had to schedule a plan with the local NCOs in the specific sector in Queens to coordinate the cat's retrieval. Mr. Holloway recounted how exasperated he was: "I said, 'Man, why don't y'all just go there and get the man's cat? Please.'" Ultimately, it was the Brooklyn DA's office that physically retrieved the pet.

Mr. Holloway wanted to recognize the DA's office at the next community council meeting: "I'm definitely bringing them in, because I want to honor the DA, the assistant DA." Publicly recognizing the DA's office was not merely to put a capstone on Ezra's case; it was a future-oriented act: "See, that's why they love us so, because we pay close attention . . . they gonna never forget that. That's strategy, that's strategy, to make sure when we need something for the next family, we can get it." As planned, at the November 2018 community council meeting, investigators and prosecutors from the Brooklyn DA's office—not the police department—were presented with a community award (Eightieth Precinct Community Council, November 2018). The next day, reminiscent of the NYPD's Twitter posts, the Brooklyn DA's office tweeted photos from the community council meeting that showed its staff posing with the community plaques.

After Ezra's cat came home, however, the precinct still minimized animal-related issues. That prompted the Eightieth Precinct Community Council to request involvement from local elected officials and the NYC Parks Department. For the September 2018 meeting, the council invited as guest speaker a resident who had emailed the council about her dog, who had been attacked twice by an off-leash dog in Eagle Park; the first attack resulted in $16,000 in veterinary expenses, and the second required that her dog be put down (Eightieth Precinct Community Council, September 2018).

President Holloway explained to me how he "spent all day on the phone with the Parks Department" and persuaded a sergeant from Parks Department Enforcement to answer questions at the meeting. Mr. Holloway also purposefully invited elected officials, to make sure their offices were aware of the community council's concern. At the front of the room, he openly pressured the commanding officer (CO) sitting next to him on the podium: "I know a lot of people look at animals like property, there's no real laws that protect them because they're animals, and I'm just being very candid with everyone, I have to be to make changes in our community—I think our police department needs to get educated more about pets." In an interview afterward, I asked the president why he made the comment, and he explained: "I wanted to let [the police] know, I'm not letting them off the hook. And the CO, he got a little disgusted with that, but I didn't care, because these are these people's loved one" (Holloway, interview, September 21, 2018).

The public pressure worked. Various state agencies began coordinating with the community council to resolve the issue. In the October 2018 meeting, the CO spent time during his monthly report to specifically discuss Eagle Park:

> We've been proactive with Eagle Park, so over the last twenty-eight days since I saw you last, officers have issued eight summonses. . . . Sergeant Bernard, my NCO sergeant, has reached out to the ASPCA, and ASPCA doesn't do dog off the leash enforcement, but they do have other abilities, so they're gonna come out and visit with us at Eagle Park so we can team up and just kind of show our presence there. I also met with the Parks Department at our last community board meeting, and again, we're just trying to be proactive to find the solution to that problem because that was a pretty terrible tragedy. (Eightieth Precinct Community Council, October 2018)

Two months after the issue was first publicized, I attended an ad hoc community meeting moderated by Mr. Holloway to discuss various proposals to change Eagle Park's leash regulations (field note, November 2018). Not only was the precinct's CO present, but he participated on a panel along with representatives from other city agencies that Holloway had invited: the borough president's office, the Brooklyn NYC parks commissioner, the community board, the health department, the school principal, and the ASPCA. When it was time for the CO to speak, he listed the most important things for audience members to do: call 911 or 311 so that the precinct can stay updated on "what is going on out there," attend community council meetings, attend Build the Block meetings, and, pointedly, follow the Eightieth Precinct on Facebook and Twitter. While the CO used his time to advance the Policing Machine, his presence and participation on the panel nonetheless reflect Mr. Holloway's ability to motivate some level of police responsiveness when it initially refused.

Pursuing services from nonpolice providers enabled the Eightieth Precinct Community Council to exert the necessary pressure to contest the police's inaction. But the complaints from Ezra and other pet owners were amplified and acted on only because the council pursued resistance on their behalf. When community councils instead choose to rely on the Policing Machine, it's the residents themselves who must organize to reestablish democratic oversight.

REESTABLISHING DEMOCRATIC OVERSIGHT

A key priority of the Policing Machine is to reorganize police accountability around the constituents they have cultivated and empowered rather than the democratic institutions designed to regulate them (see chapter 2). Community councils are integral in this shift, as they are represented as *the* authentic neighborhood representatives. When these councils choose to rely on rather than resist the Policing Machine, residents themselves acquire the onus of resistance, especially if they want to motivate police action in partner and department channels. In these cases, resisting the Policing Machine involves organizing at the block level to acquire evidence of police inaction, submitting complaints about police to elected officials, and other strategies that reestablish democratic oversight but require much volunteer labor.

Andre, from the vignette that opened this chapter, believes that

police-community meetings are a "waste of my time," since the officers there "aren't the ones that's gonna make the decisions on police
brutality cases" (Andre, interview, July 19, 2018). Nonetheless, he still
attends in order to contest or contextualize the information distributed within the meetings. When he is not at these meetings, his primary strategy is to target elected officials: "I rather be at a city council
hearing and talking about legislation, or on [Mayor] de Blasio's door-
step, or at Gracie Mansion [the mayor's residence] talking about police
brutality." Andre understands the classic tools and strategies of democratic mobilization as the optimal way to resist the Policing Machine.

Reestablishing democratic oversight is necessary because, under
the Policing Machine, community councils are encouraged to screen
or silence oppositional community complaints. President Pessod of
the Fifty-Fifth Precinct Community Council explained to me how she
screens complaints based on what she deems appropriate. For example, she often chooses not to help an "antagonistic person in the community" (Lela Pessod, interview, March 7, 2019) and tells people who
have brought complaints on behalf of others to "let them come here"
(Fifty-Fifth Precinct Community Council, October 2018). In an interview, she reiterated that she tries to help everyone, but "then we have
some people in the community who I don't want to help because of
the fact of their persona, their attitudes—I don't want to get involved
with them. So I say, 'You know what? Call the Community Affairs
office, this is their number. Call them and ask, let somebody there tell
you what it is.'" For these "antagonistic" residents, Pessod abdicates
to police leadership her role as a facilitator of community concerns,
making the calls the responsibility of residents—who often complain
that the Community Affairs Bureau does not return their calls. Rather
than an advocate representing the diverse interests of the community,
the Fifty-Fifth Precinct Community Council more often serves as a
gatekeeper to actual access to police leadership.

Regulating the issues that residents want to raise in public meetings shields the Policing Machine from democratic critique. At the
Fifty-Fifth Precinct Community Council meeting immediately following the annual Carnival celebration in 2018, a group of six older
men attended for the first time. Brooklyn's Carnival features two
parts: the West Indian Day parade, which happens during the daytime
on Labor Day Monday, and the predawn festivities called J'Ouvert
(originated from the French *jour ouvert,* "daybreak"). In contrast to

the bright costumes and orderly pageantry of the daytime Labor Day parade, the darker dress and symbolism of J'Ouvert represent both a celebration of, and a challenge to, the exclusion of the enslaved from French masquerades. Starting around 2:00 or 3:00 a.m. on Labor Day Monday, hundreds of thousands of celebrants dance, sing, and shout as they make their way down the designated route. DJs and steel bands on floats and trucks sustain the soundtrack along the entire way. No two outfits are the same: people masquerade in a variety of homemade costumes accentuated with a mix of face paint, baby powder, body oils, chains, and macabre costumes to invoke the imagery of devils, witches, and ghosts. Over one million people assemble in Brooklyn each year to channel the essence of J'Ouvert, which lies in its defiance of formal control.

Toward the end of the Fifty-Fifth Precinct Community Council meeting, one of the six older men, Stuart Hill, stood, requested to speak, and began: "My name is Stuart Hill, and we have a few people here to complain about Labor Day weekend" (Fifty-Fifth Precinct Community Council, September 2018). Immediately, President Pessod got on the microphone and interrupted: "Excuse me, hold on. You already discussed it with him [the CO] before.... It was discussed there, and everything was settled, sir. We're not gonna rehash that. I'm sorry." Stuart pushed back, saying that "the community should know—that's why we have a community meeting," but the president refused to let the men speak. All six stood and left the meeting.

I followed up with Stuart to learn what happened. During J'Ouvert for the past seven years, he and his group of approximately forty senior citizen friends from a soccer club had gathered to celebrate. They would pool $5,000 to rent the yard of a private home, hire a DJ, and order catering and liquor. But at 9:20 p.m. on the Sunday night preceding this year's Labor Day holiday, Stuart recounted that the precinct sent "about ten squad cars and a truck and a helicopter overhead" (Stuart Hill, interview, October 3, 2018). It turned out that the precinct was responding to complaints from neighbors. Nonetheless, after coming out with "such force" and confirming no threats, Stuart believed that the precinct should have allowed his group to resume their celebration after seeing "the crowd in there, people all from their seventies and above—not a bunch of youths, which is a different scenario altogether." Because one of the group members' wives knew President Pessod of the Fifty-Fifth Precinct Community Council, they got the opportunity to explain the situation to her. In response, she arranged a meeting for them with the precinct CO. At the meeting, the CO explained that "with the incidents they had before [at that address], they came out with such a force." Stuart understood, and the CO encouraged the group to let the precinct know about similar events beforehand in the future. Nonetheless, Stuart and his friends—who live in another precinct and traveled an hour to come to the meeting that night—wanted to tell their story publicly. However, after the police shutdown and being silenced at the community council meeting, he said that he could no longer even think about celebrating J'Ouvert in future years.

The NYPD chief of Community Affairs directly confirmed that the president's response to Stuart was appropriate. The chief happened to be present at the community council meeting to swear in the reelected board (Fifty-Fifth Precinct Community Council, September 2018). President Pessod revealed in an interview afterward how Chief Hoffman called her after the meeting and said, "I like the ship that you run over there" (Lela Pessod, interview, March 7, 2019). In fact, when NYPD Commissioner James O'Neill visited a Fifty-Fifth Precinct Community Council meeting, a resident whose daughter was active on the community board with Pessod explained: "Lela made it very clear, she told us at the executive meeting . . . that he wasn't here to hear our dissatisfactions with the inspector, or anything like that" (Marcia, interview, April 30, 2019). Attendees at the meeting were not to "ask those kinds of issues or ask those kinds of questions," because it was supposed to be a "happy" meeting. Operating meetings in this manner is precisely why the Policing Machine seeks to restructure police accountability away from elected officials and toward community councils as an alternative system of neighborhood representatives.

Strategic resistance in these situations involves reestablishing the democratic oversight that the Policing Machine seeks to circumvent. A first step for residents is to collect the information and evidence needed to empower elected officials to take action. Neighbors under the jurisdiction of the Fifty-Fifth Precinct Community Council have formed a collective to do just that. The collective shares the burden of attending council meetings, documenting submitted complaints, and returning to follow up. It includes two lawyers who help share legal information about the administrative codes authorizing officers to enforce the neighborhood issues the collective wants resolved. Mary, a vocal African American senior citizen in the group, told me that there are about twelve of them who share, log, and save their NCO and 311 requests (Mary, interview, March 11, 2019). In fact, she has been so insistent that the CO's open-door policy is now closed to her: a Community Affairs officer told her that any questions she has for the CO should be directed to him first.

After realizing that they were not getting called on during community council meetings even with their hands raised, members of the collective began coordinating "new faces" to submit issues on their behalf. Mary connected me to Carmella, a fifty-nine-year-old Italian American woman in the group who is an informal representative of the residents of her block. Because they lack a formal block association, neighbors come to Carmella and ask her to submit complaints on their behalf; she is familiar with navigating the administrative bureaucracies of the NYPD, community councils, 311, and other city agencies (Carmella, interview, April 10, 2019). By submitting and documenting complaints for her neighbors, she can provide police supervisors, elected officials, and other stakeholders with evidence of unanswered grievances from the community.

The collective began to see results when it raised its concerns to its community board. In New York City, members of the fifty-nine community boards covering the community districts of the city's five boroughs are appointed by democratically elected borough presidents. These boards manage local issues within their neighborhood, including land use and zoning, sanitation, transportation, and public safety. Given that specific complaints were screened or silenced at community council meetings, Mary started urging the CO to attend community board meetings. Past COs had done so, and this represented an opportunity to raise complaints outside police-influenced community council meetings. Mary's advocacy culminated in a joint meeting between the community board's Transportation Committee and its Public Safety Committee. In response to her complaints about illegally parked freight trucks occupying blocks of parking spots, the city Department of Transportation provided a presentation on the regulatory landscape and enforcement strategies that its officers could pursue in collaboration with the precinct. After the presentation, the CO's liaisons explained that he "wanted us to let you [Mary] know personally" that he "took your message" and was in the process of coordinating enforcement action (field note, February 27, 2019).

Reestablishing democratic oversight is a promising strategy, even if residents want to collect evidence and submit complaints *about* police to elected officials. Marcus, who raised issues about overpolicing and gentrification in chapter 1, explained that he would return to Build the Block meetings only if he could start a committee with "people who have been victims, who have had experiences with law enforcement that have been unjust—whether ticketing, pulled over, their son or daughter, whatever" (Marcus, interview, June 20, 2019). The committee would "go to every meeting and take notes and present this to the mayor: 'You've organized this, nothing's been done.'" By independently tracking complaints raised at meetings, Marcus envisioned that his committee could then present its case to NCOs, elected officials, and the general public: "Now we got you saying for two years, [yet] you didn't do anything. And now we got witnesses, we got notes, we got names of people who said it, list of phone calls we made, letters we wrote."

Forming a record of requests positions residents to demand a substantive response. Otherwise, according to Marcus, if residents tell NCOs, "You said last time, so-and-so," NCOs emptily respond, "You're right," and then record the issue on the meeting whiteboard but fail to take further action. Also, NCOs often exchanged contact information with residents, promising, "I'm gonna get back to you," but they never did. Marcus contended that police purposefully drag out complaints as "a play they use to discourage you," since after months of waiting, you will "get frustrated and move on with your life." In contrast, by forming a committee to track complaints, Marcus and his neighbors could build a case and hold police accountable.

Marcus's vision was one strategy that Eva pursued with success. As discussed in chapter 2, Eva wanted police to take enforcement action against cars double-parking on her street during church services; but the NCOs did not want to because of their institutional relationship with the pastor and the personal relationship between the church and the officers who attended it (Eva, interview, May 14, 2019). First, she drafted a letter with the tenants in her building. It described how every weekend, the double-parking trapped residents' vehicles; prevented deliveries; blocked fire hydrants; impeded Access-a-Ride pickups for senior citizens; and caused excessive horn blowing. It explained how for over a decade, neighbors have raised this issue to the church, the community board, the police department, and 311. After Eva emailed the letter to the borough president's office and forwarded the email to the NCO supervisor, she was contacted by investigators for the Americans with Disabilities Act to see whether any violations had occurred. A few weeks later, cars were no longer double-parked outside her building. While she could not confirm, she was told that one vehicle was fined $50,000 for the violation.

Whether seeking to consume police services or transform policing as an institution, residents can better hold police accountable by organizing neighbors, documenting submitted complaints, pressuring officers for substantive responses, and presenting nonresponses to state actors beyond the police that can reestablish democratic oversight. These strategies emphasize the strength in numbers, the significance of consistent engagement, the onus of independent documentation, and the struggle inherent in holding police accountable. Nonetheless, they represent a valuable starting point for residents seeking any type of police action to begin expressing both input *and* influence in how policing proceeds in their neighborhoods.

FORMING NONSTATE PROTECTIVE SERVICES

The first time I met Phil, whom you met in chapter 1, I heard his presence before I saw it. A small Bluetooth speaker clipped to his belt was playing Childish Gambino's "This Is America." Based on our conversation, this first impression could not have been more fitting. Phil is a twenty-seven-year-old Brooklyn native who describes himself as an "activist on standby"—he is a core organizer for an organization affiliated with Reforms Advancing Long Lives for our Youth (RALLY) but, despite his degree from Morehouse College, has not had paid work for months. He offered to provide a walking tour after I emailed his organization asking whether I could learn more about its mission. We walked around Brooklyn Gardens, where Phil pointed out several apartment buildings and sidewalks where police had killed residents experiencing medical emergencies. In many of these cases, it was actually parents or other family or friends who had contacted the police. They sought medical assistance for their loved one but were met with police violence. Phil explained how policing is connected to housing, as landlords often request police presence as backup during evictions. And he told illustrative stories, such as the time his bicycle was stolen and he decided not to contact police about it, because "I can't control what happens to the person who stole my bike" (Phil, interview, June 7, 2018). According to him, interactions with police are so often problematic because they proactively enforce compliance with the law, even though many times no law has been broken.

Besides showing me noteworthy spots, Phil had offered the walking tour because he was on copwatch patrol. Every time he heard sirens or saw a police car drive by, he perked up and either walked over or followed the car with his eyes until it disappeared. The primary goal of copwatching is to provide documentation of police interactions that can be used by community members as evidence in their legal cases. Copwatching is also a form of community empowerment, because "when people see us recording, they realize that it's okay for them to record too." Copwatchers also distribute information, including alternatives to calling police, since "police obviously won't advertise alternatives."

As we walked, I got the opportunity to see Phil in action. An older woman wearing ripped clothes that barely hung onto her frame approached and asked whether we could give her change. Phil apologized on behalf of the both of us, and we continued on our way. Not ten seconds later, we heard confrontational yelling. Phil looked behind him, where the woman was now yelling at another woman. A young male had gotten in between the two, trying to separate them. Phil ran over and demanded forcibly, "Hey! Hey, chill out." His demand startled them as much as we had been startled when the argument began. Then he directed the young man to take the woman away and to "keep walking." The woman, who appeared to be the young man's mother, mumbled something about how "these people are stealing all our coffee beans and reselling them."

When the commotion settled down, Phil explained to me: "See, that's community policing—that's the community doing the policing." In other words, it mattered in this situation that he is a community resident, just like those involved in the confrontation. Copwatchers are not just intervening when police arrive on the scene—they are trying to de-escalate situations to avoid police being notified in the first place: "I was scared that a police van would pull up, and if that happened, you know who's getting arrested? All three of them, especially the young man." His point was that police interventions are often too indiscriminate and overinclusive, sweeping up even those trying to de-escalate the dispute based on generalized perceptions of guilt. Whether distributing information or resolving disputes before police are even needed, copwatching represents a nonstate form of protective services that operates as a form of resistance against the Policing Machine.

Phil's organization distributes a fact sheet, "Alternatives to Calling 911." The informative document emerged from a community forum at which residents, social workers, and other trained professionals gathered to devise "community solutions to problems that are often addressed by police intervention" (Corey, interview, August 31, 2018). One of the easiest things that residents can do, they determined, is to get to know their neighbors. This can help clarify miscommunications and establish a sense of shared interests that can resolve issues such as loud music, trash left on doorsteps, and other situations that are annoying but do not require police intervention, thereby abating the threat that police pose. These types of complaints are the same ones that NCOs prime residents to submit during Build the Block meetings. A typical NCO introduction during a Build the Block might go, "In the past month, we've done several things: we've had locks put on the fence in the park, we've had abandoned houses sealed up and the residents kicked out that was inside of them, we've had cars towed, people that have derelict vehicles on their block, we've had neighbor disputes that we've helped mediate and resolve, and we've had speed bumps put in. If it's not within our realm to help you, we'll try and lead you to the source that would be able to help you" (55B, August 8, 2018). RALLY groups do not reject the validity of these complaints, nor that police are willing to respond; they just believe that these situations can be resolved without police intervention, thus avoiding overreliance on the police and the fatal consequences that can transpire when they are called for minor issues.

Building relationships with neighbors promotes the formation of community associations as another source for nonstate protective services. Carmella and her neighbors' informal block association documents police inaction and tries to motivate police services for issues ranging from illegally parked trucks to noise abatement at local establishments. Associations like theirs, however, can instead provide protective services as alternatives to police intervention. For example, while trying to evict an elderly Black tenant, a local landlord illegally broke into the tenant's apartment and threw her things out in the street. A confrontation erupted, and the landlord's son punched the tenant in her stomach. The tenant called police, but when they arrived, they refused to arrest the landlord for breaking into the tenant's apartment or his son for assault. The officers even refused to write a police report documenting the tenant's claims. At her wits' end, she called Nasir, the founding director of a RALLY-affiliated organization, who helped organize a tenant association in the building to oversee and mediate these tense interactions in the future. This is particularly important because, in addition to evictions, landlords often encourage tenants to contact police whenever they have disputes among themselves. Contacting neighbors, community leaders, and family members instead of the police to intervene in disputes can avoid situations—whether accidental, purposeful, or somewhere in between—in which police kill.

All these activists understand that police might have to be contacted for emergency services. In these cases, they recommend explicitly telling the 911 operator that "it is a medical emergency, and I need an ambulance." Callers, they say, should carefully describe the physical issues to the operator, then gather community members, copwatchers, and tenant or block association members to provide support to the affected person until and even after the first responders arrive. Callers and neighbors should meet the first responders before police encounter the individual with the emergency, and they should accompany that community member or loved one to the emergency room if it is safe to do so and the person consents. Community members throughout the Fifty-Fifth and Eightieth Precincts have Nasir's phone number, and they can contact him and the lawyers his organization coordinates with whenever they need assistance.

These examples describe resistance through the formation of nonstate sources of protective services, but it's crucial to note that the Policing Machine actually makes it quite difficult to identify which protective services are composed of nonstate actors. Across New York City, the NYPD has formed public safety patrols comprising representatives from the dominant religious or ethnic population in a given neighborhood. In the Jewish areas of Brooklyn, for instance, the Shomrim has conducted civilian patrols and provided emergency responses since back in the 1970s. Their badges, uniforms, patrol cars, and mobile command centers are all directly modeled after the NYPD's equipment. The Boro Park Shomrim alone has 130 volunteer members, 15 dispatchers, and a twenty-four-hour hotline.[1] More recently, in 2014 the NYPD approved a civilian patrol group in Brooklyn's Chinatown (Valentine and Harshbarger 2014). Like the Shomrim, this patrol group has walkie-talkies and NYPD-style patrol cars, and members wear security-like uniforms and jackets emblazoned with Brooklyn Asian Safety Patrol. These groups are presumed to have the neighborhood knowledge, language capacity, and cultural awareness to provide protective services to specific populations. However, they are *not* nonstate alternatives to the police. By default, the Shomrim is supposed to forward information to the police, but it has also been accused of withholding information about sex crimes, kidnappings, and excessive-force incidents victimizing non-Jewish residents (Feuer 2016). Like Neighborhood Watch and other volunteer police patrols, these groups are components of the Policing Machine rather than alternatives.

The NYPD has similarly deputized the Fifty-Fifth Precinct Clergy Council to conduct street patrols and emergency responses, even as that council has purposefully blurred its police connection. Selecting appropriate attire for its members' watch and response roles requires balance. Whereas white collars and other formal clerical attire might deter community residents from speaking to them on the street, casual attire would insufficiently distinguish them as clergy. Clergy council members also want to make sure that officers in the street recognize their affiliation: "[We] want the police to be able to identify who we are too, so they can give us the level of respect that is needed for the work that we are going to do, who we are, and what we're about" (Young, interview, September 19, 2018). The Fifty-Fifth Precinct Clergy Council has thus introduced its own uniforms. Initially, its brightly colored jackets featured "55th Precinct Clergy Council Crisis Team" in block letters, along with a logo resembling a formal police badge. Then, Pastor Maurice explained, they "actually changed the design of the jacket so they did not look like police jackets" (Maurice, interview, March 7, 2019). The new jackets erase any references to the precinct and now only read, "Clergy Response Team." This strategic decision presents the clergy council members as nonstate actors, even if they are not. Such a distinction matters for whether residents would seek clergy council help in the first place, what information they would be willing to share, and what recourse would be available if things go awry.

All residents desire and deserve protective services, yet those provided by the Policing Machine and its affiliated entities can bring harm to requests for help. Introducing nonstate forms of protective services resists the Policing Machine by offering community members alternative sources of organized help in times of need. For everyday disputes, residents can resolve disagreements with neighbors by initiating a relationship with them before a dispute erupts or by contacting a family member, associate, copwatch team, or tenant or block association to mediate. When residents do call on police in emergency situations, these organizations teach them how to do so (more) safely by explicitly informing the emergency operator that a medical crisis exists and an ambulance is requested. Contacting police always requires copwatchers—whether formal patrol people or associates informally documenting interactions—to help oversee the police response. The goal of introducing nonstate forms of protective services is to reduce reliance on police by empowering community sources of social control.

—

Past chapters identified how, under the Policing Machine, police ascribed neighborhood problems, cultivated constituents, distributed power and privilege, and induced public endorsements. This chapter finds residents resisting their roles in that machine by infusing scarce resources with community significance; pursuing services from nonpolice providers; reestablishing democratic oversight; and forming nonstate protective services. These strategies account for the complicated realities of resistance—that disengagement can enable the Policing Machine, and that the Policing Machine can still deliver services that people need and deserve. They also focus on finding ways to motivate police action or introduce substitutes for it. While other forms of resistance undoubtedly exist, these four strategies emerged from my fieldwork as some of the most promising approaches applicable across the variety of visions that residents expressed toward policing. In other words, regardless of whether one seeks greater police enforcement or wholesale transformation, these alternative strategies can be tailored to advance community goals of safety without sacrificing justice.

From Machine to Movement

On May 25, 2020, Minneapolis police officer Derek Chauvin suffocated George Floyd by kneeling on his neck for nearly ten minutes. The murder, which was recorded by a young woman in the crowd that had formed, mobilized one of the largest social protests in American history. Throughout the summer of 2020 and beyond, demonstrators took to the streets to voice their visions of the institutional changes needed for police transformation. These protests revealed the range of public preferences toward police, which needed to be vocalized on pavement precisely because they have been silenced within the indoor settings described in previous chapters.

Exactly one week later, then-president Donald Trump walked from the White House to St. John's Church in Washington, DC, Bible in hand, for a photo op—one intended to show the strength of the law and religion against the unruly crowds protesting throughout the country. The religious context was no coincidence, given how readily state actors like the police in previous chapters incorporate organized faiths into projects of state legitimation—regardless of whether clergy cooperate. Many senior law enforcement and military officials accompanied Trump, including Attorney General William Barr, Defense Secretary Mark Esper, and General Mark Milley, chairman of the Joint Chiefs of Staff. The photo was possible only because peaceful protesters had been violently removed: law enforcement officers from four different agencies used horses, batons, pepper spray, and tear gas to clear demonstrators from Lafayette Square, the area abutting the church. Having just declared in a Rose Garden speech, "I am your president of law and order," this, too, seemed appropriate. With the square emptied, Trump smiled and displayed the spine of the Bible for the press.

Many things are noteworthy about this series of events, but subsequent comments from our nation's top military official proved particularly remarkable. Two weeks later General Milley, who was part of Trump's entourage that day, gave the keynote address to the graduating class of the National Defense University. In it, he apologized unequivocally. "I should not have been there. My presence in that moment, and in that environment, created a perception of the military involved in domestic politics. As a commissioned, uniformed officer, it was a mistake" (Milley 2020). Milley's use of the phrase "domestic politics" pointed to the pair of egregious errors he made by appearing with Trump—the military must abstain from both domestic *and* political matters. "We must hold dear the principle of an apolitical military."

As an institution, the US military cannot claim an apolitical history (Mills 1956; Go 2020; Schrader 2019). Nonetheless, General Milley's public apology reflected a continued recognition of the underlying wisdom of distancing the military from domestic politics. Democracy does not work when partisan views are backed by coercive force. Protection becomes contingent rather than equal and guaranteed, and society's capacity for change is strained by politicized forces invested in a particular state of affairs. In fact, while the first piece of advice General Milley gave to graduates was to maintain "situational awareness," since they would always be watched as military leaders, the second was to "embrace the Constitution." This is crucial, because "the freedoms guaranteed to us in the Constitution allow people to demand change, just as the peaceful protesters are doing all across the country." Remaining apolitical in domestic affairs means that armed representatives of the state must guarantee the conditions that permit social change without weighing in on its particular direction.

—

In the past five chapters, I have shown how the NYPD, the largest police department in the United States and a primary role model for policing nationwide, is trending in the opposite direction of these apolitical ideals. The Policing Machine, as a concept and in the form of this book, describes how police cultivate political capital by engaging in a strategic politics of distribution—one where public resources, regulatory leniency, and coercive force are deployed to guarantee police power regardless of demands for social change.

Police pursue the Policing Machine as both legitimacy optimizers and political mobilizers. They cultivate and rely on a set of tools, strategies, and relationships—many beyond the scope of classic law enforcement—that enable them to maximize public legitimacy without sacrificing organizational independence. An illusion of public input emerges as police amplify constituents and silence alternatives. Rather than pursue apolitical ideals, let alone publicly apologize when they have transgressed, the NYPD has eschewed the apolitical stance required for democracy's armed forces. Instead, it has deployed its force and resources to build a machinery of police-community relations that can be mobilized to resist accountability, transformation, and ultimately, social justice.

This concluding chapter does not merely conclude. It presents a look forward, as the Policing Machine evolves into a broader political movement, by connecting the local consequences of this machine to its emergence onto the national stage. I will begin by looking at the consequences of the normal operation of the Policing Machine, which include the creation of a new system of police accountability in which democratic governance is used as a shield against public scrutiny, and the rise of an urban political regime in which police permeate informal social controls. Then I detail the emergence of the Policing Machine as a national political movement with an ideology, identity, and infrastructure cohering around what it means to be police. National political movements seek to advance an overarching set of principles, a goal that need not be accomplished solely through participation in electoral politics. Finally, I close with a series of first steps toward dismantling the Policing Machine. I encourage cities to interrogate existing practices, not only in enforcement interactions with the public, but in the key areas of regulatory power, social media, community sentiments, and public resources.

THE LOCAL CONSEQUENCES OF
THE POLICING MACHINE

At the local level, the Policing Machine transforms democratic governance into a shield against public scrutiny and establishes an urban political regime with police permeating informal social controls. These consequences emphasize that community nonprofit organizations do not necessarily strengthen democracy or informal social controls. Instead, the Policing Machine deploys democratic initiatives and neighborhood organizations as shields and swords in their resistance to police transformation.

Democratic Governance as a Shield against Public Scrutiny

The Policing Machine establishes a new system of police accountability. As classic Weberian bureaucracies, most urban police departments are held accountable to the public through democratically elected public officials (Crank and Langworthy 1992). Police are supposed to derive power "from above" through appointment, not "from below" through constituents.

For instance, in cities like New York and Chicago, mayors appoint police chiefs and city councils determine police department budgets. In places like Los Angeles, elected officials appoint and confirm a board of police commissioners—five civilians who determine overall departmental policies—and the chief of police, who manages the department's daily operations. By design, policing agencies are supposed to execute the mayor's vision. When departments diverge from the mayor's agenda, then community members can activate democratic mechanisms to demand new police leadership, new legislation, departmental policy changes, or new elected officials who will pursue police accountability on their behalf.

However, the Policing Machine feeds into our democratic impulses to instead circumvent these traditional lines of public accountability (Cheng 2020; Cheng and Qu 2022). Democratic governance refers to regulatory systems, agencies, organizations, and other mechanisms that empower citizens with a decision-making role in the practices of state institutions. While policing scholars have envisioned various forms of democratic governance (Manning 2010), they are united in their commitment to expanding public input as a mechanism for civilian oversight and police accountability (Kleinfeld et al. 2016; Walker 2016). The logic underlying these participatory initiatives is that public input can help direct police decision-making and curb unchecked incentives. Recent proposals for either full community control over policing decisions (Simonson 2020) or representative control through an intermediary like a police auditor (Ponomarenko 2019) have diagnosed the problem as one of institutional design: cities have yet to achieve democratic governance over police departments because they have yet to design the optimal entity, board, or process to achieve it.

That diagnosis is turned on its head when we look closely at the Policing Machine, which welcomes the participatory initiatives of democratic governance—because they actually empower police to cultivate and curate preferred sources of accountability. For instance, police channel heterogeneous community complaints toward department channels like Build the Block meetings (see chapter 1). This preference is rooted in the department's asymmetrical control over the recording and representation of complaints raised within these meetings. Exercising such control enables police to curate these grievances, elevating in particular those from the constituents they have cultivated. Outside these meetings, police can establish and empower alternative systems of neighborhood representatives (see chapter 2), such as community councils and clergy councils. Police can then claim accountability to these alternative representatives, represented as *the* authentic representatives of their communities (unlike traditionally elected officials, over whom police exercise less influence).

These initiatives are designed to infuse democratic input into policing practices either through direct attendance at open community meetings or indirectly through residents elected to community councils. But whatever their design, participatory initiatives repeatedly become part of police's "legitimacy regime" (Rocha Beardall 2022). As police's institutional priorities endure and their discretion shifts, they devise new strategies to account for the changes in the regulatory environment. These new strategies focus on mobilizing and empowering the specific parts of the public to which the department *wants* to be held accountable. Such optimization will continue positioning police to contest the necessity of institutional change as they selectively distribute public resources to constituents willing to endorse current policing as quality, in-demand policing. The Policing Machine, which cultivates autonomy from traditional sources of oversight, maintains the illusion that representative forms of public input can actually emerge, free from police influence, and substantively transform departments in ways unwelcomed by police.

The Policing Machine makes it more difficult to hold police accountable regardless of whether that accountability involves punishing officer misconduct or finally motivating enforcement action. It is not that the demands for more police services are any less valid than any other community preference. Instead, the fundamental insight is that police accountability is undermined because police proactively curate what exactly counts as a community demand in the first place. Community complaints do not automatically direct NCOs to resident-identified issues—NCOs refused, for instance, to take enforcement action against a church where Build the Block meetings are held and which officers attend (see chapter 2). Instead, NCOs selectively engage with community complaints as raw material to advance institutional priorities under the Policing Machine.

The pursuit of the Policing Machine makes police a unique city agency when it should *not* be. Imagine peer agencies pursuing these strategies. What if New York City's Department of Buildings advocated for a particular set of zoning laws or built political alliances to shape land use based on institutional beliefs about how different municipal areas should be regulated? Stakeholders may leverage public planning meetings as opportunities to approve projects (Levine 2017), but that is wholly different from representatives of the state shaping the direction of development in pursuit of political capital to resist institutional change.

When the armed representatives of the state shape public input about themselves, communities become even more vulnerable to unaccountable state violence. State violence can take a number of forms, from the police killing of Saheed Vassell described throughout this book to the unjustified stopping of Black motorists like Marcus discussed in chapter 1. As people like Marcus and Vassell's family members seek recourse, they realize the illusion—department and partner channels do not hold police accountable. Then, when they try to participate in independent channels to amplify concerns about police violence and overpolicing, police exercise enforcement to contain these demands. When the state's coercive force engages in strategic politics under the guise of democratic governance, participatory initiatives delay institutional change in ways that ultimately deepen inequalities and foment injustices.

Urban Political Regime with Police
Permeating Informal Social Controls

Existing conceptions of police as either law enforcers or order maintainers are insufficient for analyzing how police manage intensifying organizational threats such as calls for oversight and defunding. These threats are rooted in the public's growing realization that physical violence is not, in fact, police's last resort but a frontline response to community problems of all kinds.

Problematizing police violence is often paired with community alternatives featuring interventions led by nonprofit organizations. These local nonprofits are presented as alternatives, intermediaries, or even resource competitors to police (Jones 2018; Vargas 2016). Forman (2004, 37) describes the promise of intermediary organizations like "churches, schools, and community nonprofits" that can help initiate communication, bridge relationships, and form working partnerships. Whereas police epitomize formal social controls (enforcing rules defined by the state and law), reformers cast community nonprofits as resident-driven, service-oriented, and ultimately informal social controls that are implicitly less lethal. The President's Task Force on 21st Century Policing (2015, 46) reported, "Community policing is . . . about the civic engagement and capacity of communities to improve their own neighborhoods." Police and community are often presented as foils: unlike police forces, which are viewed as community outsiders, community nonprofits represent "informal sources of social control internal to communities" (Sharkey, Torrats-Espinosa, and Takyar 2017, 215).

This classic dichotomy overlooks how the Policing Machine establishes an urban political regime that dissolves any clean distinction between police and nonprofits as formal and informal social controls. Under the Policing Machine, encountering police as an organization—as the arbiters of the permissible—is unavoidable. Community groups must interact with the police for even basic regulatory approvals like amplified sound permits. Police also proactively seek to control community organizations by policing in both cooperative and coercive ways. To their preferred partners, police offer meeting spaces, officer volunteers, and other organizational resources that might ease the pressures of scarce resources. To independent channels amplifying demands for police transformation, police wield coercive force to control and silence. As political mobilizers, police have responded to their legitimacy crisis by distributing power and privilege to the constituents they have cultivated (see chapter 3) and accruing endorsements in exchange (see chapter 4). Police in my study sought to increase not the influence *of* informal social controls but rather their influence *over* informal social controls.

Although studies have found that the concentration of organizations framed as "community" or defined as "nonprofit" may decrease violent crime (e.g. Sharkey, Torrats-Espinosa, and Takyar 2017), the mechanism may not necessarily be through informal social controls. The broader policing infrastructure within cities encompasses not only the department itself but also the police union, police media channels, and as the previous chapters highlighted, a range of community nonprofits committed to public safety through police partnership. For instance, if police direct clergy council members to assist in an enforcement action against a problematic building or to quell a large street demonstration (see chapter 3), social control is blurred in ways that entrench the role of police in neighborhoods. As the Policing Machine comes to dominate community life, the presence of neighborhood nonprofits organized around safety, violence, and policing may be a better indicator of the omnipresence of formal social controls rather than their absence.

THE POLICING MACHINE ON THE NATIONAL STAGE

The Policing Machine is emerging from its foundation in urban politics to take shape on the national stage. While this study focused on the NYPD, police departments across the United States are navigating intensifying public scrutiny. Policing Machines are materializing in these cities too, albeit in locally inflected forms. Instead of community councils, Los Angeles has established Community-Police Advisory Boards, which scholars have similarly found enhance police power at the expense of community agency (Gascón and Roussell 2019). The Chicago Police Department's Neighborhood Policing Initiative is actually modeled after the NYPD's Neighborhood Policing, reflecting the precedential power of NYPD programs. In other cities, it's likely that police departments are establishing tailored but complementary sets of tools and strategies to advance Policing Machines. For instance, the Policing Machine is empowered as neighborhood boundaries are redistricted to establish a racial geography wherein police constituents can be either concentrated and amplified or concentrated and silenced (Gordon 2022; Vargas et al. 2022). As Policing Machines across cities strengthen, policing is emerging as a national political movement with an ideology, identity, and infrastructure cohering around what it means to be police.

Many examples exist of national political movements with coherent ideologies that did not necessarily prioritize electoral politics. The Black Panther Party advocated for a particular vision of society, one that emphasized Black nationalism, anti-imperialism, and armed self-defense (Seale 1970). It viewed the Black community as a colony within the United States and the police as an occupying army; thus, it sought independence rather than incorporation into American society (Bloom and Martin Jr. 2013). While the long-term goal may have been election to positions of leadership, the Black Panther Party pursued its vision more immediately through community programs like free breakfasts, copwatching, and medical clinics (Bloom and Martin Jr. 2013; Nelson 2011; Seale 1970).

National surveys already indicate divergences between police and the public on fundamental social visions. These are not mere differences of opinion. A 2017 Pew survey indicated that 38 percent of rank-and-file officers between the ages of eighteen and thirty-four agreed that "very few or none of the people in the neighborhoods they routinely patrol share their values and beliefs" (Morin et al. 2017). In the same survey, 67 percent of officers characterized the "deaths of [B]lacks during encounters with police in recent years" as "isolated incidents" as opposed to the 31 percent who viewed them as "signs of a broader problem." For the public, the percentages were reversed: 60 percent characterized the law enforcement–related deaths of Black Americans as signs of a broader problem versus 39 percent as isolated incidents. The survey also reported divergence in equal rights more broadly: 80 percent of officers agreed that "our country has made the changes needed to give [B]lacks equal rights with whites," whereas 50 percent of the public agreed that "our country needs to continue making changes to give [B]lacks equal rights with whites." While policing agencies and unions have long lobbied for policies at all levels of government (Broadwater and Edmondson 2020), police as a national political movement describes a different process—one where police seek to coalesce power around their particular social vision beyond legislative policy proposals.

Recent evidence from police departments across the United States shows how national politics and political ideology mobilize police to deploy coercive force. Economists found that after a Trump rally during the 2015–16 campaign, the probability that a motorist experiencing a traffic stop was Black increased by 5.75 percent (Grosjean, Masera, and Yousaf 2022). This effect, which lasted for up to two months after the rally, was specific to Black drivers and more pronounced among the officers and geographic areas with historically greater racial resentment. The findings were unique to Trump rallies, as the other leading opponents from the Republican Party (Ted Cruz) or the Democratic Party (Hillary Clinton) did not generate similar changes in police behavior. This evidence emphasizes how local police are providing coercive support for national political ideologies.

A key component of the national political movement centered on police is symbolic ideology, such as the Blue Lives Matter flag. This flag is an American flag rendered in black and white, with a single blue stripe directly underneath the stars. This "thin blue line" represents the belief that police are the only thing standing between order and chaos (Williams 2021). The flag is not only worn by officers on T-shirts and as patches on bulletproof vests but also displayed by citizens on car bumpers and in front yards. For many, it is a symbol specifically deployed against Black and other racialized people in the United States, given its ties to white supremacist groups and its positioning as a counterprotest to the Black Lives Matter movement. Various agencies across municipalities have begun prohibiting the display of the Blue Lives Matter flag. After the January 6 insurrection at the US Capitol and the public backlash when a Twitter photo showed the flag being displayed on the department wall, the University of Wisconsin–Madison's police chief banned officers from public displays of the flag while on duty. The police chief explained the decision by saying that the symbol holds "a very different meaning" for the public than it does for police (Griffith 2021), a nod to the fact that it is imbued with significant meaning for both its owner and its observers.

The contemporary diffusion of the flag across police departments indicates that it captures meaning for officers beyond the policing symbols that already exist. If the police badge represents an officer's duties and responsibilities, then the decision to wear a Blue Lives Matter flag in addition to it communicates a set of commitments that transcend the formal duties encapsulated by the badge. Furthermore, the Blue Lives Matter flag is distinct from material symbols like challenge coins, which feature an insignia, a logo, and a motto that help build a sense of shared identity around the mutual challenges officers face.

Displaying the Blue Lives Matter flag proclaims allegiance to the community that police rely on to motivate their public service. After San Francisco's police chief ordered officers to stop wearing face masks featuring the Blue Lives Matter design while on duty, the San Francisco Police Officers Association began selling them online to people across the country. In an editorial, the police union president and twenty-six-year veteran Sergeant Tony Montoya characterized the masks as a "morale booster" intended to show support to officers, akin to officers wearing pink for breast cancer awareness and rainbow patches during Pride Week. Even so, Montoya referenced a broader set of principles that the flag represents—and which its detractors reject when problematizing its display: "The anti-police fringes and criminal apologists, the extremes of our political community . . . continuously attempt to drive a wedge between police officers and the community we serve. In doing so, however, they only make our communities less safe, erode the communal value of personal responsibility, and perpetuate hate" (Montoya 2020). Such insistence on this issue reflects its stakes. The flag not only represents the fundamental values of community safety, personal responsibility, and public unity but, in the "thin blue line" iteration, expresses one's alignment with those values and commitment to police in the pursuit of them.

Today, other state institutions must contend with the political symbolism behind the Blue Lives Matter flag, which not coincidentally rose to prominence quickly after the first wave of record-setting Black Lives Matter protests in 2020. In Maryland district courts, court employees from bailiffs and sheriffs to clerks and judges are prohibited from displaying the flag, because it "may be perceived as showing bias or favoritism to a particular group of people and could undermine the District Court's mission" (Williams 2021). Across school districts, heated debates have consumed and divided communities over whether the flag represents an impermissible political statement—as would expressing support for Black Lives Matter—or simply a memorial to officers who have sacrificed their lives in the line of duty (Gold 2020).

The power of the Blue Lives Matter flag as symbolic ideology is advanced through an information infrastructure with the same name. On Twitter, Blue Lives Matter is (and was, before recent changes to the platform) a verified account with over seventy-nine thousand followers. The account is run by a "news publication" that changed its name from Blues Lives Matter to the *Police Tribune* in June 2020. Christopher Berg, listed as editor in chief, describes how Blue Lives Matter started after the 2014 assassination of NYPD officers Rafael Ramos and Wenjian Liu in "retaliation for perceived police injustices against [B]lack people" (Berg 2020). Blue Lives Matter thus began on social media to communicate to officers that their "lives matter too, and they have a right to self-defense" (Berg 2020). Police officers began publishing anonymized opinion pieces sharing "their side" of stories. This was important, because "one of the biggest frustrations of law enforcement officers [is] that the public did not understand why police officers may be required to use force" (Berg 2020). In 2017, the Blue Lives Matter account reestablished itself as a "police news publication" by hiring professional journalists, adopting editorial guidelines, and no longer publishing opinion-based pieces. Regardless of the name change, however, the *Police Tribune* promises to continue "produc[ing] the same content that informs people about facts and context which are under-reported in the mainstream media" (Berg 2020).

The rise of news outlets like the *Police Tribune* simultaneously reflects and enables the emergence of police as a national political movement. The *Police Tribune* does not merely engage in information distribution—the information distributed is motivated by the "cause" of Blue Lives Matter rooted in a particular worldview. This worldview includes prioritizing officers' right to self-defense, correcting the "lies" about police diffused by media and politicians, and helping the public understand why police may be required to use force—not whether force was necessary in the first place. The *Police Tribune* collects local news stories from police departments like the NYPD, whose accounts help socialize audiences and legitimate violence (Cheng 2021). Aggregating these stories amplifies the processes of the Policing Machine to a national audience by presenting a curated set of community voices—those showing demand for more police services, not more police reform and oversight.

DE-MONOPOLIZING THE POLICING MACHINE

Underlying the Policing Machine is the monopoly that police exercise on public safety resources, information, and authority. Demonopolizing these areas and empowering alternative entities can provide a more secure and just approach to help communities thrive. There are a number of strategies that city officials and local policy makers can prioritize in this effort, and I explore them below; but I caution that these policy-arena changes must be pursued in addition to investments in the resident-driven resistance strategies like those discussed in chapter 5. Further, given the range of community preferences regarding police, I realize that these initial strategies will inevitably fall short in satisfying all stakeholders. They are starting points offered for consideration as cities reckon with the ongoing crisis of American policing.

Regulatory Power

Police departments should not be the agency in charge of granting permits for public events. There is a fundamental conflict of interest in voicing public critiques against police when it requires permission from police to do so. Police's authority over other administrative decisions, like street closures and traffic patterns, further deepens their conflicts of interest. Distributing police power and privileges across community organizations and their public events shapes the organizational landscape of police support in ways that sustain the illusion of public input.

Police power over event permits is just one area addressed by a broader set of questions about first principles: What regulatory powers actually belong within policing's domain? What are police *for* (Meares and Tyler 2020), and are there alternative institutions that can fulfill the same functions? Cities that have begun to interrogate the role of police in different domains have realized that armed representatives of the state are unnecessary to enforce administrative regulations. Cities like Berkeley, California, and Lansing, Michigan, have begun to remove armed officers from low-level traffic enforcement (Vaughn 2021). Eliminating or reducing the occasions for routine police contact by definition decreases the opportunities for escalated violence and fatal policing. It also shrinks police's regulatory reach into domains of neighborhood life that are simply better suited for alternative entities to oversee.

Social Media

Police departments as an organization should not have an active public presence on social media. Proponents of police departments maintaining a public presence on social media usually advance three justifications. First, proponents point to the potential for enhancing police-community relations. The idea is that police can build legitimacy and trust through online outreach to new audiences and through replying to their comments, sharing updates of police news, and engaging through other forms of digital content. But the Policing Machine captures exactly why the community building that occurs on police social media is problematic. Social media channels like Twitter enable police departments to self-publish curated information to self-selecting online audiences. It facilitates the Policing Machine by providing police with the technological capacity to publicize endorsements, which are either unrepresentative because they are from cultivated constituents or misrepresentative because support is implied rather than verified (see chapter 4). Any audiences reached and community built, especially through the use of digital omissions, are fundamentally unlikely to advance efforts toward police accountability.

Second, like many defenses of historically questionable criminal justice policies, proponents raise the wide distribution of information during emergencies and "god forbid" scenarios. The President's Task Force on 21st Century Policing (2015, 37) cited the effectiveness of the Boston Police Department in publicizing updated information through social media during its Boston Marathon bombing response. However, emergency information can be more widely and reliably distributed through centralized crisis systems, such as Amber Alerts or those maintained by the mayor's office and emergency management services. Residents should not have to "follow" police department social media accounts to receive such information. Residents from a Sector 80A meeting I attended explained why. A parent mentioned a recent shooting near a daycare center that occurred at about the same time he was picking up his own child. The parent knew nothing of the shooting until a week later, prompting him to ask, "Is there a way for us to learn about this a little more practically?" The man's neighbors had been using Citizen, a mobile app that sends safety alerts to users based on their location in real time, but the parent wanted an option that provided "official" information. The NCO replied, "Follow the precinct on Twitter." But the parent did not regularly use Twitter and asked for other options. The NCO replied with an option that did not actually provide alerts-based notification: "You can reach out to us. I'll tell you straight up."

During crises, social media should not be the primary mode of information distribution. Instead, cities should prioritize more centralized methods of information distribution. Nonetheless, even if an exception were to be made for police departments to distribute emergency information through their social media channels, that is far from the active daily presence they maintain today to advance the Policing Machine.

Third, proponents of the police using social media point to the supposed crime-fighting advantages of doing so. Police can use their social media pages to distribute information on wanted suspects and new developments on major crimes. Yet even such crime-fighting content is curated in ways that reinforce racial stereotypes and punitive preferences. Researchers analyzing all Facebook posts from fourteen thousand law enforcement agencies in the United States found that followers are overexposed to posts of Black suspects by 25 percent relative to local arrest rates (Grunwald, Nyarko, and Rappaport 2022; see also Cheng 2022b). It is unclear why police departments need to distribute such information themselves when media outlets, subject to professional journalistic norms and accountability, have traditionally done so. As the fourth pillar of democracy, mass media have always played a vital role in overseeing how information is framed and what information is published. These traditional outlets have their own set of problems, such as privileging police narratives (Moreno-Medina et al. 2022), but are still preferable to social media that amounts to state media. Instead, a diversity of media sources, including outlets like the *Police Tribune*, is necessary to hold state institutions accountable by demanding that additional information be released, challenging and confirming the information that is released, and alerting the public when institutions fall short.

An important dimension of strengthening media oversight of police departments is that police cannot be the regulatory agency issuing press credentials. As in many cities, the NYPD has historically decided which members of the media are permitted to take crime scene photos or continue reporting outdoors past curfew (Robbins 2021). The latter has been particularly important in recent years in light of protest-related urban curfews. Transferring the power of issuing and revoking press credentials to another agency, such as the mayor's office, and establishing a process by which reporters could contest revocations would strengthen the media as an oversight mechanism to police and other public officials.

Community Sentiments

Cities must invest in infrastructure to collect and publicize data on community sentiments toward police, much as they do for crime rates. Several police departments in the United States have begun collecting data on public perceptions toward police, promising to hold supervisors accountable for the shifts within their neighborhoods—a CompStat, but for community sentiments instead of crime rates. Major cities have contracted a company named Zencity (formerly Elucd) to help collect community sentiment data using representative surveys administered via pop-up advertisements on cell phones. Zencity collects data on residents' perceptions of safety and trust in their neighborhood, as well as their answers to an open-response question about their top concerns. The multiyear and multimillion-dollar contracts that major cities have agreed to with Zencity indicate the feasibility of this enterprise of collecting representative surveys each month.

However, the commitment to community surveys must contend with the Policing Machine. While measures of community sentiments can help shift police culture in ways that prioritize the range of community opinions more than it currently does, police discretion will foreseeably shift to limit the promise of these initiatives (Kohler-Hausmann 2017). In New York City, the NYPD signed a multimillion-dollar contract with Zencity, but in the end, it never publicly released any of the data collected for over three years. It ended the contract in 2020. In other words, in response to an initiative to increase public accountability of police to reflect evolving community sentiments, police discretion shifted upstream to withhold the data wholesale. In contrast, the Chicago Police Department releases select data through a public "sentiment dashboard." Nonetheless, it is important to remember that police do not "own" these data. Making all the data publicly available is critical to equipping the public—local residents, elected officials, oversight agencies, and academic researchers—with the information needed to hold police accountable.

Investing in representative community surveys of resident perceptions toward police and public safety will provide a better gauge of community priorities. An important insight from this book is that public input arises in specific channels. For example, identifying community preferences based on complaints from Build the Blocks meetings or primarily from RALLY events would mask the sorting and decision-making that unfold before a complaint is voiced inside a church to an NCO or on the street with other protesters. Divergent preferences regarding police emerged in and from different channels, and this context was often omitted when reporting and claims-making about community priorities. A representative community survey administered monthly, unaffiliated with the police department and providing the option to remain anonymous, can provide more accurate insights into the dynamic priorities of community members.

Public Resources

Cities must distribute resources more equitably so that the organizational capacity of police is not so disproportionate to that of other community entities. This priority aligns with the idea behind calls to "defund the police"—the movement to invest in community alternatives, even at the expense of police budgets. Since the discretion of street-level bureaucrats like police can only be shifted rather than eliminated (Lipsky 1980), efforts to control how police use their resources will be less effective than organizational-level redistribution of those resources. A more equitable resource distribution may specifically release existing entities from their dependence on police resources. For example, funding community councils would provide them with greater independence, financial and otherwise, from police precincts—perhaps allowing the Fifty-Fifth Precinct Community Council to operate with the greater autonomy of the Eightieth Precinct's (as seen in chapter 5). Increased independence may also attract new participants and help transform community councils into a more representative space for community input.

Allocating city budgets more equitably across neighborhood institutions may also disincentivize strategies by social service providers to partner with police to gain funding. Community and clergy councils were not the only neighborhood nonprofits encountered in this study. Safe Horizon is "New York's largest and most comprehensive victim service provider" for cases ranging from domestic violence to child abuse (NYPD 2016a). In October 2016, it announced an initiative placing 157 crime victim advocates *inside* police precincts across New York City. The partnership reinforces the role of police in such cases: "The underlying rationale for the program is that the sooner the NYPD provides a response that addresses many of crime victims' needs and concerns, the more likely victims will feel safe, recover from the trauma of the crime, regain a sense of control of their lives, and participate in the criminal justice process" (NYPD 2016a). The Safe Horizon representative is often present at Build the Block and community council meetings, distributing the organization's contact information.

Corey, a campaign director for a RALLY-affiliated organization (see chapters 1 and 2), explained why the placement of these advocates within precincts is problematic: "It's really twisted—like the only way you can get services as a victim of domestic violence is at the police precinct. Maybe you don't actually want to go there" (Corey, interview, August 2, 2018). It is no stretch to imagine victims of police violence, specifically, as unlikely to feel that they are regaining a sense of control by going to the police for victim advocacy. Yet, as Commissioner James O'Neill explained in the press release announcing the partnership, "Victims are our partners during these investigations" (NYPD 2016a). In other words, the partnership will foreseeably reinforce the role of police by making victim services difficult to access without encountering an officer. Policy makers should use funding as a lever to encourage Safe Horizon and other service providers to move toward enabling victims to access police services as an option—

rather than an expectation, or even an obstacle, to obtaining social services. Adequately funding alternatives service providers beyond the police will provide residents with more options to obtain high-capacity, well-equipped, and appropriate services (Bell, Beckett, and Stuart 2021).

Equalizing funding across community groups also represents an important symbolic investment in independent channels. By providing resources to grassroots initiatives that facilitate community voice outside department channels, policy makers recognize the perspectives and stakes of those left with no resort but to organize independent channels. Efforts like copwatching, political protest, and other initiatives must be understood as legitimate articulations of public voice, with any adversarialism they evince reflective of the vigorous pursuit of justice. Just in 2018, Mayor Bill de Blasio's press secretary responded to criticisms of the mayor's hands-off approach to the NYPD by characterizing those critiques as coming from "fringe" activists (Pazmino 2018). However, as legal scholar Jocelyn Simonson reasons, "if we truly want to make our criminal justice system democratically accountable, we must accept feedback not just through formal state-structured mechanisms but also through means of feedback and accountability that are designed by the people" (Simonson 2016, 397). Rather than discounting these activist campaigns, policy makers should view them as legitimate, valued, and valuable forms of public participation and community input.

These efforts will help strengthen the top-down lines of public accountability over police departments that the Policing Machine seeks to weaken. Policy efforts curbing police influence over existing channels for public input will help clarify community preferences in terms of police and when and how they should be deployed, if at all, in ways that advance safety and justice. Recognizing and investing in all the different channels for public input on the police will help ensure that decisions about public resource distribution, regulatory leniency, and coercive force may be *informed* by police but not *made* by them.

—

The primary goal of this book has been to name and deconstruct the Policing Machine. By understanding how it operates and endures, communities can better determine how to begin to resist and de-monopolize police power in their own local contexts. Doing so begins by understanding gaps between the promise and the practice of community initiatives—not as shortcomings in execution but rather as revealed preferences. Strong police-community relations are not something that police departments like the NYPD lack. Nor are they some emergent property achieved as a by-product of increasing the frequency of police interactions with the public. Instead, this book showed how the Policing Machine *runs* on police-community relations—the strength of which accelerates the production of political capital and sustains resistance to institutional reforms.

Whether you are a policy maker, a community stakeholder, or even a police supervisor, this study emphasizes the importance of approaching legitimacy-enhancing initiatives in ways that account for police's independence-maximizing incentives. As future research further unpacks police roles and strategies in the public sphere, we will continue gaining a greater sense of the expansive yet subtle politics and inequalities of policing institutions, and that awareness will continue to motivate needed public scrutiny. Reimagining police is not a stage of reform but a reform-oriented process best secured when public input is voiced without the influence of the very institution targeted for transformation. Achieving this goal will require concerted efforts to convert mechanisms of structural inequality into ones of structural inclusion and community vitality.

ACKNOWLEDGMENTS

I am deeply grateful to all those who allowed me to share time and space with them during data collection for this book. Oftentimes with both open arms and an inquisitive eye, those I interviewed were patient in explaining the complicated history and local dynamics of policing in their communities to someone who took the train there on evenings and weekends. Apart from the times my life converged with theirs, these residents also worked as educators, counselors, social workers, healthcare professionals, and other occupations that formed the backbone of their neighborhoods. Their willingness to sit down for interviews and invite me into their homes and other parts of their lives reflects their commitment to their communities and the changes they wanted to see there. No matter their vision of policing, their engagement and accessibility made this book possible.

While the introduction details the methodological challenges of gaining access to the NYPD, several individual officers I encountered were eager to participate in this study. Our informal and off-the-record conversations were valuable in providing a sense of relevant stakeholders to interview, upcoming events to observe, and public records to request. Not all the community members and police officers I encountered will agree with this study's conclusions, but I hope that my concept of the Policing Machine provides a framework to articulate and undertake the institutional changes expressed by residents and officers alike.

This book is also the product of a community of supporters in both my professional and my personal lives. My graduate school experiences were defined by interactions with Andrew Papachristos, Tracey Meares, and Michael Sierra-Arévalo. They provided opportunities and mentorship in formative ways that they will never realize. They made me feel valued as a team member, and I will forever appreciate the examples they set for me. Professor Papachristos always manages to find the time to provide advice, and he remains the first person with whom I share all my academic news. Issa Kohler-Hausmann fundamentally shaped my ideas and interests in the sociology of law and organizations. No matter how confident I am before each meeting with Issa, I leave them bumbling—a testament to how she transforms my thinking each time we talk. It was Issa who suggested that I think and write about the politics of policing more explicitly, and Issa deserves full credit for the introductory vignette in the concluding chapter. Additional cornerstones of my graduate school experience include Frederick Wherry and Christopher Wildeman in my earlier years; Julia Adams, Rene Almeling, Jonathan Wyrtzen, Rourke O'Brien, and Emma Zang in my later years; and Philip Smith throughout. I learned a lot about ethnography as a craft from Elijah Anderson's Urban Ethnography Project. This study also benefited from conversations with Monica Bell and feedback from Sarah Brothers and Philip McHarris. I am grateful to Jacob Hacker and the Yale Institution for Social and Policy Studies, which provided funding for parts of my project.

My legal education for one year at Berkeley Law and then at NYU Law would not have been possible without Calvin Morrill, Jonathan Simon, Barry Friedman, and Maria Ponomarenko. Calvin and Jonathan are two of my academic idols who have supported my research in ways I do not know how to "repay" except by passing that encouragement forward to future law and society scholars. Jocelyn Simonson, whose scholarship has long shaped my thinking in important ways, provided comments on multiple versions of this project.

I have also been fortunate to find community from chance encounters that have turned into some of the most fulfilling relationships I have in academia. Since the summer of 2021, I have met almost weekly with Theresa Rocha Beardall and Collin Mueller as a writing group—one that has evolved into so much more than that. They have been constant sources of learning and inspiration, especially on how to navigate academia and live a fulfilling life outside it. I cherish my friendship with Johann Koehler, whose company is a joy and whose brilliance makes collaboration easy. I leave weekly meetings with Johann a better scholar and person. For additional feedback and support, my thanks go to Robert Vargas, Michelle Phelps, Justin Nix, Bocar Ba, and Noli Brazil.

I am indebted to colleagues in UCI's Department of Criminology, Law and Society. All were so welcoming and provided the support necessary to begin the tenure track during the pandemic. I appreciate the coffees, meals, and advice from Mona Lynch, Charis Kubrin, Nancy Rodriguez, Elizabeth Loftus, Keramet Reiter, Susan Coutin, Naomi Sugie, Sora Han, Brandon Golob, and Christopher Seeds. I owe particular gratitude to Emily Owens, my faculty mentor who affirmed my place as a faculty member at the university; Amanda Geller, the first colleague whom I met in person and got to know on a family level; and Valerie Jenness, who went above and beyond to promote my research as a senior faculty member. The transition was made easier by staff in the department—especially Mary Underwood and Lori Metherate—and fellow junior faculty who started around the same time: Nicole Iturriaga, Carolina Valdivia, and Miguel Quintana-Navarrete.

This book benefited from presentations and feedback at the following institutions and conferences: UC Berkeley, University of Nebraska–Omaha, UC Irvine, Northwestern University, Duke University, University of Chicago, Lund University, Yale University, University of Wisconsin–Milwaukee, University of Alberta, the American Sociological Association, the American Society of Criminology, the Law and Society Association, and the Society for the Study of Social Problems.

In the tradition of classic urban ethnographies, I have always wanted to publish at the University of Chicago Press. Elizabeth Branch Dyson made my publication experience smoother than I could have ever imagined. I appreciate the assistance from everyone at the press, especially Mollie McFee, Sandra Hazel, and Carrie Olivia Adams. Letta Page provided excellent copyediting and added life to the prose. I also thank the anonymous reviewers of the manuscript as well as those who edited and reviewed a related paper in the *American Journal of Sociology*.

Finally, I thank my family most of all, especially Shelley Liu.

NOTES

INTRODUCTION

1. NYPD n.d., "Neighborhood Policing," https://www1.nyc.gov/site/nypd/bureaus/patrol/neighborhood-coordination-officers.page (date accessed: February 25, 2023).

2. Introduced by the NYPD in 1994, CompStat is a system for police departments to keep track of crime rates and hold officers accountable for their assigned areas (see Weisburd et al. 2003).

3. NYPD n.d., "Precinct Community Council Handbook," https://www.ojp.gov/pdffiles1/Digitization/145633NCJRS.pdf (date accessed: February 26, 2023).

4. NYPD n.d., "Clergy Liaisons," https://www1.nyc.gov/site/nypd/bureaus/administrative/clergy-liaisons.page (date accessed: February 26, 2023).

5. To minimize repetition, I provide the relevant citation to field notes, interviews, or meetings only at the first instance within a paragraph.

CHAPTER ONE

1. While NCOs may have also omitted complaints from other substantive categories, those demanding police reform are the most relevant, because Neighborhood Policing was introduced with the promise of increasing police accountability. Neighborhood Policing is specifically a police reform program—not, for instance, a traffic reform program.

2. Meeting precincts and sectors are referred to in shorthand by the precinct number followed by the sector letter. All precincts and names are anonymized, and specific meeting dates are excluded to preserve precinct anonymity.

3. Copwatching is the systematic observing, monitoring, and recording of police activity to guard against police misconduct.

CHAPTER TWO

1. NYPD n.d., *Precinct Community Council Handbook*, https://www.ojp.gov/pdffiles1/Digitization/145633NCJRS.pdf (date accessed: February 26, 2023).

2. NYPD n.d., *Precinct Community Council Handbook*, https://www.ojp.gov/pdf files1/Digitization/145633NCJRS.pdf (date accessed: February 26, 2023).

3. NYPD n.d., *Community Council Guidelines*, http://prtl-drprd-web.nyc.gov/ html/nypd///downloads/pdf/community_affairs/communitycouncilguidelines2016 .pdf (date accessed: February 26, 2023).

4. NYPD n.d., *Patrol Guide: Community Affairs Officer*, https://www1.nyc.gov/ assets/nypd/downloads/pdf/public_information/public-pguide1.pdf (date accessed: February 26, 2023).

5. Whereas members of the Eightieth Precinct Community Council referred to their president as Mr. Holloway, members of the Fifty-Fifth called Lela simply by her first name. I follow this naming convention in presenting the evidence.

6. NYPD n.d., *Precinct Community Council Handbook*, https://www.ojp.gov/pdf files1/Digitization/145633NCJRS.pdf (date accessed: February 26, 2023).

CHAPTER THREE

1. NYPD n.d., *Community Council Guidelines*, http://prtl-drprd-web.nyc.gov/ html/nypd///downloads/pdf/community_affairs/communitycouncilguidelines2016 .pdf (date accessed: February 28, 2023).

2. NYPD n.d., "Clergy Liaisons," https://www1.nyc.gov/site/nypd/bureaus/ administrative/clergy-liaisons.page (date accessed: February 28, 2023).

3. NYPD n.d., "Clergy Liaisons."

CHAPTER FOUR

1. NYCLU n.d., "Stop-and-Frisk Data," https://www.nyclu.org/en/stop-and-frisk -data (date accessed: January 1, 2023).

2. NYPD n.d., "Neighborhood Policing," https://www1.nyc.gov/site/nypd/bureaus/ patrol/neighborhood-coordination-officers.page (date accessed: March 9, 2023).

3. In this case, Pastor Campbell attested that police invite him and other clergy to initiatives that have nothing to do with religious institutions because of the explicit endorsements they can provide to their audiences back in their home churches: "Since we have people that we minister to every day, we can better let them know this is a place they can go for the cops" (Campbell, interview, September 17, 2018).

4. Chief Rodney Harrison (@NYPDChiefPatrol), Twitter, November 14, 2018, 12:10 p.m., https://twitter.com/NYPDChiefPatrol/status/1062754779015847937.

5. In an interview with the *New York Times*, an NYPD veteran sergeant explained, "It used to be 'How many summons did you write?' . . . Now it's, 'How many community visits did you have? How many uploads to Twitter or Facebook do you have? Did you go into the dry cleaner's and shake his hand and put it on Twitter?'" (Wilson and Goldstein 2019).

CHAPTER FIVE

1. Boro Park Shomrim n.d., "Boro Park Shomrim," https://bpshomrim.org/ (date accessed: March 9, 2023).

REFERENCES

Armenta, Amada. 2017. *Protect, Serve and Deport: The Rise of Policing as Immigration Enforcement.* Oakland: University of California Press.

Auxier, Richard. 2020. "What Police Spending Data Can (and Cannot) Explain amid Calls to Defund the Police." *Urban Institute.* https://www.urban.org/urban-wire/what-police-spending-data-can-and-cannot-explain-amid-calls-defund-police.

Auyero, Javier. 2000. "The Logic of Clientelism in Argentina: An Ethnographic Account." *Latin American Research Review* 35 (3): 55–81.

Bail, Christopher. 2016. "Cultural Carrying Capacity: Organ Donation Advocacy, Discursive Framing, and Social Media Engagement." *Social Science and Medicine* 165:280–88.

Balto, Simon. 2019. *Occupied Territory: Policing Black Chicago from Red Summer to Black Power.* Chapel Hill: University of North Carolina Press.

Banfield, Edward, and James Wilson. 1963. *City Politics.* Cambridge MA: Harvard University Press.

Barman, Emily, and Heather MacIndoe. 2012. "Institutional Pressures and Organizational Capacity: The Case of Outcome Measurement." *Sociological Forum* 27 (1): 70–93.

Beck, Brenden, Joseph Antonelli, and Gabriela Piñeros. 2022. "Effects of New York City's Neighborhood Policing Policy." *Police Quarterly* 25 (4): 470–96.

Beckett, Katherine, and Steve Herbert. 2009. *Banished: The New Social Control in Urban America.* New York: Oxford University Press.

Bell, Monica. 2017. "Police Reform and the Dismantling of Legal Estrangement." *Yale Law Journal* 126:2054–2150.

———. 2019. "The Community in Criminal Justice: Subordination, Consumption, Resistance, and Transformation." *Du Bois Review: Social Science Research on Race* 16 (1): 197–220.

Bell, Monica C., Katherine Beckett, and Forrest Stuart. 2021. "Investing in Alternatives: Three Logics of Criminal System Replacement." *UC Irvine Law Review* 11 (5): 1291–1326.

Berg, Christopher. 2020. "Introducing The Police Tribune." Police Tribune, June 11, 2020. https://policetribune.com/introducing-the-police-tribune/.

Berrien, Jenny, and Christopher Winship. 2003. "Should We Have Faith in the Churches? Ten-Point Coalition's Effect on Boston's Youth Violence." In *Guns, Crime, and Punishment in America*, edited by B. Harcourt, 222–48. New York: New York University Press.

Bittner, Egon. 1990. *Aspects of Police Work*. Boston: Northeastern University Press.

Blau, Peter. 1963. *The Dynamics of Bureaucracy: Study of Interpersonal Relations in Two Government Agencies*. Rev. ed. Chicago: University of Chicago Press.

Bloom, Joshua, and Waldo Martin Jr. 2013. *Black against Empire: The History and Politics of the Black Panther Party*. Berkeley: University of California Press.

Bourdieu, Pierre. 1986. "The Forms of Capital." In *Handbook of Theory of Research for the Sociology of Education*, edited by J. G. Richardson, 241–58. New York: Greenwood Press.

Braga, Anthony, David Hureau, and Christopher Winship. 2008. "Losing Faith? Police, Black Churches, and the Resurgence of Youth Violence in Boston." *Ohio State Journal of Criminal Law* 6:141–72.

Bratton, William. 2016. "William J. Bratton: How to Reform Policing from Within." *New York Times*, September 16, 2016.

Broadwater, Luke, and Catie Edmondson. 2020. "Police Groups Wield Strong Influence in Congress, Resisting the Strictest Reforms." *New York Times*, June 25, 2020.

Brown, M. Craig, and Charles Halaby. 1987. "Machine Politics in America, 1870–1945." *Journal of Interdisciplinary History* 17 (3): 587–612.

Brunson, Rod, Anthony Braga, David Hureau, and Kashea Pegram. 2015. "We Trust You, but Not That Much: Examining Police–Black Clergy Partnerships to Reduce Youth Violence." *Justice Quarterly* 32 (6): 1006–36.

Burstein, Paul. 1991. "Legal Mobilization as a Social Movement Tactic: The Struggle for Equal Employment Opportunity." *American Journal of Sociology* 96 (5): 1201–25.

Campbell, Andrea Louise. 2003. *How Policies Make Citizens Senior Political Activism and the American Welfare State*. Princeton, NJ: Princeton University Press.

———. 2012. "Policy Makes Mass Politics." *Annual Review of Political Science* 15 (1): 333–51.

Campeau, Holly. 2015. "'Police Culture' at Work: Making Sense of Police Oversight." *British Journal of Criminology* 55 (4): 669–87.

Carr, Patrick. 2005. *Clean Streets: Controlling Crime, Maintaining Order, and Building Community Activism*. New York: New York University Press.

Center for Popular Democracy, Law for Black Lives, and Black Youth Project 100. 2017. *Freedom to Thrive: Reimagining Safety and Security in Our Communities*. Brooklyn, NY, and Washington, DC: Center for Popular Democracy.

Chaskin, Robert. 2003. "Fostering Neighborhood Democracy: Legitimacy and Accountability within Loosely Coupled Systems." *Nonprofit and Voluntary Sector Quarterly* 32 (2): 161–89.

Cheng, Tony. 2020. "Input without Influence: The Silence and Scripts of Police and Community Relations." *Social Problems* 67 (1): 171–89.

———. 2021. "Social Media, Socialization, and Pursuing Legitimation of Police Violence." *Criminology* 59 (3): 391–418.

———. 2022a. "The Cumulative Discretion of Police over Community Complaints." *American Journal of Sociology* 127 (6): 1782–1817.

———. 2022b. "Racialized Policing in the Social Media Age." *Proceedings of the National Academy of Sciences* 119 (49):e2216978119.

Cheng, Tony, and Jennifer Qu. 2022. "Regulatory Intermediaries and the Challenge of Democratic Policing." *Criminology and Public Policy* 21 (1): 59–81.

City Hall Press Office. 2014. "Transcript: Mayor de Blasio Hosts Roundtable on Police-Community Relations." July 31, 2014. https://www1.nyc.gov/office-of-the-mayor/news/379-14/transcript-mayor-de-blasio-hosts-roundtable-police-community-relations#/0.

Council of the City of New York. 2017. *Report to the Committee on Finance and the Committee on Public Safety on the Fiscal 2018 Executive Budget for New York Police Department.* New York: Council of the City of New York.

Crank, John. 1994. "Watchman and Community: Myth and Institutionalization in Policing State Theory, Myths of Policing, and Responses to Crime." *Law and Society Review* 28 (2): 325–52.

Crank, John, and Robert Langworthy. 1992. "Institutional Perspective on Policing." *Journal of Criminal Law and Criminology* 83 (2): 338–63.

Cress, Daniel, and David Snow. 1996. "Mobilization at the Margins: Resources, Benefactors, and the Viability of Homeless Social Movement Organizations." *American Sociological Review* 61 (6): 1089–1109.

de Blasio, William. 2018. "Mayor de Blasio Makes Announcement at 71st Precinct." Brooklyn, NY. YouTube video, 34:03, published August 23, 2018. https://www.youtube.com/watch?v=egYZ_q_7dtE&t=13s.

Devereaux, Ryan. 2012. "Stop-and-Frisk Protesters in New York March on Mayor's House." *Guardian*, US ed., June 18, 2012.

DiMaggio, Paul, and Walter Powell. 1983. "The Iron Cage Revisited: Institutional Isomorphism and Collective Rationality in Organizational Fields." *American Sociological Review* 48 (2): 147–60.

Dobbin, Frank. 2009. *Inventing Equal Opportunity.* Princeton, NJ: Princeton University Press.

Doering, Jan. 2020. *Us versus Them: Race, Crime, and Gentrification in Chicago Neighborhoods.* New York: Oxford University Press.

Du Bois, W. E. B. 1903. *The Negro Church.* Atlanta: Atlanta University Press.

Edelman, Lauren. 1990. "Legal Environments and Organizational Governance: The Expansion of Due Process in the American Workplace." *American Journal of Sociology* 95(6):1401–40.

———. 1992. "Legal Ambiguity and Symbolic Structures: Organizational Mediation of Civil Rights Law." *American Journal of Sociology* 97(6):1531–76.

Eisinger, Peter. 2002. "Organizational Capacity and Organizational Effectiveness among Street-Level Food Assistance Programs." *Nonprofit and Voluntary Sector Quarterly* 31(1):115–30.

Ellis, Rachel. 2021. "What Do We Mean By a 'Hard-to-Reach' Population? Legitimacy Versus Precarity as Barriers to Access." *Sociological Methods and Research.*

Ewick, Patricia, and Susan Silbey. 1998. *The Common Place of Law: Stories from Everyday Life.* Chicago: University of Chicago Press.

Fassin, Didier. 2013. *Enforcing Order: An Ethnography of Urban Policing*. Cambridge: Polity Press.

Felker-Kantor, Max. 2018. *Policing Los Angeles: Race, Resistance, and the Rise of the LAPD*. Chapel Hill: University of North Carolina Press.

Feuer, Alan. 2016. "Brooklyn's Private Jewish Patrols Wield Power. Some Call Them Bullies." *New York Times*, June 17, 2016.

Fitzgerald, Scott, and Ryan Spohn. 2005. "Pulpits and Platforms: The Role of the Church in Determining Protest among Black Americans." *Social Forces* 84 (2): 1015–48.

Flamm, Matthew. 2019. "NYPD Boss on the Keys to Neighborhood Policing." *Crain's New York Business*, July 9, 2019.

Forman Jr., James. 2004. "Community Policing and Youth as Assets." *Journal of Criminal Law and Criminology* 95:1–48.

Gascón, Luis Daniel, and Aaron Roussell. 2019. *The Limits of Community Policing: Civilian Power and Police Accountability in Black and Brown Los Angeles*. New York: New York University Press.

Gill, Charlotte, David Weisburd, Cody Telep, Zoe Vitter, and Trevor Bennett. 2014. "Community-Oriented Policing to Reduce Crime, Disorder and Fear and Increase Satisfaction and Legitimacy among Citizens: A Systematic Review." *Journal of Experimental Criminology* 10 (4): 399–428.

Go, Julian. 2020. "The Imperial Origins of American Policing: Militarization and Imperial Feedback in the Early 20th Century." *American Journal of Sociology* 125 (5): 1193–1254.

Gold, Michael. 2020. "What Happened When a School District Banned Thin Blue Line Flags." *New York Times*, November 21, 2020.

Goldstein, Herman. 1979. "Improving Policing: A Problem-Oriented Approach." *Crime and Delinquency* 25 (2): 236–58.

Goldstein, Rebecca. 2021. "Senior Citizens as a Pro-police Interest Group." *Journal of Political Institutions and Political Economy* 2 (2): 303–28.

González, Yanilda, and Lindsay Mayka. 2023. "Policing, Democratic Participation, and the Reproduction of Asymmetric Citizenship." *American Political Science Review* 117 (1): 263–79.

Gordon, Daanika. 2022. *Policing the Racial Divide: Urban Growth Politics and the Remaking of Segregation*. New York: New York University Press.

Gordon, Jon. 2020. "The Legitimation of Extrajudicial Violence in an Urban Community." *Social Forces* 98 (3): 1174–95.

Grattet, Ryken, and Valerie Jenness. 2005. "The Reconstitution of Law in Local Settings: Agency Discretion, Ambiguity, and a Surplus of Law in the Policing of Hate Crime." *Law and Society Review* 39 (4): 893–942.

Griffith, Janelle. 2021. "Police Chief Bans 'Thin Blue Line' Imagery, Says It's Been 'Co-opted' by Extremists." NBC News, January 29, 2021.

Grosjean, Pauline, Federico Masera, and Hasin Yousaf. 2022. "Inflammatory Political Campaigns and Racial Bias in Policing." *Quarterly Journal of Economics* 138 (1): 413–63.

Grunwald, Ben, Julian Nyarko, and John Rappaport. 2022. "Police Agencies on Facebook Overreport on Black Suspects." *Proceedings of the National Academy of Sciences* 119 (45): e2203089119.

Guest, Avery, and R. S. Oropesa. 1986. "Informal Social Ties and Political Activity in the Metropolis." *Urban Affairs Quarterly* 21 (4): 550–74.

Halpern, Stephen C. 1974. "Police Employee Organizations and Accountability Procedures in Three Cities: Some Reflections on Police Policy-Making." *Law and Society Review* 8 (4): 561–82.

Harcourt, Bernard. 2001. *Illusion of Order: The False Promise of Broken Windows Policing.* Cambridge, MA: Harvard University Press.

Herbert, Steve. 2006. *Citizens, Cops, and Power: Recognizing the Limits of Community.* Chicago: University of Chicago Press.

———. 2008. "The Trapdoor of Community." *Annals of the Association of American Geographers* 95 (4): 850–65.

Herbst, Susan. 2011. "(Un)Numbered Voices? Reconsidering the Meaning of Public Opinion in a Digital Age." In *Political Polling in the Digital Age: The Challenge of Measuring and Understanding Public Opinion,* edited by K. Goidel, 85–98. Baton Rouge: LSU Press.

Herring, Chris. 2019. "Complaint-Oriented Policing: Regulating Homelessness in Public Space." *American Sociological Review* 84 (5): 769–800.

Hicken, Allen. 2011. "Clientelism." *Annual Review of Political Science* 14 (1): 289–310.

Hinton, Elizabeth. 2016. *From the War on Poverty to the War on Crime: The Making of Mass Incarceration in America.* Cambridge, MA: Harvard University Press.

———. 2021. *America on Fire: The Untold History of Police Violence and Black Rebellion Since the 1960s.* New York: Liveright.

Holland, Alisha. 2016. "Forbearance." *American Political Science Review* 110 (2): 232–46.

Holland, Alisha, and Brian Palmer-Rubin. 2015. "Beyond the Machine: Clientelist Brokers and Interest Organizations in Latin America." *Comparative Political Studies* 48 (9): 1186–1223.

Jackson, Sarah J., and Brooke Foucault Welles. 2015. "Hijacking #myNYPD: Social Media Dissent and Networked Counterpublics." *Journal of Communication* 65 (6): 932–52.

Jones, Nikki. 2018. *The Chosen Ones: Black Men and the Politics of Redemption.* Oakland: University of California Press.

Jorgensen, Jillian. 2015. "Bill Bratton: City Council NYPD Reform Bills Are 'Overkill.'" *Observer,* July 6, 2015.

Kanno-Youngs, Zolan. 2018. "Latest Spike Lee Joint: Paid NYPD Consultant." *Wall Street Journal,* August 16, 2018.

Katzenbach Commission. 1967. *The Challenge of Crime in a Free Society.* Washington, DC: President's Commission on Law Enforcement and Administration of Justice.

Kelling, George, and James Wilson. 1982. "Broken Windows: The Police and Neighborhood Safety." *Atlantic,* March 1982. https://www.theatlantic.com/magazine/archive/1982/03/broken-windows/304465/.

Kelly, Kimbriell, Sarah Childress, and Steven Rich. 2015. "Forced Reforms, Mixed Results." *Washington Post,* November 13, 2015.

Kitschelt, Herbert, and Steven Wilkinson, eds. 2007. "Citizen-Politician Linkages: An

Introduction." In *Patrons, Clients and Policies: Patterns of Democratic Accountability and Political Competition*, 1–49. Cambridge: Cambridge University Press.

Kleinfeld, Joshua, Laura Appleman, Richard Bierschbach, Kenworthey Bilz, Josh Bowers, John Braithwaite, Robert Burns, R. A. Duff, Albert Dzur, and Thomas Geraghty. 2016. "White Paper of Democratic Criminal Justice." *Northwestern University Law Review* 111:1693–1706.

Kohler-Hausmann, Issa. 2017. "Jumping Bunnies and Legal Rules: The Organizational Sociologist and the Legal Scholar Should Be Friends." In *The New Criminal Justice Thinking*, edited by S. Dolovich and A. Natapoff, 246–71. New York: New York University Press.

———. 2018. *Misdemeanorland: Criminal Courts and Social Control in an Age of Broken Windows Policing*. Princeton, NJ: Princeton University Press.

Kohler-Hausmann, Julilly. 2015. "Guns and Butter: The Welfare State, the Carceral State, and the Politics of Exclusion in the Postwar United States." *Journal of American History* 102 (1): 87–99.

Lane, Jeffrey. 2018. *The Digital Street*. New York: Oxford University Press.

Legewie, Joscha, and Jeffrey Fagan. 2019. "Aggressive Policing and the Educational Performance of Minority Youth." *American Sociological Review* 84 (2): 220–47.

Leonardi, Paul, and Emmanuelle Vaast. 2017. "Social Media and Their Affordances for Organizing: A Review and Agenda for Research." *Academy of Management Annals* 11 (1): 150–88.

Lessing, Benjamin. 2021. "Conceptualizing Criminal Governance." *Perspectives on Politics* 19 (3): 854–73.

Levine, Jeremy. 2016. "The Privatization of Political Representation: Community-Based Organizations as Nonelected Neighborhood Representatives." *American Sociological Review* 81 (6): 1251–75.

———. 2017. "The Paradox of Community Power: Cultural Processes and Elite Authority in Participatory Governance." *Social Forces* 95 (3): 1155–79.

Lincoln, Eric, and Lawrence Mamiya. 1990. *The Black Church in the African American Experience*. Durham, NC: Duke University Press.

Lipsky, Michael. 1980. *Street-Level Bureaucracy: Dilemmas of the Individual in Public Services*. New York: Russell Sage Foundation.

Little Edwards, Korie, and Michelle Oyakawa. 2022. *Smart Suits, Tattered Boots: Black Ministers Mobilizing the Black Church in the Twenty-First Century*. New York: New York University Press.

Manning, Peter. 2010. *Democratic Policing in a Changing World*. New York: Routledge.

Marwell, Nicole. 2004. "Privatizing the Welfare State: Nonprofit Community-Based Organizations as Political Actors." *American Sociological Review* 69 (2): 265–91.

Mays, Jeff. 2015. "Council's Police Reform Laws Are 'Unprecedented Intrusions,' Bratton Says." *DNAinfo New York*, June 29, 2015.

McGregor, Shannon. 2020. "'Taking the Temperature of the Room': How Political Campaigns Use Social Media to Understand and Represent Public Opinion." *Public Opinion Quarterly* 84 (S1): 236–56.

McRoberts, Omar. 2003. *Streets of Glory: Church and Community in a Black Urban Neighborhood*. Chicago: University of Chicago Press.

Meares, Tracey. 2002. "Praying for Community Policing." *California Law Review* 90:1593–1634.

Meares, Tracey, and Tom Tyler. 2020. "The First Step Is Figuring Out What Police Are For." *Atlantic*, June 8, 2020. https://www.theatlantic.com/ideas/archive/2020/06/first-step-figuring-out-what-police-are/612793/.

Mettler, Suzanne, and Joe Soss. 2004. "The Consequences of Public Policy for Democratic Citizenship: Bridging Policy Studies and Mass Politics." *Perspectives on Politics* 2 (1): 55–73.

Meyer, John, and Brian Rowan. 1977. "Institutionalized Organizations: Formal Structure as Myth and Ceremony." *American Journal of Sociology* 83 (2): 340–63.

Milley, Mark. 2020. "Gen. Mark Milley's Keynote Address to National Defense University Class of 2020 Graduates." YouTube video, 13:13, published June 11, 2020. https://www.youtube.com/watch?v=7AKmmApwi0M&ab_channel=JointStaff PublicAffairs.

Mills, C. Wright. 1956. *The Power Elite*. New York: Oxford University Press.

Monahan, Terence. 2019. "News Closeup: Inside the NYPD—Keeping New Yorkers Safe and Addressing Challenges Facing the Department." Pix11 News. Posted and updated February 22, 2019.

Montoya, Tony. 2020. "San Francisco Police: The Thin Blue Line Mask Ban in Our City Exposes Anti-police Bigots." *Law Enforcement Today*, May 12, 2020.

Moreno-Medina, Jonathan, Aurelie Ouss, Patrick Bayer, and Bocar Ba. 2022. "Officer-Involved: The Media Language of Police Killings." NBER Working Paper no. 30209.

Morin, Rich, Kim Parker, Renee Stepler, and Andrew Mercer. 2017. *Behind the Badge*. Washington, DC: Pew Research Center.

Moskos, Peter. 2008. *Cop in the Hood: My Year Policing Baltimore's Eastern District*. Princeton, NJ: Princeton University Press.

Muir, William. 1977. *Police: Streetcorner Politicians*. Chicago: University of Chicago Press.

Musso, Juliet, Christopher Weare, Nail Oztas, and William Loges. 2006. "Neighborhood Governance Reform and Networks of Community Power in Los Angeles." *American Review of Public Administration* 36 (1): 79–97.

Nelson, Alondra. 2011. *Body and Soul: The Black Panther Party and the Fight against Medical Discrimination*. Minneapolis: University of Minnesota Press.

New York State Office of the Attorney General. 2019. *Report on the Investigation into the Death of Saheed Vassell*. Albany: New York State Office of the Attorney General, Special Investigations and Prosecutions Unit.

New York Times. 1944a. "New Units Fight Delinquency Here." February 25, 1944.

———. 1944b. "Single Unit Urged to Cut Delinquency." August 4, 1944.

NYPD. 2016a. "NYPD Adds 157 Advocates to Assist Victims of Crime." New York Police Department press release, October 28, 2016. https://www1.nyc.gov/site/nypd/news/p00030/nypd-adds-157-advocates-assist-victims-crime.

———. 2016b. *The Police Commissioner's Report: 2016*. New York: New York Police Department.

———. 2018. "Press Release: Neighborhood Policing Now in Every Neighborhood in New York City." http://www1.nyc.gov/site/nypd/news/pr1022/neighborhood-policing-now-every-neighborhood-new-york-city.

Ocasio, William, Jo-Ellen Pozner, and Daniel Milner. 2020. "Varieties of Political Capital and Power in Organizations: A Review and Integrative Framework." *Academy of Management Annals* 14 (1): 303–38.

O'Neill, James. 2015."NYPD Neighborhood Policing | James O'Neill | TEDxThacherSchool," November 22. YouTube video, 21:59, published November 22, 2015. https://www.youtube.com/watch?v=XxHuJopPK60.

Owens, Michael Leo. 2007. *God and Government in the Ghetto: The Politics of Church-State Collaboration in Black America*. Chicago: University of Chicago Press.

Page, Joshua. 2011. *The Toughest Beat Politics, Punishment, and the Prison Officers Union in California*. New York: Oxford University Press.

Page, Joshua, Victoria Piehowski, and Joe Soss. 2019. "A Debt of Care: Commercial Bail and the Gendered Logic of Criminal Justice Predation." *RSF: The Russell Sage Foundation Journal of the Social Sciences* 5 (1): 150–72.

Pattillo, Mary. 2007. *Black on the Block: The Politics of Race and Class in the City*. Chicago: University of Chicago Press.

Pattillo-McCoy, Mary. 1998. "Church Culture as a Strategy of Action in the Black Community." *American Sociological Review* 63 (6): 767–84.

Pazmino, Gloria. 2018. "De Blasio Facing Consternation on the Left for Silence on NYPD." Politico.com, posted and updated December 14, 2018. https://www.politico.com/states/new-york/city-hall/story/2018/12/14/de-blasio-facing-consternation-on-the-left-for-silence-on-nypd-746345.

Pegram, Kashea, Rod Brunson, and Anthony Braga. 2016. "The Doors of the Church Are Now Open: Black Clergy, Collective Efficacy, and Neighborhood Violence." *City and Community* 15 (3): 289–314.

Peyton, Kyle, Michael Sierra-Arévalo, and David Rand. 2019. "A Field Experiment on Community Policing and Police Legitimacy." *Proceedings of the National Academy of Sciences* 116 (40): 19894–98.

Phelps, Michelle, Anneliese Ward, and Dwjuan Frazier. 2021. "From Police Reform to Police Abolition? How Minneapolis Activists Fought to Make Black Lives Matter." *Mobilization: An International Quarterly* 26 (4): 421–41.

Pierson, Paul. 1996. "The New Politics of the Welfare State." *World Politics* 48 (2): 143–79.

Ponomarenko, Maria. 2019. "Rethinking Police Rulemaking." *Northwestern University Law Review* 114 (1): 1–64.

Powell, Amber Joy, and Michelle Phelps. 2021. "Gendered Racial Vulnerability: How Women Confront Crime and Criminalization." *Law and Society Review* 55 (3): 429–51.

President's Task Force on 21st Century Policing. 2015. *Final Report of the President's Task Force on 21st Century Policing*. Washington, DC: Office of Community Oriented Policing Services.

Rahman, K. Sabeel, and Jocelyn Simonson. 2020. "The Institutional Design of Community Control." *California Law Review* 108:679–742.

Rim, Nayoung, Bocar Ba, and Roman Rivera. 2020. "Disparities in Police Award Nominations: Evidence from Chicago." *AEA Papers and Proceedings* 110:447–51.

Rios, Victor. 2011. *Punished: Policing the Lives of Black and Latino Boys*. New York: New York University Press.

Rivera-Cuadrado, Wayne. 2021. "Crafting Charismatic Cops: Community Policing and the Faulty Reputations Paradigm." *Social Problems*, September 2021. https://doi .org/ 10.1093/socpro/spab054.

Robbins, Christopher. 2021. "The Mayor's Office—Not the NYPD—Will Now Issue NYC Press Credentials." Gothamist.com, March 26, 2021. https://gothamist.com/ news/the-mayors-officenot-the-nypdwill-now-issue-nyc-press-credentials.

Rocha Beardall, Theresa. 2022. "Police Legitimacy Regimes and the Suppression of Citizen Oversight in Response to Police Violence." *Criminology* 60 (4): 577-765.

Rodríguez-Muñiz, Michael. 2017. "Cultivating Consent: Nonstate Leaders and the Orchestration of State Legibility." *American Journal of Sociology* 123 (2): 385-425.

Schrader, Stuart. 2019. *Badges without Borders: How Global Counterinsurgency Transformed American Policing.* Berkeley: University of California Press.

Schradie, Jen. 2019. *The Revolution That Wasn't: How Digital Activism Favors Conservatives.* Cambridge MA: Harvard University Press.

Scott, James. 1969. "Corruption, Machine Politics, and Political Change." *American Political Science Review* 63 (4): 1142-58.

Seale, Bobby. 1970. *Seize the Time: The Story of the Black Panther Party and Huey P. Newton.* New York: Random House.

Selznick, Philip. 1949. *TVA and the Grass Roots: A Study in the Sociology of Formal Organization.* New York: Harper and Row.

Sharkey, Patrick, Gerard Torrats-Espinosa, and Delaram Takyar. 2017. "Community and the Crime Decline: The Causal Effect of Local Nonprofits on Violent Crime." *American Sociological Review* 82 (6): 1214-40.

Sierra-Arévalo, Michael. 2021. "American Policing and the Danger Imperative." *Law and Society Review* 55 (1): 70-103.

Simon, Jonathan. 2007. *Governing through Crime: How the War on Crime Transformed American Democracy and Created a Culture of Fear.* New York: Oxford University Press.

Simonson, Jocelyn. 2016. "Copwatching." *California Law Review* 104 (2): 391-446.

———. 2020. "Police Reform through a Power Lens." *Yale Law Journal* 130:778-1049.

Skogan, Wesley. 2006. *Police and Community in Chicago: A Tale of Three Cities.* New York: Oxford University Press.

Skogan, Wesley, and Susan Hartnett. 1997. *Community Policing, Chicago Style.* New York: Oxford University Press.

Small, Mario. 2009. *Unanticipated Gains: Origins of Network Inequality in Everyday Life.* New York: Oxford University Press.

Small, Mario, and Leah Gose. 2020. "How Do Low-Income People Form Survival Networks? Routine Organizations as Brokers." *ANNALS of the American Academy of Political and Social Science* 689 (1): 89-109.

Smith, Chris, and Andrew Papachristos. 2016. "Trust Thy Crooked Neighbor: Multiplexity in Chicago Organized Crime Networks." *American Sociological Review* 81 (4): 644-67.

Stokes, Susan, Thad Dunning, Marcelo Nazareno, and Valeria Brusco. 2013. *Brokers, Voters, and Clientelism: The Puzzle of Distributive Politics.* New York: Cambridge University Press.

Stuart, Forrest. 2011. "Constructing Police Abuse after Rodney King: How Skid Row

Residents and the Los Angeles Police Department Contest Video Evidence." *Law and Social Inquiry* 36 (2): 327–53.

———. 2016. *Down, Out, and Under Arrest: Policing and Everyday Life in Skid Row.* Chicago: University of Chicago Press.

———. 2020. "Code of the Tweet: Urban Gang Violence in the Social Media Age." *Social Problems* 67 (2): 191–207.

Suchman, Mark. 1995. "Managing Legitimacy: Strategic and Institutional Approaches." *Academy of Management Review* 20 (3): 571–610.

Swidler, Ann. 1986. "Culture in Action: Symbols and Strategies." *American Sociological Review* 51 (2): 273–86. https://doi.org/10.2307/2095521.

Thacher, David. 2001. "Equity and Community Policing: A New View of Community Partnerships." *Crime Justice Ethics* 20 (1): 3–16.

Thai, Mai. 2022. "Policing and Symbolic Control: The Process of Valorization." *American Journal of Sociology* 127 (4): 1183–1220. https://doi.org/10.1086/718278.

Tiry, Emily, Ashlin Oglesby-Neal, and Kim KiDeuk. 2019. *Social Media Guidebook for Law Enforcement Agencies: Strategies for Effective Community Engagement.* Washington, DC: Urban Institute.

Treem, Jeffrey, and Paul Leonardi. 2013. "Social Media Use in Organizations: Exploring the Affordances of Visibility, Editability, Persistence, and Association." *Annals of the International Communication Association* 36 (1): 143–89.

Trojanowicz, Robert, and Bonnie Bucqueroux. 1990. *Community Policing: A Contemporary Perspective.* Cincinnati: Anderson.

Tyler, Tom. 2004. "Enhancing Police Legitimacy." *ANNALS of the American Academy of Political and Social Science* 593 (1): 84–99.

Valentine, Leonica, and Rebecca Harshbarger. 2014. "'Brooklyn Asian Safety Patrol' Has NYPD's Go-Ahead." *New York Post*, August 4, 2014.

Vargas, Robert. 2016. "How Health Navigators Legitimize the Affordable Care Act to the Uninsured Poor." *Social Science and Medicine* 165:263–70.

Vargas, Robert, and Philip McHarris. 2017. "Race and State in City Police Spending Growth: 1980 to 2010." *Sociology of Race and Ethnicity* 3 (1): 96–112.

Vargas, Robert, Chris Williams, Philip O'Sullivan, and Christina Cano. 2022. "Capitalizing on Crisis: Chicago Police Responses to Homicide Waves 1920-2020." *University of Chicago Law Review* 89 (2): 405–39.

Vaughn, Joshua. 2021. "After Daunte Wright's Death, Advocates Press Leaders to Get Police Out of Traffic Enforcement." *Appeal*, April 14, 2021.

Vera Institute of Justice. 1988. *CPOP: Community Policing in Practice.* New York: Vera Institute of Justice.

Vollmer, August. 1933. "Police Progress in the Past Twenty-Five Years." *Journal of the American Institute of Criminal Law and Criminology* 24 (1): 161–75.

Walker, Samuel. 2016. "Governing the American Police: Wrestling with the Problems of Democracy." *University of Chicago Legal Forum* 2016:615–60.

Weisburd, David, Stephen Mastrofski, Ann Marie McNally, Rosann Greenspan, and James Willis. 2003. "Reforming to Preserve: Compstat and Strategic Problem Solving in American Policing." *Criminology and Public Policy* 2 (3): 421–56.

White, Michael. 2014. "The New York City Police Department, Its Crime Control

Strategies and Organizational Changes, 1970–2009." *Justice Quarterly* 31 (1): 74–95. https://doi.org/10.1080/07418825.2012.723032.

Williams, Clarence. 2021. "'Thin Blue Line' Masks, Clothing Banned for Staff in Maryland District Courts." *Washington Post*, May 7, 2021.

Wilson, Michael, and Joseph Goldstein. 2019. "After Pantaleo, Wary N.Y.P.D. Officers Say No One Has Their Backs." *New York Times*, August 22, 2019.

INDEX